INSIGHT GUIDES

COSTA RICA

Discovery CHANNEL

APA PUBLICATIONS

Part of the Langenscheidt Publishing Group

INSIGHT GUIDE
CosTa RiCa

Editorial
Project Editor
Paul Murphy
Managing Editor
Huw Hennessy
Editorial Director
Brian Bell

Distribution

UK & Ireland
GeoCenter International Ltd
The Viables Centre, Harrow Way
Basingstoke, Hants RG22 4BJ
Fax: (44) 1256 817988

United States
Langenscheidt Publishers, Inc.
36–36 33rd Street, 4th Floor
Long Island City, New York 11106
Fax: 1 (718) 784 0640

Canada
Thomas Allen & Son Ltd
390 Steelcase Road East
Markham, Ontario L3R 1G2
Fax: (1) 905 475 6747

Australia
Universal Publishers
1 Waterloo Road
Macquarie Park, NSW 2113
Fax: (61) 2 9888 9074

New Zealand
Hema Maps New Zealand Ltd (HNZ)
Unit D, 24 Ra ORA Drive
East Tamaki, Auckland
Fax: (64) 9 273 6479

Worldwide
Apa Publications GmbH & Co.
Verlag KG (Singapore branch)
38 Joo Koon Road, Singapore 628990
Tel: (65) 6865 1600. Fax: (65) 6861 6438

Printing
Insight Print Services (Pte) Ltd
38 Joo Koon Road, Singapore 628990
Tel: (65) 6865 1600. Fax: (65) 6861 6438

ABOUT THIS BOOK

This guidebook combines the interests and enthusiasms of two of the world's best-known information providers: Insight Guides, whose titles have set the standard for visual travel guides since 1970, and Discovery Channel, the world's premier source of non-fiction television programming.

The editors of Insight Guides provide both practical advice and general understanding about a destination's history, culture, institutions and people. Discovery Channel and its website, www.discovery.com, help millions of viewers explore their world from the comfort of their own home and also encourage them to explore it first-hand.

How to use this book

The book has been carefully structured both to convey an understanding of Costa Rica and its culture and to guide readers through its many sights and natural attractions:

The **Features** section, with a yellow color bar, covers the country's **history** and **culture** in lively authoritative essays written by specialists.

The **Places** section, with a blue bar, provides full details of all the sights and areas worth edited by **Paul Murphy**, assisted by managing editor **Huw Hennessy**. Harvey and Dona contributed most of the book's historical pieces, with the feature on the Nicaraguan influx by **Carol Weir**. Carol also did much valuable updating work on many other parts of the book.

Marine biologist and long-time Central America expert **Henry Genthe** wrote the Sports article and several of the Places chapters. **Cindy Hilbrink** wrote on rural aspects of Costa Rica. **David Burnie**, a biologist and natural history writer, wrote features on the flora and fauna.

Other writers whose expert text has been adapted and updated from earlier editions include **Moisés Leon**, **John McPhaul**, **Juan Bernal Ponce**, **Tony Avirgan**, **Martha Honey**, **Marjorie Ross-Cerdas**, **Mary Sheldon**, and **Alexander Skutch**.

Glyn Genin provided many of the photographs, as did Henry Genthe. In San José, **John Skiffingham** also delved deep into his vast picture library. Other photographers who contributed were **Michael** and **Patricia Fogden**, **André Bärtschi**, **Chip** and **Jill Isenhart**, and **Buddy Mays**. **John Leach** indexed the book. In 2004 the book was updated by **Dorothy MacKinnon**, a Canadian who lives in Costa Rica and writes for *The Tico Times*. **Suzanna Starcevic**, editor of the Weekend section of the *The Tico Times*, updated and expanded the Travel Tips. The book was edited by **Alyse Dar** and proofread by **Sylvia Suddes**.

seeing. The chief places of interest are coordinated by number with specially drawn maps.

The **Travel Tips** listings section, with an orange bar at the back of the book, offers a convenient point of reference for information on travel, accommodation, restaurants and other practical aspects of the country. Information may be located quickly by using the index printed on the back cover flap, which also serves as a handy bookmark.

The contributors

This new edition, which builds on the earlier edition edited by **Harvey** and **Dona Haber**, was

Map Legend

— ·· —	International Boundary
— — —	Province Boundary
⊖	Border Crossing
— • —	National Park/Reserve
— — — —	Ferry Route
✈ ✈	Airport: International/Regional
🚌	Bus Station
P	Parking
ⓘ	Tourist Information
✉	Post Office
† †	Church/Ruins
☾	Mosque
✡	Synagogue
🏰	Castle/Ruins
∴	Archaeological Site
∩	Cave
⌶	Statue/Monument
★	Place of Interest

The main places of interest in the Places section are coordinated by number with a full-color map (e.g. ❶), and a symbol at the top of every right-hand page tells you where to find the map.

CONTENTS

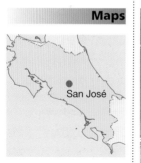

A map of Costa Rica can be found on the inside front cover, and a map of National Parks and Reserves can be found on the inside back cover.

Keeping
cool in the
shade

Insight on ...

Places

Information panels

Travel Tips

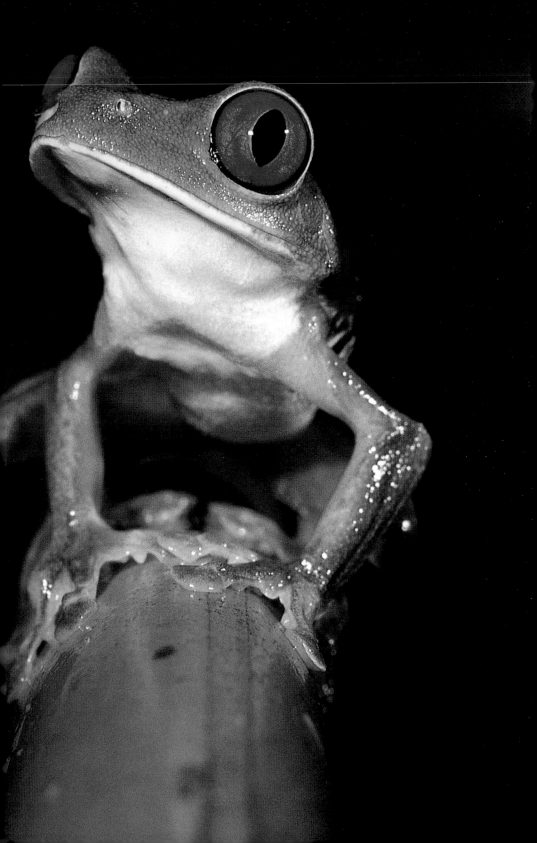

THE HAPPY MEDIUM

Amid the turmoil that often characterizes Central America

Costa Rica is a land at peace with itself and nature

N estled between Nicaragua and Panamá on the Central American isthmus, Costa Rica is a small, democratic and peaceful country, with a level of social development that always surprises first-time visitors and belies its definition as a Third-World nation. Lacking the clichéd images and iconographic characteristics of other Latin American countries, such as Mexico, Peru or Brazil, it has become famous for its natural environment and for its efforts in helping bring lasting peace to a troubled region.

Since Don Pepe Figueres abolished Costa Rica's armed forces in 1949, the government has been able to devote a large percentage of its resources to education, health and conservation. Currently about a quarter of the country is protected in national parks, biological reserves, wildlife refuges and private reserves. With more than 850 species of birds, 250 mammals, and some 6 percent of the world's total identified species, Costa Rica is a paradise for anyone who delights in the unspoiled natural world.

A land of dense jungles, active volcanoes and pristine beaches, this is a tiny country but it is full of geophysical contrasts that make it seem much bigger. A third of the country's population (total 3.8 million) live in the temperate Central Valley that houses the modern capital of San José. But as any *Tico* (Costa Rican) will tell you, the "real" Costa Rica will only be found in the *campo*, or rural areas.

It was an official at the World Bank who termed Costa Rica the Land of the Happy Medium. And while its economy is far from perfect, the standard of living is high and the climate temperate. In outlook it is often more European than Latino, and predominantly middle-class. With a per capita income of around US$4,000, Costa Rica's people rely on the state to provide quality health care, schools and other affordable services such as electricity and clean water, while its neighbors lavish equal amounts of money on national defense and putting down military coups.

Since 1994, tourism has been the country's leading industry, along with computer-chip exports, with bananas, pineapples and coffee lagging behind. More than a million visitors now arrive every year, the vast majority of them coming from North America and Europe. A sophisticated tourism industry is in place, with accommodations ranging from luxury lodges to homey bed-and-breakfasts. Eco- and adventure tourism are the buzzwords that encompass activities as diverse as birdwatching and whitewater rafting. Costa Rica has come a long way from the sleepy, agricultural land it once was, but it retains essential charm. ❏

PRECEDING PAGES: red-eyed tree frog, also called the gaudy leaf frog; cloud forest of Cerro de la Muerte; the spreading cenicero tree dots the grassy plains of Guanacaste; black-sand beach in Limón province.
LEFT: poison-dart frogs, formerly used by indigenous peoples for tipping arrows.

COAST TO COAST

Costa Rica may be small in area but it is big in diversity, with two oceans, rushing rivers, fiery volcanoes, and chilly peaks touching nearly 4,000 meters

osta Rica lies at the heart of the Central American isthmus and these days few people mistake it for an island in the Caribbean. Traveling around the countryside gives you the sense of being in a large country; geophysically there are so many things going on. There is the feeling that it would take months to really explore it all. Yet, in reality, it is quite small. From northwest to southwest it measures 460 km (285 miles) and at its narrowest point it is only 120 km (74 miles). In total, Costa Rica's land area is just 51,000 sq km (20,000 sq miles).

Neighbors

Costa Rica is bounded on the north by Nicaragua, and to the south by Panamá; situated between two countries often in the international news, for the wrong reasons, and profoundly different from this usually benevolent and peaceful land. To the east is the tranquil Caribbean Sea and to the west is the tumultuous Pacific Ocean. Costa Rica is as complex and perhaps more diverse than any place of its size on earth; divided into several distinct regions, each of them looks like an entirely separate place.

A fertile land

Perhaps it is the hot coastal plains in the tropical zones, with their rolling wild grasses and plantations of palm and banana, or the thickly forested valleys and coastlines, fringed with beaches of every description, that drew many of the early travelers here.

Or perhaps it is the fertile central plateau in the temperate zone, at 975–1,980 meters (3,200–6,500 ft), with its rich, fecund cloud forests and magical tropical jungles, which has attracted a large international community of conservationists, biologists, birdwatchers, environmentalists, naturalists, and the ecologically attuned.

Many a Northern European or *gringo* from the midwestern or northern United States or Canada has found Costa Rica to be an ideal new home, with its cool highlands of gently rolling, wooded pastureland reminiscent more of Switzerland than of a tropical country.

Running as veins of a precious ore through

the body of the country is an intricate network of waterways. They rise and fall through the mountains, flow to the sea and provide a seemingly endless source of fresh water and hydraulic power.

The soil of the Central Valley is exceptionally fertile, due primarily to the volcanic ash that has fallen through the centuries. This rich, drainable soil is ideal for producing Costa Rica's coffee, and traveling through the high country, you can view seemingly endless coffee *fincas* (estates), the bushes with their deep green, jewel-like foliage flowing up impossibly steep ridges and across the floor of great alluvial valleys.

LEFT: a prehistoric-looking mature green iguana.
RIGHT: shy but curious *Tica* welcome.

The coast

Never far away is the coastline. Indeed, there are many easily accessible points throughout this country from where you can simultaneously view both the Atlantic and the Pacific oceans. The Atlantic coast measures only 220 km (135 miles) in length, while the Pacific coast of Costa Rica, with its deep gulfs and indentations, is several times that length. On the Pacific there is the Nicoya peninsula to the north, and the Osa peninsula to the south. And, remote and mysterious, many miles off the Pacific coast, is the exceptionally beautiful, still pristine Cocos Island.

Peaks of delight

Although most of Costa Rica's volcanoes are extinct, some are still active. Poás Volcano, at 2,700 meters (8,900 ft), is located near the town of Alajuela, and is one of the world's largest craters, measuring more than a mile in diameter; and Irazú Volcano, at 3,440 meters (11,320 ft), not far from the city of Cartago, is occasionally active, and can be viewed at relatively close range.

At 1,630 meters (5,350 ft) in height, Arenal is the most consistently active of Costa Rica's

volcanoes. The rumbling, explosive spectacle of Arenal Volcano is the single most impressive pyrotechnic display in the whole country.

The highland mountains traverse Costa Rica, from the northwest to the southeast, in three ranges, rising to more than 3,800 meters (12,500 ft). These are the magnificent Guanacaste, Central, and Talamanca ranges. Chirripó Grande, at 3,800 meters (12,500 ft), and Terbi, of the same height, are the highest elevation points in the country.

Climate

Although geographically situated in what earlier travelers used to call the "torrid zone," the great majority of Costa Rica never really feel torrid at any time of year, the population living for the most part on the Central Plateau, at elevations between around 450 meters (1,500 ft) and 1,400 meters (4,500 ft), in "perennial springtime" temperatures of between 20–26°C (68–78°F), day and night.

However, near the coasts the temperatures are indeed tropical and there are distinct alternating wet and dry seasons, at different times of year, for both the Atlantic and Pacific. There are certain times here when even the local residents are overwhelmed by the too-sensuous hot and humid midday air and are driven into the shade to cool down.

Tropical downpours usually arrive with great predictability in the afternoons during the wet seasons along the coasts and are undeniably awesome. If you are caught out in one, you will never forget the experience. Over the years, millions of words have been written about these extraordinary dramas of lightning, thunder, and torrential rains.

Away from the tropical coasts, the climate is greatly determined by the altitude above sea level. At each level, daytime temperatures are fairly constant regardless of the time of year. At night, however, the heat of the coastal plains cools slightly, while high up on the mountain and volcano slopes, pleasant sun-warmed temperatures plunge at night, sometimes to just above the freezing mark.

From the edge of the almost tideless Caribbean Sea and the pounding Pacific coast, up and across the slopes of the volcanic *cordilleras*, and finally up to the highest peak of cold and brittle Chirripó, the Republic of Costa Rica is gloriously invigorating. ❏

ABOVE: birders on Tortuguero's tree-lined canals.
RIGHT: Volcán Arenal letting off steam.

Decisive Dates

12,000–4000 BC First signs of human habitation in Central America: hunter-gatherers migrating southward settle in small chiefdoms, developing diverse languages and cultures.

4000–1000 BC Establishment of earliest settlements based on crop cultivation (including maize, yucca and cotton).

1000 BC–AD 1500 Growth and expansion of organized, sedentary farming communities, who form trade and communication links with each other and as far afield as the Chibcha people of South America. By the time of

A WARRIOR OF NICOYA.

the arrival of the Spaniards, five major cultural groups of natives predominate; the Spanish name them the Carib; the Boruca; the Nahua; the Corobici, who were the oldest native group; and the most advanced group of all, the Chorotega, who inhabit the Nicoya Peninsula.

1502 Christopher Columbus drops anchor for two weeks off the island of Uvita (near Puerto Limón), where he encounters the Cariari tribe.

1519–60 The Spanish explore both coastlines of Costa Rica.

1561 An expedition from the Pacific coast finally manages to reach the Valle Central. Juan Cavallón founds the first town, Castillo de Garcimuñoz, which is relocated several times until becoming established as present-day Cartago.

1562 Juan Vazquez de Coronado explores the Valle Central and employs peaceful means to try to convert the *indígenas* (indigenous people).

1572 Beginning of Colonial Period, characterized by an almost continuous absence of labor. Costa Rica remains a poor colony for the next 250 years, largely ignored by Spain because of its lack of mineral resources.

1660–70 Atlantic coast cacao plantations bring the colony its first revenue, but they are constantly raided by pirates.

1723 The tiny fledgling capital of Cartago is wiped out by erupting Irazu Volcano.

1787 Costa Rica is the only colony in the Audiencia Guatemala allowed to cultivate tobacco.

1821 Guatemala announces independence from Spain.

1823 Civil war breaks out between the conservative imperialists in Cartago and Heredía, who want to join the Mexican Empire, and the republicans *(liberalistas)* who are in the majority in San José and Alajuela. The republicans finally secure Costa Rica's acceptance into the short-lived United Provinces of Central America, led by Guatemala. San José replaces Cartago as the national capital.

1824 Juan Mora Fernández becomes Costa Rica's first head of state (until 1833). The inhabitants of the "Partido de Nicoya" (a region governed until then by Nicaragua, and roughly corresponding to today's Guanacaste) vote to join Costa Rica.

1825 The first constitution of the free state of Costa Rica is promulgated, and the cession of Guanacaste is made official by Congress.

1832 First coffee exports to Europe, via Chile.

1835 Braulio Carrillo becomes president and uses dictatorial methods to introduce liberal reforms. Heredia, Cartago, and Alajuela all oppose these; they form a "league" and declare war on San José, eventually winning the capital.

1838 After the collapse of the United Provinces of Central America, the president announces the free and independent republic of Costa Rica.

1849 Juan Rafael Mora becomes president and is re-elected in 1853 and 1859. During his presidency coffee exports experience a sharp upswing.

1858 During the war against freebooter William Walker, who wants to turn Central America into a colony of the southern American states and introduce slavery, a decisive battle is fought near Santa Rosa. Walker is finally defeated by Costa Rica's troops in Rivas (Nicaragua).

1870 Tomás Guardia Gutiérrez takes over power after a military coup, introduces a new liberal constitution, and remains in office until 1882.

1871 Railroad construction begins.

1880 First banana exports.

1882 The death penalty is abolished.

1886 Introduction of compulsory education.

1887 Clodomiro Picado, world-acclaimed medical scientist, instrumental in discovering penicillin, vaccines and snakebite anti-venin, is born.

1890 First free and honest democratic elections in Central America bring José Joaquin Rodriguez to presidency. The Atlantic Railroad, from Cartago to Limón, is completed.

1914–18 Costa Rica loses export markets because of World War I. Economic recession.

1917 Federico A. Tinoco takes power in a coup supported by the coffee barons. A popular uprising ends his dictatorship two years later.

1932 World economic recession.

1934 A strike among banana workers in response to adverse working conditions at United Fruit Company leads to a series of concessions (including the right to strike and the minimum wage).

1939–45 World War II – coffee exports stagnate. Costa Rica declares war on Germany, Japan and Italy. German and Italian residents are dispossessed and deported.

1940–44 President Rafael Calderón successfully implements a series of social reforms.

1945 The Social Democratic Party (PSD) is founded, later to become the Partido Liberación Nacional (PLN), under (Don Pepe) José Figueres.

1948 Calderón Guardia declares election results to be annulled and reassumes the presidency. Civil war ensues. The victorious junta led by Figueres takes over government.

1949 Under the terms of the new constitution the army is disbanded and replaced by a Civil Guard. Figueres hands over power to elected president Otilio Ulate, but governs the country again from 1953 to 1958 and 1970 to 1974.

1979 The Sandinistas in Nicaragua topple the Somoza dictatorship. During the ensuing civil war, Costa Rica becomes a fallback area for guerilla groups and anti-Sandinistas. As a result of the war, hundreds of thousands of Nicaraguans seek refuge in Costa Rica.

1980 Slump in coffee and banana markets causes the onset of severe economic recession.

1983 President Luis Alberto Monge declares a state of "unarmed neutrality," leading to tensions with the United States.

PRECEDING PAGES: pre-Columbian ceramics from the National Museum, San José.

LEFT: a Nicoyan warrior, set for battle.

RIGHT: a portrait of idyllic early Amerindian life by the chronologer Figueroa.

1986 Oscar Arias Sánchez is elected president and prepares to restore peace to the region. For his efforts in instigating the Central American Peace Plan, "Esquipulas II", he is awarded the Nobel Peace Prize.

1990 The Social Christian Unity Party (PUSC) wins the elections. Rafael Angel Calderón Fournier, the son of Calderón Guardia, becomes the country's president. Costa Rica sends a national team to the soccer World Cup for the first time, and reaches the quarter finals.

1991 An earthquake strikes Limón province, killing over 60 and causing extensive damage which remains today.

1994 José M. Figueres becomes Costa Rica's youngest ever president. However, his term is dogged by scandals, including the bankruptcy and closure of

Banco Anglo-Costarricense, the nation's oldest bank.

1996 Hurricane César strikes, killing dozens of Costa Ricans and causing over US$100 million of damage.

1998 The Social Christian Unity Party (PUSC) wins general elections and Miguel Angel Rodríguez is sworn in as president. During his term he encourages foreign investment and privatizes state companies but many criticize the government's lack of transparency.

2000 Nationwide protests against proposed privatization of ICE, the government-run electricity and telecommunications monopoly.

2002 Abel Pacheco of the PUSC wins the first ever presidential run-off vote. Costa Rican astronaut Franklin Chang, crew member of US space shuttle Endeavour, goes for a walk in space. ❏

BEFORE COLUMBUS

The Amerindians' early culture was largely agrarian. Influenced by their
Mesoamerican neighbors, they learned to fashion goods from stone, jade and gold

On September 8, 1502, Cristóbal Colón (Christopher Columbus) arrived on the Atlantic Coast of Costa Rica and took refuge in the calm waters just off the coast, between tiny Uvita Island and what is now the Port of Limón.

The native population greeted the Spaniards with interest and brought out goods to trade with them. They swam out to the ship carrying cotton cloth, shirts, tumbaga pendants (an alloy made of copper and gold) and weapons such as clubs, bows and arrows.

Golden dreams

Dreaming of gold, Columbus had charted the coastal area from Honduras to Panamá and named it Veragua. He was so enamored by the golden mirrors that the Amerindians of Costa Rica wore about their necks, and by their many stories of gold and gold mines along the coast to the south, that he named the area the Rich Coast of Veragua.

Rich though it seemed to Columbus at the time, the newly discovered area was not to be a great, rich jewel in Spain's crown. In fact, the "Rich Coast" turned out to be one of the poorest of Spain's American colonies. Impassable mountains, impenetrable forests, raging rivers, unbearable heat, floods, disease, swamps, shortages of food, internal rivalries, lack of natural resources and a way to generate wealth all oppressed the settlers. They were often reduced to living like the "savages" they had come to conquer: wearing goat-hair garments or clothing made of bark; using cacao (chocolate beans) for currency; eking out a bare subsistence in the fields, using native methods to cultivate native crops.

This bleak reality was yet to come. Columbus naively returned to Spain with dreams of great riches and grandeur, to the point of asking the king to confer on him the title of Duke of Veragua.

LEFT: a ceremonial polychrome vessel.
RIGHT: gold ornament and battlewear.

Natural riches

Unrealistic visions of gold aside, what was life in the newly discovered territory really like? It was a rich land, if not in gold, then in natural resources, with forests, mountains, rivers, grasslands and abundant animal and plant life. In the Atlantic watershed area, where much of

the land is flat, navigable rivers and their tributaries were swelled in some areas by more than 400 cm (160 inches) of rain a year. In the heavy tropical vegetation grew wild rubber trees, orchids and ferns. Fish, alligators and an occasional shark lived in the rivers. Waterfowl, turkeys, iguanas, red monkeys, howler monkeys, peccaries (wild pigs) and jaguars inhabited the forests.

To the north, in the Nicoya region, were tropical dry forests, also abundant in plant and animal life: on the broad, seasonally dry plains grew the beautiful wide, green guanacaste tree; the javillo with its poisonous sap and thorny trunk; the cenicero with its flesh-colored flowers; the guapinol with its characteristic seed pods, referred to as "stinky toes;" and many varieties of cacti and spiny shrubs. White-faced monkeys, howler monkeys, red squirrels with grey tails, tapirs, coatis, deer, jaguars, mountain lions, coyotes and other small animals lived in the forests. In the trees, scarlet macaws and other parrots squawked and roosted. Avocados, papayas, guavas and countless other fruits grew wild.

And the grasslands and swamps of the southern Pacific region, also called the Diquis region, were lush with life, as were the often misty green hills and valleys of the Central High-

At the time of Columbus's arrival, the people of the Guanacaste/Nicoya region lived in well-developed settlements, some with populations as large as 20,000. These settlements, supported by the cultivation of corn, were constructed around central plazas, marketplaces and religious centers.

Guayabo city

In the Atlantic Watershed/Central Highlands area, located in the mountains near the present-day city of Turrialba, was a city with wide, cobblestoned walkways, freshwater springs bubbling out of stone-lined pools, and a stone

lands, where broadleaf evergreen forests, palms and white oaks grew on the luxuriant hillsides, harboring innumerable species of birds, animals and plants.

Native settlers

Groups of indigenous peoples with diverse languages and cultures lived throughout these areas in small chiefdoms. They were agricultural people, cultivating crops of yucca, corn, *pejibaye* (the bright orange fruit of palm) and numerous other plants. They supplemented their diets with wild fruits and game from the forests, fish and shrimp from the rivers, and crustacea and small oysters from the ocean.

WHAT'S IN A NAME?

The Spanish colonists gave the Amerindians the names by which we know them today (often the name of the chief at the time): the Chorotega, Bribri, Cacebar, Coctu, Corobicí, to name a few. We do not know the names they called themselves. Since some groups were completely wiped out before the Spanish came, we do not have names for them, or know what languages they spoke. Because of this, archeologists usually refer to Amerindian groups by the areas in which they lived: Guanacaste/Nicoya region, the Atlantic Watershed/Central Highlands region and the Diquis, or Southern Pacific region.

aqueduct system carrying fresh water to some of the stone mounds on which houses were built. This ancient ceremonial or administrative center, called Guayabo, flourished and disappeared (approximately 1000 BC to AD 1400) before the arrival of the Spaniards. From Guayabo, ancient roads of stone led to towns and may have even reached the ocean.

Other groups within the Atlantic Watershed/ Central Highlands region were less settled. They cultivated root crops and hunted what small game was available, and then moved on to new lands when the soil or supply of game became depleted.

seems, was a kind of mercantile and cultural crossroads of the Americas. Linguistic and cultural influences, not to mention a wealth of artifacts and materials, were being exchanged within the country and without, from as far north as Mexico and as far south as Ecuador. The native Costa Ricans were enthusiastic traders and prized jade pieces, ceramic ware, gold and stone carvings from Mesoamerica and South America.

The Nicoya area, with its quiet Pacific bays and safe anchorages, provided pre-Columbian commercial ports. Merchant marines from ancient Ecuador, making ports of call all along

In the Diquis region, people also hunted, cultivated root crops and lived in well-fortified villages that were strategically laid out to protect villagers from enemy attack.

Crossroads of the Americas

Influenced by some of the other great indigenous cultures of the Americas, the native peoples of Costa Rica had become skilled in the arts of ceramics, gold and metalwork, fine weaving and stone carving. Costa Rica, it

LEFT: a *mano*, or *metate* prehistoric corn grinder.
ABOVE: *conquistador* statue, San José.
ABOVE RIGHT: stone figure found at Guayabo.

the Pacific coast of Mexico, Central and South America, frequently stopped at sites in Nicoya, bringing with them the crafts and arts of those places they have visited. Perhaps it was they who introduced Olmec influences to the area – or perhaps the Olmecs (and others) came themselves. Regardless, the influence of the Olmecs was evident in the Pacific Northwest in: an impressive range of pottery styles; utilitarian articles such as grinding stones; and the practice of certain customs, such as filing human teeth into points.

Over the years, the pottery of Nicoya developed into a vigorous hybrid style that for centuries would be traded around Central America and southern Mexico. A collection of such work is on view at the National Museum. It is lively, bold, colorful work: large globular jars and vessels; figures of men and women, some with oversized genitals and physical deformities; animals of all kinds; mysterious effigies of man-birds; haunting funerary masks; and some quieter pieces, almost luminously beautiful.

Mystery of the spheres

The Diquis region is the site of one of the great pre-Columbian riddles. Spheres made of granite, andesite and sedimentary stone have been found in their thousands along river beds and arranged in cemetery sites. Some are as small as oranges while others weigh up to 14 metric tons (16 tons), and measure up to 2 meters (7 ft) in diameter. They are perfectly spherical to within a centimeter or two and are perhaps the finest example of precision stone carving in the ancient world.

The stone spheres are unique – none has been discovered anywhere else in the world. How were they made? How were they shaped to be so perfectly spherical? How were they transported more than 30 km (20 miles) from the source of the stone to the ceremonial sites where they were arranged? And what do they

THE RIDDLE OF JADE

In addition to the enigma of the country's lithic spheres *(see above)*, there is another pre-Columbian riddle in Cost Rica that perplexes historians and archeologists: it is the source of jade for the many pieces found throughout the country. No quarries have ever been found in Costa Rica. Guatemala is believed to be the principal source, although some pieces may have come from Mexico.

Many of the objects appear to have been treasured for years, passed down as heirlooms; others appear to have arrived in one form and to have been re-sculpted to the tastes of their new owners. One interesting theory holds that some of the jade was brought to Costa Rica by pre-Columbian looters of Mayan burial sites, thus explaining the presence of Mayan hieroglyphs on the jade – which apparently had no value or significance to the Costa Ricans.

The Jade Museum in San José has the largest display of jade in the Americas, with over 6,000 pieces. The exhibits are of great variety; notable oddities include a tooth with jade inset and jade breast supports, thought to have been worn by high-ranking women.

mean? Today, they stand mute in their new locations, at the National Museum and in the gardens of expensive homes throughout the Central Valley. You can also see them, undisturbed, in their original habitat, on Isla Caño, near Corcovado National Park.

Gold and cotton

The Diquis region also abounded with gold, which the Amerindians washed out of rivers, or obtained from shallow digs in the savannahs, under groves of trees on hilltops or in the plains. They became experts in the art of goldworking and employed different techniques, including the "lost wax" method, to craft all manner of items: gold headbands, arm and leg bands, collars, bracelets, beads, bells; golden ornaments sewn on clothes; gold tweezers for plucking away unwanted facial hair; gold awls, fish-hooks and needles; gold sheathing for teeth; gold to use on decorative masks.

The people of the Diquis region also wove fine, white cotton cloth, which was used to wrap the dead. Although no archeological evidence has been uncovered since cotton clothing does not survive for millennia, the cloth may also have been sewn into shirts to be worn by both men and women for ceremonial occasions.

Wars, rituals and religion

Taken in isolation, archeological evidence on village life, diet and the arts and commerce of the early Costa Rican people might suggest that life was plentiful, complete and quite idyllic. In fact it was anything but – war was almost continuous.

In the Guanacaste/Nicoya region, wars were unceasingly fought between rival groups to obtain captives, who were perhaps for human sacrifice (and even consumption). Throughout Costa Rica there were wars to capture women and youths for slaves; to obtain the heads of enemies, which were carried as trophies; and to obtain access to new land. Sometimes, as in the Diquis region, men and women warred together. Artifacts and skeletons found in unearthed graves suggest that the dead were honored. Funerals and burials of high-ranking people were elaborate affairs: people of rank

LEFT: an elated Nicoya figure.
RIGHT: stone carving of a female, found at Guayabo.

were buried with riches – and their slaves were sacrificed in order to serve their masters once again in the other world.

Spiritual life

Of their spiritual beliefs little is actually known, although much has been speculated. Phallic images and figures in pottery and stone, emphasizing male and female genitalia, suggest a religion focused on fertility. Fertility rites probably included the music of pottery drums, bone and clay flutes, trumpets, ocarinas, and rattles made of clay or gourds. Large vessels for the fermentation of corn, yucca or

palm fruit suggest ritual inebriation. And there were medicine men – shamans – with vast knowledge of the flora of the forests, who cured illness, forecast the future and dealt with supernatural matters.

The proud pre-Columbian lineages disintegrated with the arrival of the Europeans, who captured their leaders, disrupted their communities, enslaved their people and destroyed their ceremonial and religious articles. Spirited artistry gave way to a lackluster mediocrity, and dynamic spiritual beliefs were replaced by a half-hearted hybrid religion. Little by little, Costa Rica's rich pre-Columbian traditions were all but extinguished. ❏

CONQUEST

*The conquest of Costa Rica followed the sad pattern of much of Central America,
bringing disease, death and slavery in the largely fruitless quest for gold*

When Christopher Columbus set sail from Spain in 1492 on his first voyage to the New World, he was planning to find a group of islands near Japan, which he conceived to be about 2,400 nautical miles to the west of Spain. There, he determined, he would build a great city and trade gold, gems

fort and left 40 men behind to search for gold. He returned to Spain in triumph, with several captive locals.

Columbus was given a grand reception. He was named Admiral of the Ocean Sea and was ordered to organize a second voyage to further explore Hispaniola.

and spices from the Indies with the cities of Europe. He imagined himself as a rich governor, lord of it all.

His ambitions coincided with the interests of the Spanish Crown. The wars to oust the Moors from Spain had depleted the royal treasury. The promise of the wealth of the Indies was attractive indeed.

The voyages of Columbus

The first of his four voyages took Columbus to the Bahamas, where he established the first Spanish settlement in the New World, at Hispaniola, where present-day Haiti and the Dominican Republic are situated. He built a

The second expedition reached Hispaniola only to discover that the 40 settlers had been killed after mistreating the locals. Undeterred, Columbus sailed to the north coast of Hispaniola, where he attempted to establish another settlement.

Leaving his brother, Diego, in charge, he went off to explore for gold. But the settlers fought among themselves and with the Amerindians. Frustrated gold hunters returned to Spain angry; they grumbled about the disappointingly small amounts of gold and the cruelties of Columbus, who, according to historic accounts, was indeed an arrogant commander.

Nevertheless, a third voyage saw Columbus exploring the Atlantic coast of South America and claiming it for Spain. Meanwhile, Hispaniola was seething with discontent. "Not enough gold!" was the cry, and "We can't eat this Indian food!" Columbus tried to placate the rebels, as would his successors throughout Central America, by permitting them to enslave the indigenous population.

But even that measure failed to satisfy many. Large numbers of men returned to Spain demanding back pay and Columbus's head. Columbus was sent back to Spain in chains. Through the intercession of Isabella and

Limón, in a place he called Cariari. There, the local people sent out two girls to welcome the party. In a letter to King Ferdinand, Columbus wrote: "As soon as I got there they sent right out two girls, all dressed up; the elder was hardly eleven, the other seven, both behaving with such lack of modesty as to be no better than whores. As soon as they arrived, I gave orders that they be presented with some of our trading truck and sent them directly ashore."

While in Cariari, Columbus made repairs to his damaged ships – the *Capitania, Gallega, Viscaína,* and *Santiago de Palos* – as the near tideless ocean lapped on beautiful white- and

Ferdinand, he managed to secure his release and set out on his fourth voyage.

The "discovery" of Costa Rica

It was on this voyage, in 1502, sailing up and down the Atlantic Coast looking for a passage to what would later be called the Pacific, that Columbus discovered in Central America the Rich Coast of Veragua.

He spent 18 days in what was later to be called Costa Rica, near the present-day port of

LEFT: ritual drinking vessel.
ABOVE: Nicoyan phallic figure.
ABOVE RIGHT: gold breastplate, Diquis region.

black-sand beaches and coconut trees swayed in the gentle breezes. The respite was sorely needed: a violent storm off the coast of Honduras had caused considerable damage to his ships, and his men, one-third of whom were between the ages of 13 and 18, were sick and exhausted. Columbus himself, at 51 years of age, was almost crippled with the pains of arthritis.

A difficult passage home

The return voyage was difficult. Columbus's ships had been attacked by worms and were battered by foul weather: they were leaking badly. He made it only as far as Santa Gloria,

Jamaica and spent a year there, marooned, unable to get help from the governor of Hispaniola, who was worried that Columbus might usurp his position. There were food shortages and an attempted mutiny, but eventually Columbus and 100 of the original 135 men did return to Spain in 1504, shortly after the death of Queen Isabella.

Columbus spent his final years in increasingly failing health, attempting to secure for himself the governorship, trade and other benefits that had been promised to him by the queen. But the king refused even to see him, and the struggle to attain title, territory and wealth fell to his sons and in turn their sons (Columbus' grandson was finally named Duke of Veragua in 1546), and to the *conquistadores* who followed him to the Americas. As for his spiritual and material heirs, they too were to encounter hardships.

The *conquistadores*

It is tempting to characterize the conquest of South America as a brutal cartoon: greedy, ruthless *conquistadores* bungling explorations, slitting each other's throats for gold, territory or titles; murdering, stealing from and enslaving the peoples of the land.

GOLD FEVER

The Amerindians of Costa Rica, wearing gold mirrors and necklaces, guided the Spaniards around the area, and spoke of great mines of gold, pointing south.

"I have seen more signs of gold in the first two days than I saw in Hispaniola during four years," Columbus wrote to the Spanish king and queen.

Columbus thought he had struck it rich. But the riches he fantasized about never materialized. Costa Rica's gold supply was limited to small surface and river deposits.

The Gold Museum in San José is the country's best, with thousands of different examples of Pre-Columbian gold artifacts *(see page 137).*

It took 60 years from the time of Columbus's arrival at Limón until the first European settlement in Costa Rica was established. The rough terrain, the unfriendly oceans, the extreme weather and a feisty local population all played a large part in the delay. But the continuous, jealous feuding among the *conquistadores* themselves was also a major factor in the failure of the many colonization attempts.

Gold was consistently the big theme. When the *conquistadores* asked the Amerindians about the location of gold mines, they simply pointed south to the fabled mines of Veragua. It gave the Spaniards gold fever. But if the indigenous population really knew where the mines were, they never revealed their location, and to this day the great, legendary mines remain undiscovered. The *conquistadores*, spurning the gold to be found in rivers, had to content themselves with taking the locals' gold, which they did – until there was no more. Then they had to determine how to survive, let alone get rich.

More expeditions

In 1506, two years after Columbus returned to Spain, King Ferdinand sent Governor Diego de Nicuesa and a group of settlers to establish a colony at Veragua. It was the first of many ill-fated attempts to establish settlements.

dian slaves and sending them to work in the mines of Hispaniola, stealing their gold and furiously searching for a passage across the continent to the other ocean. Finally, in 1513, Vasco Nuñez de Balboa, a young stowaway escaping debts on Hispaniola, led an expedition across the isthmus and discovered the Pacific Ocean. It wasn't long before rudimentary shipyards appeared on the Pacific coast to accommodate would-be explorers who had sailed into Atlantic ports then walked across the isthmus, ready to set sail on the Pacific and continue their explorations. The unexplored Pacific had better anchorages, and was thought to have more gold.

Nicuesa's ship ran aground in Panamá and he and his group set about walking up the coast to their destination. Food shortages and tropical diseases were acute; the terrain was devastating. Indigenous peoples along the way burned their own crops rather than yield their food. By the time the settlers finally arrived, their numbers had been halved.

Around this time, expeditions from Spain were landing throughout the Atlantic coast of Central America. They were capturing Amerin-

LEFT: Columbus and *conquistadores*.
ABOVE: the *Pinta* founders in a storm.
ABOVE RIGHT: the Virgin of the Navigators.

The adventures of Gil González

The second inland expedition to Costa Rica was led by Captain Gil González in 1522, and it, too, ended without establishing a settlement. Faulty ships hastily constructed on the Pacific coast of Panamá took on water and forced González and his men to abandon the sea and move forward on foot.

The expeditions of González, which included a walk of 224 leagues (over 1,000 km/600 miles) from the south Pacific coast of Costa Rica to the north, and into Nicaragua, have a mythic quality. At the age of 65 – and suffering from arthritis aggravated by the unceasing rain – González sometimes had to be carried on a litter, but he insisted on completing the arduous trip. González rested for 15 days in the home of the Térraba chief near Boruca. According to his accounts, he baptized some 32,000 of the indigenous people here, collecting golden items of vast value.

He also encountered Chief Diríagen, who appeared out of the blue one day along with 500 Amerindians, each carrying one or two turkeys; 17 women covered from head to foot in gold disks; 10 men carrying standards; five trumpeters and other attendants bringing 200 golden hatchets. The party stopped in front of the house where González was staying, the

was aroused by the enormous amounts of gold González had collected and by González's refusal to give up his claim on Nicaragua. The affair ended with González fleeing Panamá with his treasure.

Pestilence and slavery

The people of Nicoya and Nicaragua were not so fortunate as González, who got away with his life and his treasure. His expedition had brought smallpox, influenza and plague to the area, and tens of thousands of Amerindians died. Survivors of the epidemics faced another danger: enslavement. Indigenous peoples from

trumpeters played and then the chiefs, women and lords entered. When González asked their business, Chief Diríagen replied that they had come to see the men with beards who rode upon strange beasts. Probably Diríagen had come to ascertain the strength of the Spaniards, because three days after his visit, he returned and attacked the Spaniards. It was an attack that González and less than 20 men, at least according to the legend, easily repelled.

González ran into trouble later on with the greedy Pedrarias, governor of Panamá, who was responsible for the deaths of many Spanish *conquistadores*, including Balboa, his own son-in-law, whom he had beheaded. Pedrarias's ire

the Nicoya region, who then lived in large population centers and were vulnerable to such attacks, were captured, branded with hot irons and shipped off to Panamá and Peru to be sold as slaves.

The second attempted Costa Rican settlement was at Villa Bruselas, near present-day Orotina, not far from the large port city of Puntarenas. It lasted only three years and succumbed to feuding among the settlers and Amerindian attacks.

During this period, the *conquistadores* who arrived in Central America were free to exploit the indigenous population in virtually any way they wished. The Spanish policy of *requerimiento*, which went into effect in 1510, permitted settlers to make war on those who did not become baptized, a convenient justification for killing Amerindians and plundering their gold.

Later, *encomienda*, a royal grant from the Crown, gave settlers in Central America the right to force indigenous peoples to labor without compensation – or to demand goods as tribute. It was, in effect, slavery. The Amerindians were re-located to live on the land where they worked, and were considered the property of the grant holder. Without the system of *encomienda*, the *conquistadores* could not realize their aspirations of becoming landed aristocracy. All of the rights and assumed privileges of title had no real value without Amerindians to work the land.

Encomienda was not as widely practiced in Costa Rica as it was in other Central American colonies for a variety of reasons: the Amerindian labor force in Costa Rica was smaller; the Costa Rican Amerindians, outside of the Nicoya area, were not living in as large population centers as were, for example, the Maya of Guatemala. Instead, they lived in smaller, autonomous groups spread throughout the country. Thus the Spaniards weren't able simply to move in and conquer large numbers in a single effort as they had in Mexico.

Moreover, the Costa Rican Amerindians did not adapt well to slavery and fiercely resisted its imposition. Many fought and died avoiding enslavement, and many others fled to the mountains where they could not be followed. Finally, the practice of *encomienda* was abolished well before large numbers of Spanish settlers arrived in Costa Rica.

Church intervention

The Church proved to have an uneasy time with the *encomienda* system. After forceful campaigning by many churchmen, including Friar Bartolmé de las Casas, a former *conquistador*, *encomienda* was abolished in 1542.

This set off violent protests among the settlers, who believed they could not survive without slave labor. In Nicaragua, feelings ran so high that an armed uprising of colonists murdered the bishop who had supported *encomienda*'s repeal. Settlers petitioned the king, arguing that they had invested their lives and possessions, and the Crown had derived much benefit from their sacrifices. To his credit, the king refused.

Repartimiento

Still, the Crown had to support the colonists' need for labor. *Encomienda* was replaced by a system called *repartimiento*, (meaning to divide up) which required all Amerindian men between the ages of 16 and 60 to labor one week of each month for private individuals, religious institutions, municipalities and government offices.

On paper, the system was supposed to provide indigenous peoples with compensation for their labor and leave them free to work their own fields for the remaining three or so weeks of the month. But, in practice, things were very different, and abuses became commonplace.

Locals were required to devote considerably more than a week's labor to the Spaniards, since they had to walk very long distances, sometimes for days on end, from their villages to their places of work. And they were charged for the food and any other goods they consumed – thus using up their miserably small amount of pay.

LEFT: converting the Amerindians with the cross.
RIGHT: Catholic missionaries among the locals.

Years passed and the search continued for the fabled great gold mines of Veragua. But the mines were never found. Spanish *conquistadores* plundered the coastlines, laying claim to whatever booty they could find, capturing local people and enslaving them, and fighting all the while among themselves for claims to the new lands. English pirates appeared on the scene, competing for gold and slaves.

Spain's Central American colonies were

> **DUKE OF VERAGUA**
>
> In 1546, Luis, the grandson of Christopher Columbus, was finally named Duke of Veragua. He set out with an expedition of 130 men to claim his legacy, but he was attacked by Amerindians, lost most of his men and retreated in failure.

conquistadores, since they scarcely ever attempted to escape and return to their homes.

Cavallón also brought along livestock, including horses, cows, goats, pigs, chickens and ducks, to improve the community's chances of success. It was a well-planned and well-financed expedition. Finally, 60 years after Columbus had arrived in Veragua, the first inland settlement in Costa Rica was established. It was christened Garcimuñoz, after Cavallón's place of birth.

developing, with administrative centers springing up in Panamá, Nicaragua and Guatemala. In 1539, officials in Panamá used the name Costa Rica for the first time to distinguish the territory between Panamá and Nicaragua. But still there were no permanent settlements.

In 1559, Phillip II of Spain insisted that Costa Rica be populated, this time well inland. In 1561, Juan de Cavallón arrived with a group of 90 Spaniards recruited from Guatemala and Nicaragua, along with a team of black slaves and auxiliary Amerindians from Nicaragua.

Bringing indigenous peoples from one area to another was a common practice among the

Juan Vásquez de Coronado

Hailed by some historians as the true conqueror of Costa Rica, Coronado moved the Garcimuñoz settlement to the Cartago Valley and thence to El Guarco, and it was there, for the first time, that a permanent community took root. Coronado's tactics with the Amerindians of Costa Rica were different from those of his predecessors. While he fully intended to settle their lands and take what gold he could lay his hands on, he was friendly toward them, he treated them with respect and he requested, rather than demanded, labor and tribute.

Coronado was pressured by his soldiers and the settlers, who weren't particularly interested in peace, to be more aggressive with the indigenous population. The settlers wanted food, gold and labor, or at least the promise of wealth and an easier life. During this time, they were continuously threatening to desert Costa Rica, claiming life was too difficult. Coronado's peaceful strategies were effective, however, and the colony flourished.

Pacification and punishment

Among Coronado's successes was the surrender (pacification, it was called) of a local chief named Quitao. At a meeting of all the chiefs in the area, Quitao announced that he was tired of hiding in the jungles and was ready to submit to the Spaniards. He told the other chiefs they were free to decide for themselves what they would do. The chiefs asked Quitao to decide for them and he replied that they would have to serve the king and his representative. Those who did not go along would be severely punished. Then, as a token of his submission, he sent 150 locals to serve the Spanish, an act that was "cause for great admiration among the Spaniards."

Coronado's chronicles of his explorations through Costa Rica include keen, almost affectionate observations of the Amerindians. In the Diquis region, visiting the Coctu, he wrote of the well-organized and well-developed villages, unlike any he had previously seen. He noted that the people had a lot of gold, which they acquired from tribes on the Atlantic coast and scooped from the rivers, and fine cotton clothing as well. He described them as a very good-looking people, bellicose, skillful in their manners, and very honest, "a thing rarely seen in indians."

It was among the Coctu that Coronado met the "most good-looking indian" he had ever seen, Chief Corrohore, who asked his assistance in recovering his sister, Dulcehe, who had been kidnapped by a neighboring chief. Coronado succeeded and Dulcehe was returned.

The situation was not always peaceful, however. Coronado, known for making peace among some of the warring tribes of Costa Rica, joined them in their wars against one another. There were also Amerindian uprisings in the colony. Returning after an exploration,

Coronado found that all the Amerindians of the area, including Quitao, were at war with the Spanish. (The Spanish had been stealing the locals' corn.) Amerindians in Orosi had killed eight Spaniards and their horses. His old friends, the chiefs Aserri, Currirabá, Yurustí, Quircó and Purirsí, had been made prisoners. In an attempt to calm the situation, Coronado went to speak to the Amerindians and, in a fit of temper, ordered two of them to be dismembered.

The lack of gold, food shortages and indigenous revolts imposed continuous hardships on the settlers. Supplies and new settlers were brought in from Nicaragua, but life was almost

unendurable for the Spaniards. In 1569, settlers demanded indigenous slaves, threatening to abandon the colony if their demands weren't met. Perafán de Ribera, Coronado's successor, a man of 74 years and in frail health, defied Spanish law and permitted the settlers to enslave the locals.

The late 1560s marked the end of the conquest of Costa Rica. By then the majority of the indigenous population of the new colony had been killed, had died of diseases, had submitted to the Spaniards or had fled to the forested mountains of Talamanca. The land was now available to the settlers from Spain to come and make a new life. ❏

LEFT: the return of Dulcehe by Coronado.
RIGHT: Don Juan de Cavallón.

COLONIALISM AND INDEPENDENCE

After years as a forgotten penurious colony that received news of its independence by mail, Costa Rica discovered coffee and launched a fledgling democracy

The Costa Rican colony grew slowly. In 1573, there was a total of 50 families in Cartago, and a fledgling community that would later become San José. Spanish immigrants arrived from Extremadura, in the west of Spain; from Andalucia, in the south, with its strong Moorish influences; and from Castile, the heart of old Spain. The Spanish had also founded colonies on the Pacific coast, at Espiritú Santo de Esparza and Nicoya. Although the population of Costa Rica was slowly growing, life was anything but easy.

Riches to rags

During the conquest, *conquistadores* had loaded their ships and lined their pockets with gold and had sent their obligatory percentages off to the royal treasury, which had swelled with their contributions. But by the end of the 16th century, what little gold there was in Costa Rica was gone. There was little Spanish currency available and it appeared as though there was no way to generate wealth. Cacao beans were used as money and barter became common. Even the few goods the colonists "bought" from Spain were traded for wheat flour, pigs, lard, chickens, tobacco and liquor produced on their farms. Most families lived on isolated farms in the Central Valley, using primitive methods of agriculture. Social and even church life was non-existent, and the populace lived in a state of grim impoverishment.

The forgotten colony

By now Spain was paying scant attention to its far-off colony and even the colonial governor in Guatemala made little effort to acquaint himself with the colony's concerns. It was, after all, a three-month trip from Guatemala by horse, and there was little reason to travel to Costa Rica.

Official neglect had a positive side effect, however. Without large landholdings or plentiful peon labor to work plantations, even Costa Rica's

LEFT: the infamous English pirate Henry Morgan.
RIGHT: Miskito bandits, scourge of the colonists.

governor and the aristocratic Spanish settlers were forced to work their own fields. Despite the gruelling labor, the land at least was fertile, enriched by volcanic ash and irrigated by rivers. Colonists grew wheat, vegetables and sugar, and raised livestock and poultry. Slowly but surely, the seeds of an economy began to take root.

GENERAL PETER SLAM.

The birth of commerce

The first export of the Costa Rican colony was mules. They were walked along the Mule Road to Panamá, where they were sold to hardy souls who needed beasts to bear goods from the Atlantic to the Pacific coast. Later came cacao production on the Atlantic coast, and then tobacco, in the Central Plateau. In an attempt to give Costa Rica a product to export and a dependable income that could be taxed, the Crown set up tobacco-processing plants and granted to Costa Rica sole rights within the colonies to grow tobacco. But Costa Rican tobacco was never of good quality, and there was not a large market for it.

On the Atlantic coast, piracy and slave-trading were the business of the day. The Atlantic waters were continually plundered by English pirates, including Drake, Mansfield, Morgann and Owens; and by French, Dutch and Portuguese buccaneers. They were all attempting to control the territory so they could cross the isthmus, from the Atlantic to the Pacific, and thus avoid the Spaniards in Panamá.

The *Miskitos*

In 1641 a slave ship was wrecked off the coast of Nicaragua/Honduras. The black slaves on board escaped onto the Atlantic coast. Well-

the British-controlled Jamaican governor. (The British and the Spanish were then at war.)

Protection money

By 1779 the pirate situation had gotten so out of hand that the government started paying tribute to the *Miskitos* and leaving them "gifts" of coats made of fine fabric, shiny buttons, or three-cornered French hats, to collect at Matina.

Many years later, in 1841, President Braulio Carrillo refused to continue paying tribute to, or bestow gifts upon the *Miskitos* and threatened to bring the resources of the country to war against them. Probably because cacao produc-

Saqueo y incendio de la Ciudad de Esparza por los piratas ingleses.

A D. Miguel Gómez de Lara sucedió como Gobernador y Capitán General el Maestre de campo D. Manuel de Bustamante y Vivero, nombrado por Real Cédula de 11 de mayo de [?] Tomó posesión el 28 de abril de 1693 y residenció a su antecesor. Este Gobernador era Caballero de [?]

liked by the Amerindians, they intermarried and, over the years, developed an identity and language of their own, named *Miskito*. British pirates joined forces with the *Miskitos*, and together they wreaked havoc along the Atlantic coast of Costa Rica and in the cacao plantations. For the *Miskitos*, the undefended plantations offered little resistance. They sailed in for their biannual raids, took the cacao, captured the black slaves and set off again.

In 1742, after many years of such devastation, the government built Fort San Fernando in Matina, north of present-day Limón. Only five years later, the fort was destroyed by the pirate Owens and the *Miskitos*, under orders of

tion had dwindled greatly by then, the *Miskitos* stopped raiding Matina. Traces of their influence remain in the Atlantic coast area, however, and many of the place names there come from the *Miskito* language, including Talamanca (Talamalka), Sixaola and Cahuita.

Amerindian resettlement

Owing to its mountainous terrain and inaccessibility, the Talamanca region of Costa Rica had escaped the conquest. Groups of indigenous people, some of them refugees fleeing oppressive conditions elsewhere in the country, lived there, undisturbed by the invading Spaniards. However, as more colonists arrived in Costa Rica to clear land, build roads and farm, the paltry size of the available Amerindian labor force became a serious problem. The solution was to begin raids on the Talamanca region. After numerous raids, attempts to conquer Talamanca proved unsuccessful. There were counter attacks and cruel revenges on both sides. Ultimately, hundreds of Amerindians were "re-located" to the Central Valley by the Indian Resettlement Policies of 1747.

Meanwhile, in the Central Valley, growing communities were being established. In 1706, the village of Cubujugui, which later became

Independence – by mail

Costa Ricans like to tell the story of how they received their independence from Spain by mail. In fact, a courier aboard a mule arrived in the Central Valley of Costa Rica with the news on October 13, 1821, nearly a month after colonial officials in Guatemala City had declared independence for Costa Rica from the Spanish Empire.

The news aroused ambivalence, confusion and conflict over what independence meant for the backwater region of Costa Rica. Being the province farthest removed from the colonial capital, Costa Rica came under the least influence of

Heredia, was founded; in 1737, Villa Nueva de la Boca del Monte, now San José, was born; and in 1782, Villa Hermosa, now Alajuela, was settled.

Costa Ricans, living at subsistence levels, were too busy trying to survive to be much affected by the currents of thought and the conflicts that led to Central America's struggle for independence from Spain. The discord that was brewing elsewhere in Central America, fueled by class distinctions and onerous trade restrictions, largely passed them by.

LEFT: English pirates sack a village near the Pacific.
ABOVE: a public beheading in Talamanca.

the Spanish Crown, the Catholic Church, the colonial bureaucracy and the monopolistic Guatemalan traders who dominated colonial life in the rest of Central America. Tucked away in the recesses of the country's central highlands, leaders of the four small communities of San José, Cartago, Heredia and Alajuela began a lengthy debate over what to do next.

Which way now?

Taking their cues from the 1812 Spanish Constitution – written with the participation of distinguished liberal Costa Rican Florencio de Castillo – local leaders drafted their first Constitution, the *Pacto de Concordia,* on December

1, 1821. A split quickly developed over whether or not to follow the lead of other Central American countries in joining Mexican nationalist and emperor Agustín de Itúrbide's Empire, or to opt for total independence.

Leaders of the towns of San José and Alajuela, inspired by the revolutionary ideas that were then sweeping the world, argued for independence, while those of Cartago and Heredia leaned toward the Mexican Empire. There were even those who argued passionately that Costa Rica should become a part of Colombia, at the time ruled by Simón Bolívar.

The disagreements reflected the basic disparity in the respective characters of the cities. Cartago and Heredia had been founded to create Catholic congregations out of the early settlers: these towns evolved into centers of conservative thought and were more closely linked to the Church and the old colonial bureaucracy. By contrast, San José was founded by settlers who were banished from Cartago for defying the strict colonial trading laws on smuggling. Alajuela, too, developed into a fringe agricultural center where the smuggling of tobacco flourished. Both towns developed more free-wheeling, commercially based liberal attitudes than those of their strait-laced neighbors.

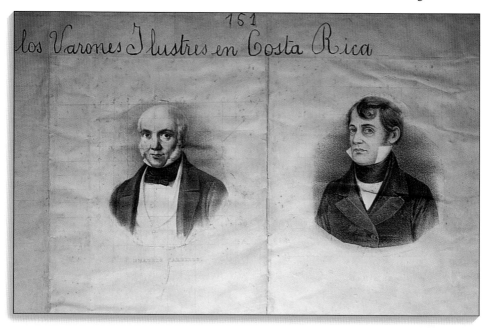

los Varones Ilustres en Costa Rica

THE OLD CAPITAL

The country's first capital of Cartago was founded in 1561 by Juan de Cavallón as Castillo de Garcimuñoz. The site and name were abandoned when Coronado moved all the inhabitants to El Guarco in the Cartago Valley. Then Perafán de Ribera moved it again, to Mata Redonda, near present-day Sabana. Later, the peripatetic city returned to the Cartago Valley, to its present location.

In 1723, Irazú Volcano erupted, covering Cartago in layers of ash. At that time, Costa Rica's capital comprised just 70 houses, a parish church and two shrines. It had no shops, no drug store, not even a resident doctor.

The issue of whether or not Costa Rica would join the Mexican Empire was settled on April 5, 1823. Two armies from the rival cities met in battle on the Continental Divide between San José and Cartago in a skirmish that left 20 men dead. The victorious independence forces, led by a former merchant seaman named Gregorio José Ramírez, took the town of Cartago.

Independence from the Mexican Empire was assured. As it turned out, they need not have bothered: the Costa Ricans belatedly learned that Itúrbide had been declared a traitor several days before the battle, and had been captured and executed. And with him had gone the Mexican Empire.

Farmers and teachers

Gregorio Ramírez set a precedent by relinquishing power in order to return to his farm, an example that would be followed by other victorious Costa Rican leaders. He later returned to put down an army coup, establishing civilian dominance over the military at a very early stage in the country's development.

Statehood was conferred upon a rather ambivalent Costa Rica by the Federal Republic of Central America. This confederation was a noble effort to create a "United States of Central America" out of the five provinces, with a capital in Guatemala City. But it was doomed to

dez distinguished himself by conducting the affairs of state with prudence and humility.

The first printing presses arrived in Costa Rica under Mora Fernández's tenure. By the time his successor, another elementary school teacher named José Rafael Gallegas, was elected, (against his will) in 1833, several newspapers were in print. One of them, *La Tertulia*, published humiliating attacks on Gallegas. Not much interested in the office to begin with, Gallegas resigned as Head of State. One of *La Tertulia*'s major complaints was the social disintegration that had befallen the community as a result of the first modest signs of prosperity

failure because of class disparities and the tenacity with which the elite class clung to the local colonial social order in other parts of Central America.

Costa Rica, on the other hand, was largely a nation of family farmers. It lacked both an elite class and a well-defined social order, so it offered neither great resistance to, nor enthusiasm for, the confederation. As a sovereign federal state, the country elected its first Head of State, Juan Mora Fernández, in 1824. An elementary school teacher, Fernán-

brought on by the planting of coffee, near San José. That limited prosperity brought with it prostitution, gambling and property theft at levels unknown during the more austere colonial era. A strong, no-nonsense authoritarian hand seemed called for, and a San José lawyer, named Braulio Carrillo, was the right man in the right place at the right time.

Braulio Carrillo

Carrillo imposed vagrancy laws, withdrew Costa Rica from the faltering Central American Federal Republic and enacted liberal reforms such as a civil and penal code. He also outlawed the church's right to tithe and earned the enmity

LEFT: 19th-century heads of state.
ABOVE: early 20th-century Nicoya group.

of Central Valley townships by imposing a tax on rural land, using the revenues to build roads and ports. Braulio Carrillo also settled Costa Rica's share of a debt to British bankers that had been incurred by the founders of the Central American Federation. Other Central American countries would have that debt hanging over them until well into the 20th century. The payback of the "English debt" eventually paid dividends in the form of good credit with which to invest in the country's new-found source of wealth: coffee.

The economic power that coffee gave to the citizens of San José, added to Carrillo's reorganizing of the country's institutions around the new source of wealth, caused resentment from the other townships. In 1837, Cartago, Alajuela and Heredia challenged Carrillo and San José in the *Guerra de la Liga*. Emerging victorious from the battle, Carrillo moved the capital permanently to San José.

When his term was up in 1837, Braulio Carrillo left office, only to return in a military

Coffee power

Carrillo had, with unabashed autocracy, reorganized public administration to support the demands of the coffee economy. Serendipitously, in 1843 William Le Lacheuron, an English seaman on his way back home with a cargo of pelts, put in to Puntarenas in Costa Rica in search of ballast for his ship, which had been battered by storms off the Mexican coast. He loaded some 500,000 pounds of coffee into his hold and the Costa Rica–Liverpool connection was established. Thus were the British Isles and, ultimately, the European continent, opened up as an important new market for Costa Rican coffee.

coup the following year, after his successor tried to roll back some of his reforms. Continuing to force the country down the road to a coffee-fueled progress, he proclaimed himself president-in-perpetuity.

General Morazán

By 1842, the new social order created by Carrillo rose up to overwhelm him. Members of the budding coffee oligarchy called on General Francisco Morazán, a hero of the Central American Federal Republic, to free them from what they perceived as Carrillo's despotism. Morazán was welcomed as a liberator when he arrived in Costa Rica, in April of 1842, with an army of 500 mostly Salvadoran volunteers. The head of Carrillo's army, Vicente Villaseñor, met up with Morazán just as the general and his men neared Alajuela on their march from the Pacific port of Caldera, and offered to join forces with him. The *Pacto de Jocote* sealed, Carrillo fell and was forced into exile in El Salvador.

A special assembly named Morazán Provisional Head of the State of Costa Rica. The General received a hero's welcome in Heredia and Alajuela, but received a somewhat restrained and cooler reception in San José.

Morazán wore out his welcome when he attempted to use Costa Rica as a base to revive his moribund Confederation. The General sent missives to the other Central American countries calling for a National Constituent Assembly to revive his dream of a unified Central American nation. He threatened to impose compliance by force of arms. When Morazán tried to conscript Costa Ricans to enforce his ultimatum, the people of San José revolted. After three days of fierce fighting, Morazán was captured and, on September 15, 1842, he was executed in San José's Central Park.

Less than three years later, Braulio Carrillo, too, was to meet a violent end, assassinated in El Salvador. Today, Costa Ricans have mixed feelings about Braulio Carrillo. He is remembered as both a despot and as a strong, sometimes benevolent leader who, perhaps, was the right man at the right time. He forced Costa Rica to break with its colonial past, placing the country firmly, if hesitatingly, on the path to nationhood.

William Walker

In 1855, a Tennessee adventurer named William Walker took control of Nicaragua. One of his aims was to institutionalize slavery there and in neighboring countries so that he could sell slaves to the United States. Certain US industrialists liked the plan and gave support to Walker. The following year, with an army of 300 mercenaries, called filibusters, he invaded Costa Rica, advancing as far as the site of the present Santa Rosa National Park. Walker and his men entrenched themselves in the fortified Santa Rosa *casona* (mansion). Costa Rican

President Juan Rafael Mora, a member of the coffee oligarchy, had been monitoring the threat and had already mustered a force of *campesinos* (farm workers) to repel Walker. The Costa Ricans were numerically superior, though many were poorly armed with little more than farming implements and rusty rifles. On May 20, 1856, they engaged Walker in a 14-minute-long battle and forced him to retreat back toward the Nicaraguan border.

The Costa Rican army pursued them and, at Rivas in Nicaragua, trapped Walker in a wooden fort. A young drummer boy named Juan Santamaría volunteered to torch the fort,

but was shot dead in the process. With the fort in flames, Walker's men were routed and his Costa Rican adventure was over. Three years later, he met his end in front of a firing squad in Honduras. The name of Juan Santamaría lives on in Costa Rican folklore as a youthful hero and symbol of national freedom, and in the country's main international airport, which is named after him.

President Mora was not such a hero. Despite his victory, his domestic policies were not popular. He rigged the elections of 1859, however, to win another term in office. He was deposed, attempted an unsuccessful coup d'état, and was executed. ❏

LEFT: a 19th-century mud-and-wattle home.
RIGHT: statue of Juan Santamaría, Alajuela.

MODERN TIMES

Economic difficulties and the rising tide of reform came to a head in civil war,
but 21st-century Costa Rica became Central America's peace broker

I n 1889, with the drafting of the country's liberal constitution and the institution of a reliable, quadrennial electoral process, Costa Rica entered an era of bucolic prosperity and political stability. Affairs of state were left in the hands of so-called "Olympian" political plutocrats who administered public affairs with a laissez-faire assurance.

The coffee coup

It was not all plain sailing, however. The presumed downward trickle of profits in the coffee economy failed to reach enough people, especially in the neglected urban centers. Faced with the closing of European coffee markets during World War I, Costa Rica's first reformist president, Alfredo Gonzáles Flores, instituted a tax on coffee. This incurred the wrath of the coffee establishment, which backed the president's own army chief, Federico Tinoco, in a successful coup on January 27, 1917. Tinoco assumed the presidency and named his brother, Joaquín, to head the army.

The warrior priest

Popular reaction to the repressive Tinoco dictatorship brought Jorge Volio Jiménez onto the country's political stage with a dramatic flourish. The pious scion of a Cartago coffee family, which bred Costa Rica several presidents, Volio began studying for the priesthood at Belgium's Leuven University in 1903. Heavily influenced by Belgian social Christian thinking, Volio returned to Costa Rica in 1910 to become pastor of the parish of Carmen de Heredia. No simple parish priest, in 1912 Volio denounced the silence of the Costa Rican government over the intervention of US marines in Nicaragua and backed up his words by leading a group of Nicaraguan revolutionaries into battle. He was seriously wounded in the battle of Paz Centro, which took place in southern Nicaragua.

PRECEDING PAGES: volunteer militiamen.
LEFT: young soldiers in a border dispute with Panamá.
RIGHT: animal trophies were once the fashion.

For his military adventure Volio was suspended from the Church, but was later reinstated and assigned to the Santa Ana parish. His passion for social justice led him to more clashes with the conservative local hierarchy, and, in 1915, he left the priesthood to devote himself full-time to working for social change.

As the Tinoco dictatorship became even more repressive, Volio and a handful of other Costa Ricans left the country and formed an armed resistance against the Tinocos, first from Panamá and then from Nicaragua. The revolutionary forces were defeated by government troops led by army chief Joaquín Tinoco in battles near the Nicaraguan border in early 1919. But the Tinoco dictatorship was brought down not by this armed resistance nor by a military one, but rather by school teachers and students who rioted after soldiers marched on them, during a demonstration, in July of 1919. On August 9, 1919, Federico Tinoco resigned the presidency. The next day,

Joaquín Tinoco was gunned down as he walked in the street. The gunman was never identified.

¡Viva Volio!

His military defeat notwithstanding, Volio received a hero's welcome on his arrival in San José and the ready cry "¡Viva Volio!" expressed the hope for change in the country's stodgy political status quo. The title of "General" was subsequently conferred on Volio by the Costa Rican Congress. But much to Volio's consternation, the fall of Tinoco meant a return to business as usual in Costa Rica. Volio established the Reformist Party in 1923, which set

indifference to strife in neighboring Nicaragua, Volio took matters into his own hands and commanded a force across the border to intervene. Concerned as to what an increasingly belligerent Volio might do with his force upon return, Jiménez ordered the General to be intercepted when he arrived in Liberia.

After a gunfight that left two government soldiers and Volio himself wounded, he was apprehended. Volio was then brought back to San José where he was examined by doctors. They diagnosed Volio as suffering from "nervous hypersensitivity." Rather than imprisoning the patriot, Jiménez, in consulta-

an agenda for agrarian reform, decent housing, job security and social protections. During the same year he ran for president on the Reformist ticket against Ricardo Jiménez and Alberto Echandi.

Volio came in a close third in a vote that gave none of the candidates the required majority. A crisis was averted when he agreed to join forces with Jiménez, accepting the vice-presidency and a seat in Congress. But Volio did not see his pact with Jiménez as one of compromise. Instead, he used his seat in Congress to bewilder his fellow congressmen with forceful attacks on the country's upper classes.

When the government once again showed

tion with Volio's family, allowed the General to be taken to Belgium for psychiatric care. Volio's promising political career came to an ignominious end.

The growth of reform

Volio's brand of reformism collapsed with his party, but the reformist movement was important in giving voice to the aspirations of sectors of society on the margins of the agro-export economy. It also inspired young intellectuals to action.

One of those intellectuals was Manuel Mora, who, in his own words, "used to follow Volio around like a puppy dog." Disillusioned with

Volio's political flirtation with Jiménez, Mora split with the Reformist Party to eventually form the Communist Party in 1931.

The Communists immediately made their presence felt in the lowland banana zones. In a strike in the banana zones in 1934, immortalized in the novel *Mamita Yunai* by labor organizer Carlos Luis Fallas, the Communists won wage guarantees and the right to unionize, but only after a heated battle with both government troops and the United Fruit Company.

Meanwhile, plummeting coffee prices during the Great Depression had created additional hardship for a great many Costa Ricans.

Calderón Guardia

The rising tide of reform finally found its champion when, as the economic crisis reached its breaking point, Costa Ricans elected Dr. Rafael Angel Calderón Guardia to the presidency in 1939. Inheritor of his father's humanitarian legacy and backed by the coffee establishment, Calderón Guardia seemed the perfect choice. He won the election with more than 80 percent of the total vote.

Calderón Guardia, also steeped in social Christian doctrine at medical school in

ABOVE: mural in Costa Rica's Museum of Art: *Cultivating the Wild New Country.*

Belgium, carried out reforms beyond the hopes of even the most fervent reformers and the fears of the most entrenched liberal, creating a social security system, a labor code and various other social guarantees.

Costa Rica declared war on Germany and Japan following the attack on Pearl Harbor – a day before even the United States. But Calderón Guardia added insult to injury for the coffee barons by using his wartime emergency powers to confiscate the lands of German families, some of whom had been in Costa Rica for generations and who had intermarried with the oligarchy.

Having alienated himself from the traditional source of political power, Calderón Guardia made common cause with Manual Mora and his Communist Party, and with the Catholic church, led by the socially-minded Archbishop Victor Sanabria. Together they defied the coffee barons and the economic liberals who had dominated Costa Rica since the end of the 19th century and set about expanding the role of the state in providing for people's needs. The nascent bureaucracies would invariably be headed by a member of the Communist Party. Manuel Mora eventually would be named head of the country's army.

When the worldwide anti-Nazi alliances – which made this peculiar Church-State-Party pact feasible – vanished, so too did the wide-based, popular support for Calderón's leadership. As the government clung to power, a disillusioned Mora was paid a visit by an old friend who offered his support. It was the elderly and ailing General Jorge Volio Jiménez.

History has shown that the winners of the ensuing 1948 Civil War, led by José (Don Pepe) Figueres, had no intention of rolling back the social guarantees. Instead, they further institutionalized the legacy of nearly 30 years of reformist struggle. It was a legacy summed up by the immortal cry: "¡Viva Volio!"

The grandfather of Costa Rica

José Figueres is best known abroad for abolishing the army, but Costa Ricans remember him for the way in which he lived his life, and for the heritage of democracy that he created and solidified.

Don Pepe was born of Catalán parents, and for many, that somehow explained his ego, his opinionated, self-righteous, impossibly principled, obstinate, courageous, unyielding, unpredictable self. He was self-educated, and as a young man, he virtually lived in the Boston Public Library, where he became infected with the new and exciting spirit of North American liberalism. He returned to Costa Rica from Boston and New York City in the 1920s with a romantic vision and deeply held belief in the nobility of the human spirit, and hope for social justice for the people of his country.

Until 1942, Don Pepe had no real political experience. Then, on July 2, the *San Pablo*, a United Fruit Company vessel, was sunk by a German submarine in the Port of Limón. All of the Costa Ricans aboard were killed. President

Rafael Angel Calderón responded to the public outcry by imprisoning the German and Italian citizens of the Atlantic region. Two days later, on July 4, a celebration planned to honor the US Day of Independence turned violent. The 20,000 people in San José's Central Park began to riot after a German-educated medical doctor's window was smashed. Looting followed, and the government not only did nothing to control the mob, but also allegedly encouraged it.

In the aftermath of the riots a climate of fear and suspicion grew. Businessmen who had been looted were afraid to seek redress; instead, cowed by fear of further reprisals, they placed paid ads in newspapers asserting their loyalty to

Costa Rica. Don Pepe Figueres blamed Calderón for failing to maintain public order and safety.

Figueres decided to express "what everyone felt but was afraid to say," and purchased radio air time on "America Latina." In strident mocking tones he accused the administration of an inability to govern. His acid denunciation of the government was interrupted mid-sentence as the director-general of the police arrived and hauled him away. The result was, perhaps all too predictably, the making of a martyr and national hero out of the imprisoned Don Pepe Figueres.

The seeds of revolution

Figueres spent the next two years in exile in Mexico. There he began to plan his revenge. Force, he was convinced, was the only way to overthrow the government of Rafael Angel Calderón. Always an avid reader, Figueres continued his personal studies. He formed mutual-help relationships and forged agreements with exiles, intellectuals and revolutionaries from other countries, and he began stockpiling arms.

In 1944, after a particularly violent and discreditable presidential election in Costa Rica – marked by fraudulent ballots, stolen ballot boxes and shootings – Teodoro Picado, Calderón's political successor, was elected president. The fraudulent election, the faltering economy, the Communist presence and widespread official corruption were just too much for Figueres. He returned to Costa Rica in May 1944. Determined to do something about Calderón, he jumped into opposition politics, but felt that the electoral process had been so badly corrupted that he would not run as the

LA LUCHA SIN FIN

Don Pepe founded a farm high in the mountains, to the south of San José, and called it *La Lucha Sin Fin* (The Endless Struggle). It was a success and he used the profits to open schools, libraries, stores, movie houses, soccer fields and medical clinics for local people.

At *La Lucha*, Don Pepe worked at liberating the *campesino* (farm laborer) from ignorance and poverty and attempting to turn some of the Utopian theories he had studied into a workable reality.

The day-to-day way of life on the farm provided lessons that in many ways he was later to apply to all of Costa Rica.

opposition candidate. He once again insisted that only a violent revolution would bring about real change.

In the fateful 1948 presidential elections, Otilio Ulate, publisher of the San José newspaper, *Diario de Costa Rica*, ran against Calderón. Ulate won by a substantial margin, but the *calderonistas* maintained control of congress. There were charges and counter-charges of fraud. And, in the midst of all the violent confrontations, a large number of ballots were set ablaze.

The Electoral Tribunal, which had been entrusted to oversee fair elections, and to which the nation was looking for an electoral verdict, failed to issue one, perhaps in the hope that the candidates themselves would reach a compromise agreement.

With no action forthcoming from the Electoral Tribunal and no compromise possible between the candidates, the *calderonista*-controlled Congress, in an unprecedented act, annulled the presidential election. Ulate was arrested by Picado's police colonel, and his closest advisor, Dr. Carlos Luis Valverde, was shot and died the following day. In San José, businesses were closed and storefronts were boarded up. It felt as though a bomb were ready to go off.

Meanwhile, Figueres was in the mountains near his ranch, *La Lucha Sin Fin* (the Endless Struggle), planning for the coming war.

Civil war

The War of National Liberation began on March 11, 1948. It consisted of a well-planned offensive carried out by men with no formal military backgrounds, who were trained by *guerrilleros* (guerrilla fighters) from the Dominican Republic and Honduras, and armed with guns flown in from Guatemala.

Forty-four days later, 2,000 men, one in every 300 Costa Ricans, had been killed during the violent, sad war of liberation. Figueres' forces were victorious, despite the efforts of the Nicaraguan dictator Anastasio Somoza, and his invasion of the north of Costa Rica. President Picado, who had never really believed an armed insurrection would occur, and who had no heart

for conflict, saw that a swiftly negotiated peace was essential; he announced his surrender.

The Second Republic

Don Pepe Figueres, as both the acknowledged winner of the battle and head of the victorious junta, entered San José five days after the ceasefire and led a triumphant parade. His National Liberation Army, festooned with flowers, marched up Avenida Central to the International Airport at La Sabana. Figueres addressed the people, outlining his goals and fundamental concepts, which he referred to as "the greatest good for the greatest number." More

precisely, he described the four main objectives of what he called his Second Republic: the re-establishment of civic ethics, elimination of the spoils system in public administration, social progress without communism, and a greater sense of solidarity with other nations.

One of Figueres' first acts was to place a 10 percent tax on wealth, a law that was resented, badly administered and, in most cases, evaded by the affluent. He expanded the social security system, enacted full voting rights for all women, created a minimum wage, established low-cost national health care services for all, passed legislation on child support, and proposed nationalizing every bank in the country. The

LEFT: Don Pepe, the country's grandfather *(left)*, and Oscar Arias, the Nobel Laureate *(right)*.
RIGHT: a pensive Don Pepe.

firing of large numbers of bureaucrats and schoolteachers, in an attempt to reorganize government agencies, exacerbated his declining popularity. And then the assets of individuals connected with the Calderón-Picado governments were frozen. Don Pepe's extreme and, to some, arbitrary politics, alienated many. Even the press became hostile to him.

Acceptance of his new vision was very difficult in what was then an atmosphere of mistrust and disharmony. Still, the constitution of 1949, when it was finally accepted by the Constitutional Congress, did reflect many of the goals of the Second Republic. It included political and

brated and memorable achievement, and one that he would point to over and over again. As he liked to explain, if a member of the family is ill, you should call the doctor. But that doesn't mean that the doctor has to continue to live with you for the rest of your life.

In a public ceremony, he delivered the keys of the Bella Vista military fortress to the Minister of Public Education, and told him to convert the old fort into a national museum. Don Pepe knew how to exploit the moment: with photographers standing by, he raised a sledgehammer and symbolically smashed at the wall of the fortress. Figueres supporters considered that

individual freedoms, and added new social guarantees. It established the principle of public regulation of private property and enterprise, and empowered the state to take actions assuring the widest distribution of wealth possible.

But arguably its finest social guarantee was to extend citizenship to everyone born in Costa Rica. This was an important issue to the Afro-Caribbean people of the Atlantic region, who until that time, had been treated as second-class persons.

The end of the military

The new constitution also abolished the military. This was perhaps Figueres' most cele-

THE PRAGMATIC REVOLUTIONARY

The junta of Don Pepe was not universally popular and he suffered criticism from all quarters. He was accused of being a Communist by the right and a Nazi by the left. Indeed, his revolution had received funding from very conservative Costa Ricans; he had accepted military aid from the United States; he had also received armaments from a group called the Caribbean Legion, who had supplied him on the understanding that this revolution was to be the first of a series that would re-create the Central American region and oust many of the dictatorial regimes that had risen to power with the aid of the United States.

dramatic act as a final blow to militarism. His enemies regarded the abolition of the military as a clever move, since lacking the full backing of the military, he simply decided to get rid of it.

Calm before storm

The 1960s and 1970s were essentially peaceful and prosperous decades for Costa Rica. The development of a welfare state and rights bills protecting indigenous peoples were just two of the highlights of a progressive regime. But in 1979, the anti-government Sandinista forces in neighboring Nicaragua toppled the Somoza dictatorship. Costa Rica became a fallback area for guerilla groups and anti-Sandinistas, largely at the behest of the United States, to whom Costa Rica was financially indebted.

Equally bad news, if not worse, was the collapse of both the banana and coffee markets in the early 1980s. Throughout the decade, debt continued to mount and by 1989 Costa Rica was in the red to the tune of a massive US$5 billion.

The silver lining on the cloud hanging over the nation was provided by its president, Oscar Arias, who was trying to mediate a peace settlement in the escalating regional conflicts. By now El Salvador, Honduras and Guatamala were also embroiled in various types of war or disputes. Costa Rica, for all its economic problems, was at least an oasis of peace. In 1987, Arias was awarded the Nobel Peace Prize for his efforts to bring peace to Central America. He also managed to accept millions of dollars of aid for his country from the United States without compromising Costa Rica's neutral position.

A family affair

Despite the success of Oscar Arias abroad, he was voted out in 1990 in favor of Rafael Calderón Fournier, the son of post-war president Dr Rafael Calderón Guardia. Following a lackluster term, he was succeeded by José Maria Figueres, son of Don Pepe, who was, of course, Calderón Guardia senior's arch rival.

An unpleasant legacy of the Calderón era was the El Banco Anglo Costariccense affair. In 1994, just after the president left office, the nation's oldest government-owned bank went

bankrupt, to the tune of more than US$100 million. The legal battles continue to this day.

Sadly, the young Figueres was unable to repeat his father's success or even improve much on the previous miserable administration, and proved to be one of Costa Rica's most unpopular presidents. In 1998 the Social Christian Unity Party (PUSC) won the election under conservative economist Miguel Angel Rodríguez, who pledged to liberalize certain key economic sectors and slash government spending. Despite attracting foreign investment such as the Intel silicon-chip plant, and signing free-trade deals with Canada and Mexico, many Costa Ricans suspected that his

privatization plans for the state-run telecommunication and energy monopolies pointed to corruption. Critics accused his government of lack of transparency, triggering the largest street demonstrations since the 1948 revolution.

In April 2002, PUSC retained power with the election of Abel Pacheco, who has placed much emphasis on tourism as the country's greatest economic priority. The first years of his tenure have been plagued by the departure of disillusioned government ministers and an intransigent, uncooperative Congress. It remains to be seen whether he will manage to stimulate the stagnant Costa Rican economy and its declining banana- and coffee-growing industries. ❑

LEFT: national flag-waving politicos.
RIGHT: former president Oscar Arias, winner of the Nobel Peace Prize, with his family.

COSTA RICA
(THE HEART OF THE AMERICAS)

FOR FURTHER INFO
THE NATIONAL TOURIST BOARD, S
OR ANY TOURIST AND TRAVEL A

WHERE THE WORLD's CHOICEST COFFEE GROWS.

ATION APPLY TO

JOSÉ, COSTA RICA, (CENTRAL AMERICA)

CY OR COSTA RICAN CONSULATE.

SAN JOSÉ – THE WAY IT WAS

Thanks to coffee, San José enjoyed a golden age in the early 1900s. It became the toast of Central America, a bourgeois paradise. But, sadly, it was not to last

In 1737, the authorities ordered the construction of a thatch-covered hermitage on the flatlands of the Boca del Monte. It was to be the centerpoint of a new village to bring together the residents of the area, whose small homes were scattered over the valley. From this humble beginning began the city of San José.

For its first 39 years, it was still just a village, with mud-covered streets and miserable little houses. Then an official ordered the construction of a tobacco factory, and it was from here that the country's tobacco industry monopoly was administered. It proved to be an activity that brought a certain degree of prosperity.

The coffee boom

Tobacco was a short-lived success, as was cacao. But then came experimentation with a new crop: coffee. It grew with such ease and it bore fruit with such abundance that this once-small Central American colony very quickly left behind the squalor that it had known.

England was interested in not only buying this coffee, but also in loaning funds, on account, against the next harvest. The surrounding areas filled quickly with orderly rows of coffee plantations and the people, with their new wealth, sought the life of San José, transforming it into a prosperous coffee-growing center.

Beside the town square there was at first only the Church of Mercy and the Town Council building. But other conveniences, created to serve the foreigners who were beginning to arrive, were soon set up. At the end of the 18th century, the Education Building was erected, as was a cathedral, at the front of which stood a beautiful central park, where both Amerindians and farmers of Spanish extraction held their weekly fairs. Money was minted at the Currency House, and, to support the nascent militia, military quarters were erected.

Social and cultural life

In 1821, Costa Rica gained its independence from the Spanish Empire and became a republic. The small village-town of San José soon grew into a city, then a capital city, and its newly installed authorities struggled to improve the streets, build bridges and open roads to the ports. Guards, armed with rusty muskets, patrolled the brick-layered streets, illuminated at night by kerosene lamps.

In the dance parlors of the bourgeoisie, the quadrille was in vogue. An actor would recite poetry and a young lady would play Chopin ballads amidst conversations concerning the price of coffee in London.

Social and economic life was rigidly defined. The indigenous population was severely depleted; the black community was excluded from the Central Valley and consigned to manual labor. Meanwhile the descendants of the Spanish lived in the central part of town where they built their large adobe houses with corridors opening onto enclosed vegetable gardens.

Cultural life centered around the Mora Theater, where fourth-rate companies would perform, along with jugglers and an occasional virtuoso musician. The ladies would sit and listen, dressed in their regal dresses, while the gentlemen stood around, robed in their Spanish capes, smoking and engaging in small-talk concerning politics.

Foreign visitors would stay in a rooming house and venture forth to see the town's sights. Some considered the possibility of entering the coffee-export business and others idly took notes for their travel diaries.

The European influence

Earnings from the export of coffee engendered an illustrious bourgeoisie. The members of this

Ever grander plantations were created in an effort to stay ahead of their competitors.

Costa Rican architects visited the Universal Exposition of Paris in 1900 and, along with other new and imported ideas, brought back metal buildings for schools. They imported finely wrought metal plates for walls, steel columns, building crests, and Italian mosaics. The homes of the coffee growers soon began to look like the mansions of the wealthy in New Orleans and Jamaica: French adobe walls; wide, inclined roofs; ornate verandahs with white balustrades and woodwork cut in the style of gingerbread. Jalousies and shades pro-

class traveled to France to have their children educated in Europe. When home in San José, the children missed the theaters, the boulevards, the cafés and the fine architecture of Europe. As they grew up, they insisted on improving the appearance of their native capital city. As coffee production engendered greater prosperity, the leading planter families increased their investments, which led to rivalries among them.

PRECEDING PAGES: an early attempt to lure tourists.
LEFT: downtown San José was conceived as a handsome place of fine buildings and grand statues.
ABOVE: First Avenue, San José, during the early years of the 20th century.

EARLY IMPRESSIONS

A German scientist, visiting during the mid-19th century, wrote: "There is not a building that calls attention for its beauty. The government buildings, the garrison and its gallery, the university and the theater are insignificant structures. The cathedral has an air of negligence and economy. There aren't even any chairs. The president of the republic has to sit with his followers on a wooden bench." By contrast a French journalist noted: "The presidential palace is an enchanting square building with an internal half-Spanish, half-Arab patio. A circular stair led to the congressional room where a ball was staged for me."

tected the windows made of colored glass through which the brilliant tropical sun shone.

The city's golden age

Toward the end of the 19th century, Monsieur Amon Faiseleau Duplantier, who received the concession to establish the streetcar system, divided his farm on the sunny slopes of the Torres River and there began the business of real-estate sales. He was successful and the best of San José society fought for the urban lots, building mansions, a few of which still survive in Barrio Amón. Soon the coffee plantations were replaced with tree-shaded streets and

the shape of a horseshoe was financed from the national budget and by a tax paid by the rich coffee growers.

By the early 1900s, the village had given way to a glowing city, which, even if it did not attain the elegant, urbane layout to which it aspired, developed a comfortable lifestyle permitted by its growing prosperity.

If the early European critics of Costa Rica had looked in the crystal ball and foreseen the amenities of San José at the turn of the 20th-century, they would surely have remained. In front of the theater was the elegant Hotel Français. Nearby, the Petite Trianon was a coffee

stately residences with large gardens. Meanwhile, Minor Keith, who was occupied with developing The United Fruit Company and the railroad system to the Atlantic coast, finished the Atlantic Railroad station in San José. At the same time, Mother Superior Barthelemy Rich was opening her prestigious girls' high school, *Colegio de Sión*, where the daughters of the bourgeoisie received their education.

On October 19, 1897, the president and a select audience entered the wide doors of the National Theater to inaugurate the building. That opening night featured a magnificent presentation of the opera *Faust*. The sumptuous building with its four levels and a floor plan in

house favored by high society, artists and diplomats; a little beyond, the windows of the Golden Eagle were filled with French wine and liquors and Spanish preserves and fine oils. *Talabarteria Inglesa* and *La Tiendita* satisfied the most demanding tastes in matters of decoration and leatherwork.

The Ford agency exhibited its 1912 model, which was priced at US$975. It competed with a number of other import agencies, along with booming real-estate businesses that offered farms, lots, beaches and Victorian residences. The streetcar ran to the limits of the city carrying great numbers of merchants, their employees and office workers.

The other side of the tracks

Not all members of San José society enjoyed a rose-colored lifestyle. The city had expanded too rapidly, with vast, obscure and sad suburbs encircling older areas. World War I and the accompanying fall in coffee demand and prices brought wide-scale unemployment to those that had previously been able to live relatively well, along with salaries that fell below the poverty level. The Society of Casas Baratas began the construction of workers' housing units of the type known as *puerta ventana*, where several families would cram in narrow and poorly ventilated rooms.

End of an era

Under the pick and sledgehammer, the magnificent National Palace, the Garrison, the National Library, the Union Club and many lovely residences disappeared. The city extended its arms beyond the suburbs; the inner city lost its sense of identity and was invaded by mediocre commercial constructions. Fast highways opened up and North American influence began to replace elegant European ideals.

San José spilled over and outward in a random fashion. Cars permitted the wealthy classes to move their residences from what had now become the depressed inner city to the

To the south and near the railroad station to the Pacific, there soon appeared barracks, warehouses and factories, where soap and candles were made. An industrial zone with beer factories, ice-making factories, printing presses, mechanics' shops and lumber mills slowly began to surround and envelop the elegant urban center. With the advent of cement structures, the arrival of the new rich, and the industrialization of the city, there also came the desire to modernize, to create new statements and to destroy the past.

LEFT: San José, around 1928.
ABOVE: the leisured class at home.

desirable suburbs of Escalante, Los Yoses, Curridabat, Paseo Colon, Sabana and Rohrmoser. By the 1960s, several satellite town centers evolved, resembling the style of suburban North America.

Certainly San José would no longer win a prize as the most beautiful Central American city. But it still possesses a certain charm. You won't find the monumental scale of Guatemala City nor the cosmopolitan quality of Panamá City; yet there is a vital quality to the hustle and sheer movement of the place, along with tangible remains of the coffee-growing bourgeoisie and their neo-classical architecture and whimsical Caribbean-colonial style. ❑

THE PEOPLE OF COSTA RICA

Costa Ricans, or Ticos, *come in all shapes, sizes and colors.*

"We are all Ticos," is the proud claim, though some Ticos *fare better than others*

Racially and ethnically, Costa Rica is not a simple place. Along with the overwhelming majority of Spanish-heritage *Ticos*, there are four other distinct ethnic groups. The people of Guanacaste have dark skin, resembling their Nicaraguan neighbors in manner and accent. In the southern, mountainous regions of the country, the Amerindians of Costa Rica, who were here long before the Spanish, belong to six discrete linguistic groups. Though they increasingly speak Spanish, they still debate whether it is more important to retain their indigenous cultural identity or to assimilate more into mainstream Costa Rican culture.

The blacks of the Atlantic Coast are the country's largest immigrant minority; they speak Caribbean-accented English and talk with pride of their Jamaican heritage. Sino-Costa Ricans are called *Chinos*. Descendents of indentured laborers, they own many of the bars, restaurants and stores, especially in small towns.

All these different races are *Costarricense*.

Indigenous people

Archeologists, using very different methods of calculating populations, estimate that anywhere from 30,000 to 400,000 native people lived in Costa Rica when Columbus arrived. Today, about 63,000 native people remain, although it is hard to establish an accurate figure since many indigenous people have had mixed marriages.

The history of the Amerindians of Costa Rica is much like that of other indigenous peoples of the American continent. The Europeans brought diseases to which the native populations had no immunity. Entire tribes were obliterated before they had even seen a white man.

In pre-Columbian times, the Chorotegas, cousins of the Nicaro, inhabited Guanacaste and the Nicoya Peninsula. They lived in patrimonial groups, grew corn and were culturally similar to groups from southern Mexico. These peoples were devastated during the Spanish Conquest by disease and by slave traders who shipped them off to Panamá and Peru. Their surviving descendants are today mostly integrated into contemporary Costa Rican life.

Other native groups spoke dialects originating in Colombia. They were divided into clans,

PRECEDING PAGES: Carnival time; ox-cart painter.
LEFT: *campesino* cultivating onions.
RIGHT: a young and carefree Afro-Caribbean boy.

A PROUD PEOPLE

"The blood that flows in the veins of the people of this Republic is too generous. The Costa Ricans are a people of such excellent mettle; ardently patriotic, they are very proud of their independence, their autonomy, and of a prosperity due almost wholly to industry. The country is one of flourishing villages. There it is that the population of Costa Rica dwells, since it is there that are found the hardy toilers who wrest from the earth the products which form the wealth of the land. An air of ease combined with antique simplicity characterizes these villages."

A.S. Calvert, *A Year of Costa Rica,* 1901

which the Spanish gave names to, and their original names are mostly lost to history: the Guaymí, for example, call themselves Ngabe, pronounced Nobe. The other clans were named the Terraba, the Boruca and, in the Talamanca mountains, the Bribri and Cabecar. These people lived in matrilineal societies in clearings in the jungles. With the coming of the Europeans, many of them fled to the almost inaccessible jungle regions of the southern mountains. Much of their culture has been preserved by their descendants, who still speak their original languages and live in the remote regions of the Talamanca mountains.

food, as well as images of the First World to these people who live without electricity and running water. The cultural imperialism of the airwaves is persistently penetrating the world of people who have resisted the *conquistadores* for 500 years. Among the young, the temptations of this high-tech world are enticing and the desire to assimilate strong.

Today, indigenous peoples live on reserves designated for their use in 1971. By law, non-native people cannot own land inside these areas, but this has been difficult to enforce and non-Amerindians have moved into these territories, which happen to contain a significant

Despite the influence of Christian missionaries, many native people have not forsaken their animistic religious traditions. The Bribri call their deity "Sibu" and use shamans, with their vast knowledge of the rainforest's medicinal herbs, to cure a range of illnesses. Farther south, along the Panamá border, the Guaymí live in their traditional areas, which span political boundaries.

Modern temptations

No matter how remote their jungle reserves, the Amerindians are still not insulated from contemporary culture. Battery-powered televisions bring pressure to consume soft drinks and junk

THE *TICO* SPIRIT

Costa Ricans call themselves *Ticos* in a reference to their common use of the diminutive ending: "*Un momentico, por favor.*" There is a sweetness to the way in which they speak Spanish.

Ticos are politically temperate, shy and unaggressive, yet, today more than ever, they are actively democratic. Once it was only a game; more of a pretense, a love of the rules and trappings of democracy. "Hey, look at me, I voted!" Today, it is stronger, more involved, more functional, more passionate. Demonstrations, protests, strikes, rallies and caucuses are common. Yet the people remain mostly prudent, respectful and discreet.

proportion of the country's mineral wealth. Encroaching contemporary society threatens indigenous peoples' language, cultural identity and way of life. Caught in time between two worlds, slowly relinquishing the old, but not yet embracing the new, native peoples are extremely vulnerable. In the 500 years since the European conquest, little has changed for the aboriginal Costa Rican people.

Black settlers

As early as 1825, Afro-Caribbeans came to Costa Rica to fish, hunt turtles and market coconuts. These immigrants were part of a

Indies came to work on building the Atlantic railroad. They proved more successful than previous laborers imported by Keith in their ability to tolerate the working conditions, which included exposure to yellow fever, malaria and poisonous snakes, as well as severe physical labor and oppressive management. The maltreatment of workers in the banana fields of the Atlantic United Fruit Company is well-documented. But the blacks were certainly not invulnerable and they, too, died in their thousands while building the tracks, the endless numbers of bridges, the docks and the wide, rectangular streets of the port city of Limón.

migration from the West Indies to the Central American Atlantic coast. From Panamá to Honduras, they came looking for ways to support themselves. Many were transient. One man might harvest cacao in Limón, then find employment on the barges in Nicaragua and next labor on the construction of the Panamá Canal; they went where there was work.

In 1872, under contract from Minor C. Keith, who was later to become the founder of the United Fruit Company, blacks from the West

Other Afro-Caribbeans came to the Atlantic coast on their own, looking for any kind of work to escape the poverty of their native islands. Some ultimately were given land along the railroad right-of-way and others, thanks to their command of English, rose from the ranks of laborers to become managers in the banana business. Most originally planned to earn whatever they could and then return to their islands.

When United Fruit left the Atlantic region and moved to the Pacific coast, the blacks were left behind, unemployed. Many emigrated for the same reason that had motivated their parents to immigrate to the country in the first place: they were again seeking work. Those

LEFT: *pipas* – drinking coconuts for sale at a roadside stand in Limón province.
ABOVE: Puntarenas schoolboys.

who stayed behind lived for the most part at subsistence level, producing what they could from small plots of land. They retained their English language and their Protestant religion, remaining proudly separate from the Hispanic Costa Ricans and enriching these coastal communities with a distinct Afro-Caribbean flavor. At the same time, they endured racist immigration and residency laws that restricted their movement until the middle of the 20th century.

When the Constitution of 1949 declared that anyone born in Costa Rica had automatic citizenship, doors finally opened for blacks. They were allowed to travel outside Limón province

two-sided racism that exists. Blacks usually consider themselves more civilized and superior to Hispanic Costa Ricans, while Hispanic Costa Ricans sometimes insist that blacks are racially inferior.

Today, less than 5 percent of the total Costa Rican population is black, and less than 25 percent of the population of the Atlantic coast is of black ancestry.

The construction of the railroad to the Atlantic coast brought other waves of immigrants during the late 19th century. Among the builders, managers and technicians of the Northern Railway Company were English, Irish

and they began to attend public schools and enter politics. When, in the 1950s, the value of cacao soared on the international market, many of the squatter-farmers were able to achieve a certain prosperity. And, in an ironic reversal of historical patterns, they hired Hispanics to work their fields.

Many members of the subsequent generation of blacks were well educated and, preferring professions to farming, left the Limón area. Indeed, many left Costa Rica entirely to find jobs elsewhere. Some middle-class, educated blacks who remained in Costa Rica married Hispanics, but their assimilation into Costa Rican society is not total, owing to the curious,

ORIGIN OF THE SPECIES

Tradition holds that most Costa Ricans descended from hard-working rural Spanish farmers; that they came from good, simple, unpretentious, egalitarian stock.

Yet among colonial immigrants to Costa Rica from the Iberian peninsula there were also Spanish Jews and Arabs, Catalans and Basques, as well as a great many people from the Middle East.

Then in the 19th century, lured by the promise of coffee prosperity, German and English settlers set up import-export trades, while Lebanese, Turks and Polish Jews became powerful local merchants. Clearly these were no simple agrarian folk.

and North Americans. But the largest group of immigrants, apart from the Afro-Caribbean workers, were laborers from southern China, who joined the blacks on the railroad, essentially as slaves, but euphemistically referred to as "indentured workers."

Chinese immigrants

The first Chinese to set foot in Costa Rica were 77 indentured servants, in 1855. Almost 20 years later, despite the existence of a law against the permanent settlement in Costa Rica of African and Asian

> **BLOOD ON THE TRACKS**
>
> After 4,000 West Indians died during the laying of the first 32 km (20 miles) of the Atlantic Railroad, businessman Minor C. Keith simply imported another 10,000 laborers.

lowed the first railroad workers benefited from those who were already established. Through work contracts and credit assistance from other Chinese, they set up commercial ventures along the railroad, in the port cities and in growing rural communities throughout the country. Their small-scale businesses required little capital investment, only a minimal acquaintance with the language, and allowed all members of the growing family network to become involved in tending the business. Chinese family traditions upheld

races, contractors for the Atlantic railroad imported "one thousand healthy, robust Chinese of good customs and addicted to work." These two groups were to become the founding fathers of the Chinese colony of Costa Rica.

Those contracted by the railroad left as quickly as they could escape, to work as cooks and domestic servants. As their fortunes improved, Chinese immigrants set up small eateries, groceries and liquor stores. The steady trickle of Chinese immigrant laborers that fol-

---

LEFT: the younger generation.
ABOVE: the ubiquitous Costa Rican *pulpería* (neighborhood store) and its proud owner.

the authority of elders and reinforced an already strong generational hierarchy. Well-defined divisions of labor, plus a strong work ethic, ensured that their businesses flourished.

Chinese colonies, headed by businessmen's associations, evolved into strong business groups in the cities and towns of Costa Rica. By the beginning of the 20th century, a number of Chinese immigrants had become wealthy, and were then able to sponsor the immigration of other family members and acquaintances.

Among the first generations of Chinese to settle in Costa Rica, many men lived with local Costa Rican white women, while retaining marriages established in China with childhood brides. The money they sent to China was often used to finance family enterprises back home.

In the last century, the successful Sino-Costa Rican businessman traveled to China to oversee his holdings, raise a family and invest toward retirement in the home of his ancestors. During his absence from Costa Rica, his business was managed by close younger kin.

With the Communist takeover of mainland China in 1949, return to their ancestral homeland became less attractive, and most Sino-Costa Ricans forsook any hopes of a permanent return to China.

Many among them have married Hispanics, and faced opposition from their parents and ostracism by the Chinese community. Nevertheless, they have retained venerable family traditions that express Chinese values of ancestral wisdom and family solidarity.

Many young Sino-Costa Ricans have now joined the ranks of the professionally educated; although they are doctors, lawyers, engineers, business administrators and university professors, many still continue to also oversee the family businesses that allowed their ancestors to achieve economic success in Costa Rica.

More recent events also reinforced this influx from the East. The prospect of the British colony of Hong Kong being transferred to Chinese hands caused a steady flow of Asian immigrants from Hong Kong as long ago as the 1970s. Today, 1 percent of the total population in Costa Rica is Chinese, and there are more than 250 Chinese restaurants in the San José area alone.

Those Chinese born of mixed Costa Rican-Chinese families consider themselves full members of Costa Rican society, identifying heartily with its ways and traditions, while, at the same time, expressing a strong sense of devotion to their immigrant forefathers.

The Italians

The Atlantic railroad had serious difficulties retaining Chinese laborers. In an attempt to find an alternative working force, in 1888 it imported 1,500 "good, humble, thrifty Italians of a superior race". The disagreeable working conditions soon led the Italians to leave the railroad project. Many remained in Costa Rica, and in the 1950s they were joined by an influx of Italian farmers who settled in a government-sponsored colony, San Vito, in the southern Pacific region of Costa Rica.

Today, San Vito still has a distinctive Italian flavor: there is a Dante Alighieri Society; there are a dozen shoe stores in town, as well as *pas-*

ticcerias serving Italian *gelato* and pastries. More recently, entrepreneurial Italians have come to Costa Rica to open restaurants and hotels all over the country, bringing a dash of style and culinary gusto.

The *gringo*

They are unmistakable in San José, their heads sticking out above the throng of people crowding the chaotic city sidewalks. *Gringos*, fairer and usually taller than the locals, easily catch the eye. A pejorative term in much of Latin America, *gringo* is a much milder moniker here, applied not only to US citizens but also

In the 1950s, Quakers from the United States came to Costa Rica looking for peace. They found it in the cloud forest of Monteverde, where they formed a community dedicated to a life of harmony with the land. They created a successful dairy and cheese industry, which today supplies much of Costa Rica's specialty cheese market.

Since the 1960s, Costa Rican laws favoring North American and European retirees have led to the establishment of a large number of comparatively wealthy *gringos* in the Central Valley area. These retirees, recently estimated at more than 35,000, are officially called *pensionados*,

to Canadians and Europeans. They have been coming to Costa Rica for a long time. Early in the 19th century, attracted by the promise of wealth from coffee, French, German and British entrepreneurs, along with teachers, scientists and professionals came to Costa Rica. Many married Costa Rican women, and most became thoroughly assimilated into the aggregate of *Tico* culture. Today, many powerful families in the arts and politics bear British or German surnames.

LEFT: growing old in Costa Rica.
ABOVE: shining sisters of devotion at a town fair in Guanacaste province.

non-nationals living in Costa Rica with a guaranteed monthly income. They come to Costa Rica for the warm climate and for the higher standard of living their dollar affords them.

Effects of tourism

The most dramatic influx of people today is the result of the country's flourishing tourism industry. Environmentally concerned young people come to carry out ecological work. For them the country is a laboratory, a place where the viability of living in harmony with the environment can be demonstrated to the world at large. Their arrival has stimulated major changes in the country's environmental awareness.

A large cadre of biologists, botanists and scientific researchers has had a huge impact on both the academic world in Costa Rica, and on research efforts into conservation.

While Costa Ricans are proud to show off their beautiful land, tourism often has a downside: the small landowner may lose his land for a biological reserve; dairy farmers can't afford to buy fresh pasture because property speculation has driven prices sky high; cattle ranchers without enough water

> ### LIMÓN CARNIVAL
>
> Chinese participation in the social life of the towns they settled is nowhere more in evidence than at the Limón Carnival, when the traditional Chinese dragon snakes its way alongside flamboyantly costumed Caribbean dancers.

Latin American newcomers

More recently, Costa Rica has become a safe haven for those fleeing violence, wars and economic problems: during the past couple of decades, onerous political conditions and deteriorating economic circumstances in their home countries have brought significant numbers of South Americans to Costa Rica, including educated Chileans, Argentinians, Uruguayans and Colombians. These groups have greatly enhanced Costa

for their livestock in the dry season watch as huge resorts build water-hungry golf courses. Profits often flow abroad to large hotel groups, and promised local benefits often amount to little more than the modest wages of waiters, hotel maids, gardeners and pool attendants.

Sustainable tourism, which benefits the local community, has become the watchword of both international conservation organizations active in Costa Rica and the Ministry of Tourism. A program that awards "green-leaf" status, according to the eco-friendliness of hotels, has been successful, along with the Bandera Azul (Blue Flag) program that promotes clean beaches around the country.

Rica's cultural sensibilities over the past 20 years. For example, the exceptional *Teatro El Angel* was virtually transplanted to San José, along with numerous dissidents, all fleeing Pinochet's dictatorship in Chile.

Absorbing poorer, more desperate illegal immigrants, especially from Nicaragua, has caused undeniable difficulties, though in general the country has accepted newcomers with a mix of grace and tolerance *(see box on Ticos and Nicas, page 77).*

Ticos today

A Latin American writer recently observed: "The problem is that the Costa Rican looks too much to the North. He should be looking to the South." But even if he did, the *Tico* would insist that he is different from most Latinos because of what he sees as his "whiteness," or European heritage. Just go to Guatemala, Panamá or El Salvador, and observe the differences. These countries are only short distances away but the Costa Rican is as different from these other Latin people as, say, the Swiss is to the Italian, or the German to the Dane. Costa Ricans revel in the difference and are unabashedly proud of it.

INVASION OF THE ANTS

Even today, the native tribes refer disparagingly to the white man as *"hormiga"* (ant), a creature that wipes out everything in its path.

from people in other Central and South American countries, yet they notice it in subtle ways. Perhaps it's because Costa Ricans have acquired the curious and skillful art of being poor and not showing it. Cardboard shanty towns that dominate the cityscape of other developing countries are less evident here. People seen on the streets of the towns and cities are, more often than not, well-dressed. Homeless people are not omnipresent as they are in other Latin and Asian countries, and, indeed, in many large US cities.

Grace under pressure

Costa Ricans have a graceful sense of the universal corruption that surrounds them. They shake their heads, lamentably acknowledging it. They know that almost endless problems beyond easy resolution abound. But despite some skeptical complaining they express confidence that their government is the most honest in Latin America.

Travelers to Costa Rica find it difficult to identify just how different Costa Ricans are

---

LEFT: heady blossoms off to market; melon seller at the 10th Avenue open-air market in San José.
ABOVE: *boyero* ("cowboy") with his Brahman oxen.

Small-town family life

To fly to Costa Rica, leaving behind the numbing babble of Los Angeles or the crowded bustle of western European cities, and to head for a small town here is like leaping backwards to an earlier time. But it is not an earlier time by North American or even European standards; it is somewhere more idealized and more precious.

In the villages and small towns of Costa Rica there is a connectedness, a familial unity. The family is still the main focus here. Young people live at home well into their twenties and thirties, and some even stay home after marrying. The pressure of life in the cities is essentially at odds with this national character. San José can feel unreal at times, as though it is out of place and time, because it represents a basic contradiction to Costa Rican ideals. So many *Ticos* live in and around San José, yet Costa Ricans are much happier living and working in a village or a small town surrounded by a familiar community.

US influence

Because the United States is by far the richest neighbor in the hemisphere, and the most powerful broadcaster of image and ideology, Costa Rica knows a great deal more about the United

States than the United States knows about Costa Rica. *Ticos* know the names of sports figures, actors and actresses, television personalities, musicians and politicians from the USA. And they know the strange collection of fact and fallacy that viewers derive from watching satellite-relayed North American television shows and subtitled Hollywood movies.

Increasingly, a bilingual education is the key to success for young *Ticos*, many of whom will have careers working for branches of foreign companies.

Costa Rica welcomes foreign investors. There are duty-free zones, tax-free incentives to foreigners setting up industry, and other incentives to build tourist facilities. Several government institutions exist to encourage people to come and view the marvels of the country and to invest here.

A fragile world

Costa Rica is fragile, book-ended by politically volatile Nicaragua and Americanized Panamá. Foreign investors buy whatever appears profitable; political and economic refugees come in from other parts of Central America; and drug dealers infiltrate the shores and ports of this relatively violence-free country.

Yet somehow you feel that Costa Rica will endure. Though Costa Ricans may not be perfect, they are essentially a democratic, benevolent and peaceful nation. There is a kind of strength in their fragility. After coming to visit, many people from all over the world are inspired to do whatever they can to ensure the survival and intelligent growth of this vulnerable country and its peaceable people.   ❏

HEALTH AND EDUCATION

The standards of health and education in Costa Rica are anything but Third World. In 1920, infant mortality was nearly 26 percent. Today it is less than 2 percent. A century ago the annual mortality rate was 41 per thousand. By 1944 it had dropped to 18 and today it is less than four.

According to a United Nations report in 2002, the average Costa Rican man lives to be over 75 years old, on a par with the average US citizen and several European nations.

This is not sheer luck, or just the quality of the air they breathe; without the burden of supporting any armed forces, Costa Rica is able to invest around 10 percent of its GNP on health care. The public system, accessible to all, is starting to show some wear and tear. But the quality of care is so high, especially in the private sector, that it is said even Beverly Hills residents come here for their plastic surgery and dental work.

Costa Rica is also an exceptionally literate nation, which claims 95 percent literacy across the population aged 10 and over. Again, this is a figure that compares favorably with the US and many European nations.

The country has always been progressive in electing teachers to high political posts and, in 1869, it was the first country in the world to make education both mandatory and free of charge.

Ticos and Nicas

Costa Rica's poor stepsister, Nicaragua, reminds *Ticos* of what their country's fortune could have been, given slightly different geographical and political conditions.

An estimated 500,000 Nicaraguans (although some action groups suggest up to a million) fleeing nearly 70 percent unemployment and harsh living conditions in their home country, work in Costa Rica, many of them illegally. Most form part of the country's growing informal sector, with low wages, under-the-table payments and no access to the country's socialized health service. Many work as maids, gardeners or construction workers, or sell snacks or trinkets in the streets. The sugar cane and coffee industries depend on Nicaraguan workers for their harvests. Perhaps it is not surprising that they are prepared to work for such low wages when you consider that the average per capita income in their own country is just US$430 per year, the lowest in the Western hemisphere.

Not all Nicaraguan refugees are poor, however. Middle- and upper-class supporters of the Somoza regime came in the 1980s seeking refuge from Nicaragua's civil war. Many run successful businesses.

When former president José María Figueres signed an accord in mid-1997 allowing all Nicaraguans in the country a five-month window to apply for work permits, thus obtaining health and other benefits, lines of applicants at the Nicaraguan embassy stretched around the block.

Always a troubling issue in Central America, the immigration debate became more polemic when the US adopted a harsh immigration law in early 1997. Though the law was later toned down and mass deportations avoided, thousands of Nicaraguans chose Costa Rica instead of the US as their destination in the search of a better life.

In March 1998, 29 Nicaraguans drowned when their overladen boat *El Cairo* overturned on the choppy waters of Lake Nicaragua, many of them on their way to Costa Rica to seek employment. Later that year Nicaragua suffered two terrible blows – after drought caused the loss of 40 percent of its crop, Hurricane Mitch hit Central America and approximately 3,000 Nicaraguans perished. The government estimated that 870,000 people were directly affected and it cost the country US$1.5 billion. A huge number of illegal immigrants fled to

Costa Rica, which, although hit badly by the hurricane, had not suffered such catastrophic losses.

Immigration officials of the southern Nicaraguan port of San Carlos estimate some 5,000 people enter Costa Rica illegally each month. The two countries share a 320-km (200-mile) border and the Costa Rican authorities have tried to stem the flow by tightening migration controls in the north.

Shanty towns full of Nicaraguan immigrants ring the capital, and many squat, rent or own farms in the Northern Zone. *Ticos* are often prejudiced against their northern neighbors, who are stereotyped as "dirty," and are unjustly accused of committing crimes. Further, "Nicas" are often blamed for the perceived social

decline of the country and for putting a burden on the health service, schools and the workplace, when in reality the immigrants are doing the work many *Ticos* refuse to do, and without them coffee, banana and sugar production would be devastated.

Thick-accented and darker-skinned than most Costa Ricans, who like to forget that the province of Guanacaste was once part of Nicaragua, *Nicas* are generally quieter and more serious than *Ticos*. They are also hard workers and many people prefer to hire Nicaraguans as domestic help. Nicaraguans also bring with them a love of poetry and music, and a tradition of camaraderie. Often it is desperation that drives so many Nicaraguans to leave their homeland and loved ones, and risk everything to come to a land where they are not wanted. ❑

Left: cellist of the National Symphony Orchestra, San José. **Right:** Nicaraguan mother and child.

NATIONAL PARKS

With so much of its land under protected status, Costa Rica is the flag bearer for the forces of conservation. But, while many battles have been won, the war goes on

An astonishing 27 percent of Costa Rica is designated as national park, biological reserve, wildlife refuge or some other category of protected area, both private and public. Increasingly, individuals and groups are purchasing tracts of Costa Rican wilderness in order to preserve it. And so, more than a quarter of the country has been set aside in some capacity or other by human beings to protect it from the potential exploitation and ravages of other human beings. No other country in the world comes even close to such a statistic.

Heroes and villains

The story of the creation of Costa Rica's parks and protected areas is one of drama, ideals, and sacrifice. One of the earliest in an international lineage of protectors was Nils Olaf Wessberg, who, with his wife, Karen Mogensen Fischer, came to Costa Rica from Sweden in 1955 and bought a farm in Nicoya near Montezuma. Fervent naturalists, they built a home of palm leaves, determined to live in harmony with the land. Yet even in this removed corner of the world they did not escape what many call progress, and they watched, dismayed, as the destruction of virgin forest took place at Cabo Blanco, on the Nicoya peninsula. Nils became an activist, working ardently to raise money to purchase the property and thereby preserve it.

After three years and 1,000 pages of letters, he raised the US$30,000 he needed to buy the 1,200 hectares (3,000 acres) that constitute the Cabo Blanco Strict Nature Reserve. Today, a plaque inside the park is a memorial to Nils, who, while trying to establish another park in the Osa Peninsula, was murdered by those who had vested interests in preventing his work. In 2004, a new reserve near Montezuma was established and named after Karen Mogensen Fischer.

Another individual, Mario Boza, a student of Costa Rican forestry, was able to put his con-

servation ideas to work in the creation of Santa Rosa, the country's first national park. In 1969, the Forestry Law trumpeted the creation of the Santa Rosa National Monument and established the National Parks Department. But with little funding and personnel to enforce it, the new law went unrecognized and the land continued

NATURAL WONDERLAND

There are many astounding statistics concerning Costa Rica's natural abundance. In a space that occupies less than 0.01 percent of the earth's surface are 6 percent of all of the scientifically identified plant and animal species on the planet. In total this numbers somewhere between 500,000 and a million species of flora and fauna including: 50,000 species of insects (some the size of small mammals!); over 1,000 species of orchids; 800 ferns (more than in all North America and Mexico); 208 species of mammals; 850 species of birds; 200 species of reptiles (half of which are snakes), and thousands of species of moths and butterflies.

PRECEDING PAGES: dusk at Braulio Carrillo; heliconias on the jungle floor; iguanas at La Orotina.
LEFT: jaguars. **RIGHT:** the *bejuquillo* vine snake.

to be used as it had been in the past, as grazing pasture for the cattle of nearby ranchers and as the homesteads of squatters who cleared the land by using the slash and burn technique.

Unable to halt the destruction through bureaucratic channels, Boza went to the people through the press. "Santa Rosa in Flames; National Park Being Ruined" read the headlines. The public was outraged and park authorities were duly authorized to move out the squatters and protect the land from the encroachment of livestock and agriculture.

Rodrigo Carazo, president of Costa Rica from 1978 to 1982, described the national parks as

country's population in the most fertile area of the country, the Central Valley – covers the land with concrete and asphalt, and it continues at a frenzied pace. Extensive soil erosion, an effect of the rapid deforestation of the country by the destructive use of land for cattle grazing, causes a phenomenal loss of topsoil.

Threats to the watershed, as well as the nation's extensive hydroelectric system, also result. Uncontrolled dumping of toxic waste from the banana, coffee, and fertilizer industries has contaminated coastal and inland waters. Agricultural chemicals used in pesticides, once employed only on the traditional export crops of

"splendid natural laboratories which we offer to the international scientific community and also to children, young people and adults who should not be denied the joy of direct contact with nature in its pristine state. All of this represents the contribution of the Costa Rican people to peace among men and goodwill among nations."

The economy versus the ecology

As admirable as Costa Rica's conservation initiatives may be, the environmental efforts of this Third World country are counter to its economic development. Parks are, after all, expensive. Urban sprawl – resulting from the concentration of more than 60 percent of the

bananas and sugar, are now being used by vegetable and flower growers; pesticide poisoning has resulted in, among other things, the virtual elimination of large species such as armadillos and crocodiles along the Tempisque River. The crazed rush to feed the demands for exotic plywood by the First World is resulting in the deforestation of the land surrounding the magnificent Tortuguero canals. And so it goes on.

In its attempts to imitate much of North America and the First World, the country experiences the inevitable conflict between consumption and conservation. Trying to balance these forces are armies of international naturalists. Environmentalists and ecologists from all over the world come to Costa Rica to join the side of "the good guys." Today, Costa Rica has environmental experts in abundance, and dozens of international conservation organizations work on behalf of the country's ecological efforts.

Conservation by education

Believing that true conservation can only be accomplished by the will of the people, the national parks system has made a great effort to educate the *Ticos* most affected by the transfer of land into parks. The co-operation of these people is necessary for the parks' survival. For example, the custom of hunting species for whom the

work and contributions to the many foundations working in Costa Rica.

Sometimes eco-projects even cross Costa Rica's borders. Current projects already in operation include the extension of La Amistad National Park, which spans the border of Panamá, and is considered one of the first Bi-National reserves; and also the proposed Peace Park, known as Sía Paz, a joint effort with Nicaragua along the San Juan River, which forms the border between the two nations. These are just two examples of the potential for national parks to engender co-operative international relations.

parks are a refuge must be changed. Large animals, such as pumas and jaguars, require an extensive amount of free territory in order to survive. Convincing people not to kill them, despite the fact that the cats are a constant threat to livestock, is an enormous and often thankless task.

Eco-tourists and traditional travelers to Costa Rica support the national parks system by coming to visit, by staying at the private reserves, by viewing and understanding some of the workings of the national parks, and through their

LEFT: the arboreal fruit-eating kinkajou (martella).
ABOVE: sometimes you have to look very carefully to penetrate the jungle's camouflage.

Future perfect?

Yet is this good news enough? The fact that Costa Rica is thought of as a safe, quiet democratic place is perhaps both the nation's great blessing and problem. Ironically the world will not be sufficiently moved to donate aid, attention and media coverage to such a gentle democratic place.

It is not clear yet as to which side will prevail, the conservationists or the economic development-at-all-costs forces; it is not predictable whether Costa Rica will become a successful environmental model for the nations of the world or just another failed experiment in ecological idealism. ❏

A Tropical Forest Watcher's Guide

Don't be disappointed if, on your first few visits to the tropical rainforest, you fail to see any of the hundreds of bird species and spectacular large cats, monkeys and sloths that are listed as living there. In fact, your first impression of the forest will probably be of a great green wall of vegetation, not the spectacular variety of colorful animals you had hoped to see. However, be assured a great diversity of organisms do inhabit the tropical

forest and their very survival, which may span millennia, depends not least on how successful they are in avoiding the attention of predators, which include humans.

Before setting off into the forest, do your homework. Study specialist guidebooks that describe animals living in the area and familiarise yourself with the characteristics that are used to identify them, such as color, shape and behavior.

Determine the time of day or night when they are most active. A good pair of binoculars is essential; they can also be used backwards as a powerful magnifying glass. Take every opportunity to charter a boat for lake or river trips; they are always worth the investment.

Observe safety tips before proceeding. Remember that even though it may look like Disneyland, it isn't. Here snakes slither, insects bite and animals may (in very rare cases) become aggressive. Notify someone of your intentions: where you are going, when you plan to arrive, when to expect you back. Take water, insect repellent, flashlight, sunscreen, umbrella or rain poncho and hat.

Look before you touch, step, sit or lean. Scan the trail for slippery rocks, mud, downed trees, ants and snakes. Then move ahead while you search the canopy for animals. Continually shift your gaze. Don't wander off into the woods following a bird without carefully looking where you step. Snakes are rare but potentially lethal. Consider carrying an antivenin kit – and make sure you know how to administer it.

A general guideline: forest wildlife-viewing is easiest and most productive along habitat "edges" next to rivers, beaches, open fields, roads and trail heads. Look for shapes, colors and behaviors that stand out and do not appear to "fit" the design of the forest vegetation.

In the dry season deciduous forests lose their leaves, opening the canopy for viewing; and water sources are frequented by thirsty animals.

Seasoned forest-watchers, like legendary animal trackers, are alert to certain small and easily overlooked clues that indicate the presence of animals or birds present in the forest. Things rustling or dropping from the forest canopy (especially on a windless day) and unexplained noises are often a sign that an animal is nearby. Seeds or leaves dropping from above are probably caused by parrots, monkeys or sloths in the canopy. Fruits, nuts, seed husks or leaf fragments in the trail mean a food tree is nearby and perhaps sustaining feeding animals or birds.

Large, dark shapes in tree crevices might be sleeping sloths, anteaters or monkeys. A hanging green tail may indicate an iguana. Logs on river banks could be crocodiles. Rotten tree sections are often home to amphibians, insects, fungi and mosses. Holes in trees might contain precious birds' nests.

When you've developed skills in seeing and identifying some of the plants and animals, think about what they eat and why they live where they do. Soon you will begin to understand the complexity that makes the forest so mesmerising. ❏

LEFT: a small colorful forest dweller.
RIGHT: birdwatchers at Monteverde.

Ecosystems of Costa Rica

For its size, this country contains a remarkable variety of natural ecosystems. A journey of a few miles is often enough to take you from one to another, each with quite different plants and animals. Much of this variety is due to the country's mountains, which create a range of "life zones" at different altitudes and rainfall patterns. Some species of plants and animals live in several zones, but many are confined to just one.

Dry tropical forest

In some parts of Costa Rica – particularly the lowlands of Guanacaste – little rain falls for four or five months of the year. Here, the natural vegetation is dry tropical forest, with most of the trees shedding their leaves soon after the dry season begins. The trees are rarely more than 30 meters (100 ft) high, and there is usually a tangled understory of spiny and thorny shrubs.

Although the trees are leafless during the dry season, few of them are fully dormant, and many burst into flower soon after their leaves have been shed. Among the most conspicuous of these dry-season flowerers is the guayacan or corteza amarilla tree, which puts on a particularly spectacular display of waxy yellow blooms. Dry tropical forest abounds with reptiles, including rattlesnakes and large lizards called ctenosaurs, which often feed on the fallen guayacan flowers and fruit.

Rainforest

Across most of the Costa Rican lowlands, the climate is wet and warm enough for trees to keep growing for much of the year. The result of this non-stop growth is generally called rainforest. Strictly speaking, though, botanists restrict this term for the wettest forests of all. Unlike the trees in tropical dry forests, rainforest trees are evergreen, and their dense crowns form a continuous canopy that casts a deep and almost unbroken shade.

In lowland rainforest, the canopy trees generally reach up to 50 meters (165 ft), and many have buttress roots called gambas. Scattered among them are emergents – giant trees that rise above the canopy, and which may reach 60 meters (200 ft) or more. With increasing altitude, the canopy height starts to drop, while rainfall levels usually rise, typically reaching a maximum at about 1,000 meters (3,300 ft). Above this height, rainfall begins to decline again. But on slopes facing the prevailing wind, the forest is often enveloped by cloud. At mid- and higher altitudes, the trees are often laden with such epiphytic plants as bromeliads, orchids and ferns.

Epiphytes use trees as living perches in their quest for light, and they generally do their hosts little harm. However, where high rainfall allows them to grow unchecked, their combined weight sometimes brings branches crashing to the ground.

Costa Rica's rainforests – both on low ground and at high altitude – harbor an immense variety of life. But actually seeing wild animals is not as easy as it sounds. With the exception of monkeys and agoutis, most forest mammals are nocturnal. Some birds feed on or near the forest floor, and a number specialize in following columns of army ants, snapping up small insects that flee the ants' advancing front. However, the full richness of rainforest wildlife is in the canopy overhead, where a complex community of species lives with minimal contact with the ground.

Páramo

On Costa Rica's highest peaks, the forest gives way to a treeless landscape known as *páramo*. Cold and frequently swathed in cloud, *páramo* seems a world away from the warmth and lushness of lower altitudes. This ecosystem is dominated by tough, low-growing shrubs that can withstand strong winds. *Páramo* is also found in the Andes, and Costa Rica's scattered patches of it – for example, in the Talamanca Mountains – are the northernmost in the Americas.

Freshwater wetlands

Costa Rica's topography means that its rivers are generally short and fast-flowing, quickly completing their journey from the interior to the sea. Sudden fluctuations in water level – brought on by tropical downpours – are a common event, and freshwater animals are experts at taking cover when flow levels abruptly increase. On lower ground, where the flow is more sluggish, river wildlife is more varied. Animals of particular note include caimans, which often bask on the banks. One of the world's few bipedal lizards, the basilisk, escapes danger by running across the water on its back legs, thus earning its nickname, the Jesus Christ lizard.

Small forest streams usually flow beneath a continuous overhead canopy, but most rivers are broad enough to allow light to reach the forest floor. The result is a linear "light gap," and a profusion of plant growth of the kind rarely seen inside forests themselves. Some of the most eye-catching species are heliconias, or lobster-claws, which are pollinated by hummingbirds. They often spring up on mudbanks and sandbars, but rarely grow in deep shade.

Costa Rica's largest body of freshwater – Lake Arenal – has a distinctly highland feel, and while it teems with fish, its bird life is unexceptional. By contrast, the shallow lakes and marshes of Palo Verde National Park and Caño Negro are much more productive ecosystems. These seasonal wetlands attract a wide variety of wading birds, particularly when water levels are low, and prey is more easy to catch.

Mangrove swamps

Mangroves are the natural vegetation of muddy, low-lying coasts throughout the tropics. In Costa Rica, there are five species of mangrove, and they form extensive forests on both the Caribbean and Pacific shores. None of the five species is closely related to each other, but they have all evolved a collection of adaptations for surviving in seawater and saline silt. Known to botanists as halophytes, these trees have mechanisms for getting rid of excess salt and elaborate roots that anchor them in the shifting mud.

Although they are often inaccessible, smelly and hot, Costa Rican mangrove swamps abound with life. Crabs are a particular specialty, including hordes of fiddler crabs, which pick over the mud for

particles of food, fist-sized land crabs and the mangrove tree crab, which feeds on mangrove leaves and leaps acrobatically from branch to branch. Even mangrove mud makes an important contribution to the marine food chain for the nutrient-rich algae and other small organisms it produces.

Coasts and coral reefs

Apart from mangrove swamps, Costa Rica's coastline consists largely of extensive beaches – often of dark volcanic sand – low-lying rocks and a small number of offshore islands. Although the two coasts are never far apart, their marine life is quite different, and their physical differences also affect other animals. Brown

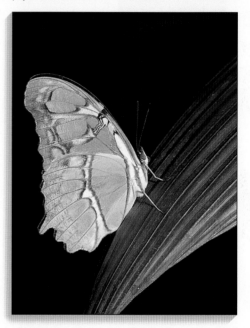

pelicans, for example, feed on both coasts, but they only breed on the Pacific, where the rocky islands give them the protection that they need. The spectacular frigatebird is also a much more common sight in the Pacific Ocean than in the waters of the Caribbean.

Costa Rica has a number of small coral reefs on its Pacific coast, but only one significant area on the Caribbean, at Cahuita. Reef-building corals need sunlight to grow, and they can only survive in clear water. This limits them to areas well away from the mouths of silt-laden rivers, but it also makes them vulnerable to any increase in silt run-off. Unfortunately, in recent years the Cahuita reef has been affected by deforestation, which has increased silt levels in the surrounding water. ❑

LEFT: the density of the rainforest, seen from above.
RIGHT: malachite butterfly in Braulio Carillo Park.

A PASSION FOR PLANTS

From the beautiful to the bizarre, Costa Rica's many species of flora offer a vibrant introduction to the kaleidoscopic plant wealth of the tropics

For many visitors to Costa Rica, first contact with the country's spectacular plant life comes at the hotel reception desk. As likely as not, the desk will be adorned by a vase of heliconias – strikingly angular red or orange flowers, also known as lobster claws, which grow in the country's forests.

Heliconias are typical of the outsize blooms that flourish in Costa Rica's warm and humid climate. As a rule of thumb, the biggest and most robust flowers – including heliconias – are pollinated by birds or bats, while more delicate flowers are pollinated by insects. This second category includes most of the country's orchids – another group of plants for which Costa Rica is justly famous.

INTRODUCED PLANTS

Costa Rica has a vast number of native plants, including about a thousand different species of trees. To add to this botanical richness, many other species have been introduced from different parts of the tropics, either for food or for ornament. The food plants include bananas, which arrived in the Americas in the early 1500s, coffee, mangoes and sugar cane, and also the African oil palm, first cultivated on a large scale in the 1960s. Many of the showiest garden and roadside plants are from distant parts of the world. Among the most eye-catching are jacarandas, South American trees that produce a mass of purplish-blue flowers.

▷ **GIANT LEAVES**
Elephant ear takes its name from its enormous leaves, over 1.2m (4ft) long. Originally from southern and southeast Asia, they are common on marshy ground by streams. Also known as giant taro, these plants have edible roots and stems.

◁ **LANDING PLATFORM**
Popular garden plants throughout Costa Rica, bird-of-paradise flowers are pollinated by birds. The flower has a built-in perch.

◁ NATIONAL FLOWER

Like most orchids, *Guarianthe skinnerii*, the national flower (Guariamorada in Spanish) lives high up on trees, and is very difficult to spot from the ground. Visiting an orchid garden is the easiest way to see it.

▷ PRIZED ORNAMENTALS

Named after a 19th-century German naturalist, kohlerias have hanging tubular flowers and live in damp, shady places on the forest floor. The family that they belong to is widespread throughout the tropics, and includes many popular indoor plants, such as African violets and gloxinias.

◁ BLUE BLOOMS

The blue passionflower (*Passiflora caerulea*) is found throughout Costa Rica. Like other passionflowers, it produces juicy berries, and its seeds are spread by animals.

▷ SYMBOLIC FLOWERS

Legend has it that Spanish missionaries named the red passionflower after Christ's crucifixion: the flower's three stigmas, for example, represent the three nails.

△ LOBSTER CLAWS

The flowers of heliconias, or lobster claws, are clasped by brilliantly coloured flaps. In some species, the flower head stays upright, but in others it gradually topples over as it grows.

▽ NECTAR STATION

The nectar-rich flowers of ginger lilies have a magnetic effect on butterflies and on nectar-drinking birds. These shoulder-high relatives of edible ginger come from India and southeast Asia and are widely grown in Costa Rica as garden plants.

THE PLANTS THAT GROW ON PLANTS

Costa Rica's forests are home to an immense variety of epiphytes, or plants that grow on the shoulders of other plants, often far above the ground. Epiphytes manage this remarkable feat by collecting rainwater and by scavenging nutrients from any organic debris that is washed or blown their way.

Of all the country's epiphytes, bromeliads are the most conspicuous. Tank bromeliads, like the one shown above, collect water by funneling it into a central reservoir formed by their leaves. These plants can be over 1 meter (3 ft) across, and their tanks can hold several liters of water. Other epiphytes, including most orchids, have specialized roots that absorb water and nutrients before they have a chance to drain away.

In forests, a different collection of plants – including philodendrons and the Swiss-cheese plant (*Monstera deliciosa*) – start life rooted in the ground, but soon head for the sunlit treetops. In the wild, the cheese plant and its relatives have a bizarre growth pattern. If the plant climbs up a tree that turns out to be too short, it simply drops back to the forest floor and searches for another one.

THE SPORTS SCENE

Activity holidays are booming in Costa Rica. Getting wet – whether
by spilling out of a raft or falling off a board – is usually part of the game

Sport is a much-loved pastime in Cost Rica, and *Ticos* are always happy to have visiting foreigners join them in watching an important game of soccer or basketball. In the past decade a fitness craze has swept the country – joggers and cyclists are a common sight puffing up the hills of the Central Valley in the early morning. On weekends, the enormous La Sabana Park, on the west side of San José, is filled with thousands of athletes: soccer teams, basketball players, swimmers, volleyball players, roller-blade teams and baseball enthusiasts. On the Central Valley plateau, private golf and tennis clubs with complete health spas cater for wealthy suburbanites.

The country's burgeoning watersports, however, are the main attractions for the increasing number of visitors who are coming to Costa Rica to surf isolated beaches, to windsurf on magnificent Lake Arenal, and to enjoy some of the best whitewater rafting in the world.

Whitewater rafting

The brightly colored inflatable raft rushes down a chute of cascading whitewater, then plunges over and through waves that are nearly 2 meters (6 ft) high. Those in the raft gleefully dig their paddles into the frothing water, and then shriek with delight as they maneuver the raft between boulders the size of small cars. After a while, a calm spot on the river is reached, an eddy, and from there the raft passengers pause and look up from the roaring river course to inhale and appreciate the beauty of the Reventazón Gorge. The scenery includes the colossally broad panorama of the canyon, rolling fields of coffee, sugar-cane, wild grasses and radiant flowers blooming unexpectedly in the canopy of trees that lean over the river.

Whitewater rafting is relatively new to Costa Rica, and it is rapidly growing in popularity.

PRECEDING PAGES: rafting on the Reventazón River.
LEFT: surf's up at Playa Dominical.
RIGHT: a windsurfer enjoys a breezy, late-afternoon sail on Lake Arenal.

Costa Rica has more accessible whitewater rivers and rapids than any other place in the world. It is, of course, the unique geography of the country that makes it one of the world's great destinations for rafters. To have the right kind of rapids, you need a river that descends in a fairly steep gradient. The four mountain

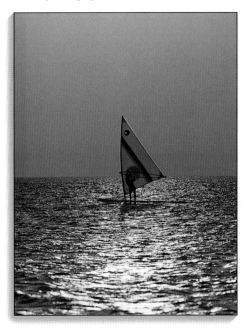

chains that wind down the axis of Costa Rica provide the perfect conditions. The Talamanca range and the Cordillera Central have many steep, wide, perennial rivers that are regularly supplied with bounteous rainfall.

The variety of these rivers provides an enormous range of wilderness experiences. Some offer idyllic float trips through luscious landscapes with abundant wildlife, while others contain explosive whitewater and raging rapids that challenge the most experienced rafter.

The Sarapiquí

The Sarapiquí River flows through the lowlands of Heredia, providing stunning scenery and exceptional whitewater. About a two-hour drive from San José, the upper portion of the Sarapiquí contains moderate rapids that are suitable for novice paddlers. On the calm, lower section of the river, the jungle closes in and gives rafters the opportunity to relax for a while and view the monkeys, otters and abundant water fowl of the area.

The Reventazón

The head of the Reventazón River is a 90-minute drive from San José and offers some of Costa Rica's most challenging whitewater and spectacular scenery. Rafting companies run four sections of the river. The first, which is just below the hydro-electric power plant of Cachí, is steep and contains continuous rapids of moderate to high difficulty. The second section, from Tucurrique to Angostura, is suited to novice paddlers and provides splendid views of the surrounding volcanoes.

The final two sections of the Reventazón, from Angostura to Siquirres, have some of the most challenging whitewater in the world.

The Pacuare

Many consider Costa Rica's most famous whitewater river to be the Pacuare. Accessible

WHITEWATER RAFTING – THE MAJOR PLAYERS

Despite its perilous appearance, whitewater rafting, also known as river running, is a relatively safe sport. And it offers anyone in moderately good health an exhilarating way to observe the scenery and wildlife of the country. Several professional outfitters provide all of the necessities: life preservers, helmets and rafts. Guides have been through training in the classroom and on the rivers. Most Costa Rican head guides have been trained at whitewater schools in the USA and many have worked with the world's best.

The first whitewater exploration of Costa Rican rivers was made by Costa Rica Expeditions on the Reventazón River in 1978. The following year the same company pioneered commercial whitewater rafting in Central America. Ríos Tropicales, founded in 1985, started rafting on the Sarapiquí and Sucio rivers, and local graduates of their kayaking school have represented Costa Rica at the World Championships of Whitewater Racing. Aventuras Naturales is the third major company in this field. Others of varying expertise have also sprung up in San José, Turrialba, and elsewhere.

Many offer day-trip packages from San José, including transportation, breakfast and lunch, at very reasonable rates.

from the Central Valley via Turrialba, it passes through a deep gorge in dense jungle that contains rich flora and wildlife. Most groups spend two or more days descending this river from Tres Equis to Siquirres, and camping in riverside sites within view of thundering waterfalls and great flocks of birds.

On the Pacific side of Costa Rica, the river system offers the longest of the uninterrupted stretches of whitewater in Costa Rica. Most rafting parties take around four days to travel the 80 km (50 miles) from Chiles to Crujo, allowing time for exploring the waterfalls and for relaxing in camp.

Surfing

During the past few years, Costa Rica's unending beaches have been discovered by surfers from North America, Australia and Europe. They generally concur that the quality of Costa Rica's surf is firmly in the top four – along with California, Hawaii and Australia. Moreover, they find that the surf here is plentiful and relatively uncrowded, the water temperature is a comfortable 27°C (80°F) throughout the year, and there is still the rare experience of having a wave all to yourself, just offshore a pristine and empty beach.

A map of Costa Rica reveals what may not be

The Corobicí

This is the gentlest of Costa Rica's rafting rivers and is ideal for rafters who are also birdwatchers. In the adjacent Palo Verde National Park, over 300 species of birds have been observed and the majority can be seen from rafts on the Corobicí. Because the river's perennial flow is controlled by a dam on Lake Arenal, it becomes an oasis that attracts birds, monkeys and lizards during the dry season in Guanacaste.

LEFT: surfers appreciate the beautifully shaped waves on the Pacific seaboard.
ABOVE: wave jumping on Lake Arenal.

too obvious from driving on the highway up or down the coasts: there are masses of beaches and, often, few access roads to many of them. In fact, there are some 200 km (120 miles) of Atlantic coast and 1,000 km (630 miles) of Pacific shore, sculpted with sandy beaches, rocky headlands, offshore reefs and river mouths near coastal jungles.

There is also a great number of open beaches that are exposed to ocean swells coming from many directions. Much of the coastline is removed from civilization, so there may be no facilities, food or emergency services within many miles. A four-wheel drive vehicle is often essential, especially during the rainy season.

Popular surf spots

With hundreds of miles of coastline, there are many undiscovered, nameless surfing beaches. But among the favorites are the following:

Jacó, a Pacific beach town southeast of the Gulf of Nicoya, is less than two hours by car or bus from San José. It is a long, silty beach trapped between two jungle-covered rocky points, with waves that are particularly good for body surfing or boogie boarding. The surf is easily accessible, just beyond the patios of many of the hotels and *cabinas*. For non-surfers, however, the beach is unattractive and the currents and riptides are strong.

Just under 3 km (2 miles) to the south of Jacó is Playa Hermosa. It is possible to hitchhike, rent a bike or take a bus with a surfboard around the point south of Jacó to this beach. South from Jacó to Playa Panamá are many superb unexploited surfing spots. North of Jacó, near Puntarenas, the sandspit at the mouth of the Barranca River produces what is reputed to be one of the world's longest left-breaking waves.

Far to the north, the beaches of Guanacaste province have some of the best surf anywhere, particularly during the dry season when steady offshore winds help to create the waves. The break near Roca de la Bruja (Witch's Rock; *see*

SWELLS AND BREAKS

Wave-making conditions are complex in Costa Rica. On the Pacific coast, swells originating from storms in the north and central Pacific Ocean occur frequently from November through March. South swells from distant storms prevail for the remainder of the year.

Pacific beaches are shaped by sediment carried to the sea by major rivers. The silt migrates up and down the coast on strong onshore currents. Sandbars produce beach breaks with long and fast right and left rides along much of the coast. Sandspits form at the river mouths, and create long, and often clean, point breaks. But because the sand floor is unstable, bars and sandspits change with the season. Tides and winds also strongly influence wave shape.

From December to April, large swells caused by winds and storms originating in the Caribbean arrive at Costa Rica's east-coast beaches. The steep, fast-moving waves break over shallow coral reefs, often in shapes and sizes that rival those of the north shore of Oahu in Hawaii. Smaller west swells from tradewinds originating in the West Indies prevail from June through August. The only time when there is generally little or no surf on the east coast is September through November.

To check on conditions visit www.surfingcr.com

page 195) at Playa Naranjo, in the Santa Rosa National Park, is one of the most spectacular waves; the number of surfers is officially limited to 25 daily. Surfers need to book ahead with one of the many local surf shops and travel to Playas del Coco where officially designated boats transport them to this surfing spot.

The Nicoya Peninsula to the south of Guanacaste is scalloped with beaches, many of them with rideable waves. Some of the best surfing in the country is found in remote Pavones on the Golfo Dulce coast.

Near Limón, 2½ hours east of San José, are playas Blanca and Portete, both of which are good, popular surfing beaches. Approximately 1 hour south of Limón, Puerto Viejo, a tranquil Caribbean village, is the site of the sometimes awesome Salsa Brava, a surf break that seems to have acquired an international reputation; from December through March, consistent, large north swells hit the coral reef with tremendous force.

Windsurfing

In January 1991 a television sports network hosted and filmed Costa Rica's first windsurfing contest. The event served as an announcement to the world that the country warranted recognition as an outstanding destination for international windsurfers. During the competition, strong tradewinds whipped the picturesque Lake Arenal into a sea of white water and waves, creating ideal windsurfing.

The few pioneers who have sailed Arenal compare this lake favorably with the world's best windsurfing locations, such as the Columbia River Gorge in Oregon and Maui in the Hawaiian Islands (with the only caveat that the waves are sometimes rather choppy).

Almost every other day between January and April, consistent winds of around 20 knots whip the waves to a metre-high swell along the length of Arenal, creating excellent short-board sailing conditions. For the rest of the season, lighter winds predominate and are ideal for longboard sailing. Lake Arenal is not a suitable place for beginners. Sideshore winds are consistent and blow across the full width of the lake. During high winds, steep swells provide the right conditions to practice acrobatic speed runs, jumps,

and loops. The water is a comfortable 18–21°C (64–70°F) year-round. Hotel Tilawa and River Rock Lodge are good places to hire equipment.

Another excellent windsurfing destination is nearby Coter Lake. If you are looking for the "funnel effect," try Bahía Salinas, near La Cruz, in the far north west of the country.

Golf

Golf is growing in popularity in Costa Rica. The Hotel Cariari and Country Club, northwest of San José, was the country's first championship course. Since the 1990s, famous golf architects have been designing new courses in Costa Rica.

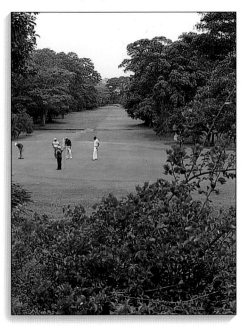

There are excellent courses on the Nicoya Peninsula, including the par-72 Garra de León, designed by Robert Trent Jones Jr in the Paradisus Meliá Playa Conchal Hotel, and the par-72 courses at Hacienda Pinilla, designed by Mike Young. The newest course opened in 2004 at the new Four Seasons Papagayo Resort at the north end of the peninsula. There is also a Ted Robinson-designed course at the Marriott Los Sueños Hotel in the Central Pacific zone.

There are fairly good nine-hole courses at Tango Mar, which overlooks the Gulf of Nicoya; Costa Rica Country Club in Escazú; the Los Reyes Country Club, La Guácima; and the El Castillo Country Club, above Heredia. ❑

LEFT: divers explore Isla del Caño's beautiful coral reef. **RIGHT:** bougainvillea frames the fairways at Cariari Country Club golf course.

BIG FINS AND FRESH FISH

Costa Rica is a paradise for both fresh and saltwater fishing. It's quiet, too:
you'll run into other fishing folk only if you really want to

The king of game fish swims calmly toward Costa Rica's Caribbean coast. At around 70 kilos (150 lbs), he fears no predators, except sharks, as he cruises toward the mouth of the Colorado River.

Where the tarpon has come from is a mystery. He could have been off the coasts of Flor-ida, South America or West Africa. Or he might have been in local waters the entire time.

But now he is with an ocean school of 100 fish of the same size. Suddenly they spot a school of titi, a small sardine-like fish, and chase them to the surface. The tarpon cause an acre of the Caribbean to explode as they churn

RULES OF ENGAGEMENT

In tarpon fishing, the rules of angling must be suspended or reversed. Otherwise there's no chance of success. The first trick that goes against all that you've ever learned is to retrieve the lure with the rod tip low – at water level or, better yet, in the water. That way, when it's time to set the hook, the rod tip can be brought up and backwards in a long arc. The maneuver must be repeated rapidly at least three times with a force that would tear the hook out of the mouth of almost any other fish.

Tarpon sometimes strike like a rocket, hurtling 5 meters (16 ft) straight up as they hit the plug. At other times it is hard to tell whether or not one of these giant fish is even on your hook. If you react fast enough, and if you're lucky, the tarpon will be hooked before it makes its first jump. If you're not so lucky, you'll see your lure thrown into the air as the great silver fish seems to explode out of the water and reach for the clouds. A tarpon's jump is like no other in fishing. They reach incredibly high; twist right, twist left, flip over, fall back on the line and do everything possible to get free.

Usually the tarpon succeeds and you lose. The success rate of experts is to land about one out of every 10 hooked. though try telling that to your friends when you go back after a day's tarpon fishing empty-handed.

the water and devour the titi. If you are lucky enough to witness this scene, it's simply a matter of casting into the chaos to get into contact with what many consider the most exciting aquatic quarry on earth.

Tarpon enter the river mouths all along the Caribbean coast of Costa Rica, from the Colorado River in the north to the Sixaola River, which forms the border with Panamá. In most rivers, they swim a few hundred meters upstream in search of food and then return to the sea.

Only in the Río Colorado do they keep going upriver, following the titi, in an incredible journey of more than 200 km (124 miles) to Lake Nicaragua, close to the Pacific Ocean.

Freshwater "lakes"

As the tarpon begin their long swim, they pass a series of thin fingers of water stretching north-ward almost to the border with Nicaragua. These freshwater "lakes" are full of a variety of exotic fish that make great sport on light tackle. One of the most fascinating is the alli-gator gar, known in Costa Rica as *gaspar*. Looking like a holdback to prehistoric times, this fish has a long, narrow snout as full of sharp teeth as an alligator's. Its coffee-colored body is covered with tough skin and large scales. Its tail is broad and powerful. The meat of the *gaspar* is firm and sweet, not unlike that of shrimps. But the eggs should never be eaten as they are highly toxic to humans.

The tarpon is not alone in his upriver swims. Snook also make the long journey following the titi. And following them all are bull sharks.

The sharks, like the tarpon, continue all the way to Lake Nicaragua. Their presence has led many people to believe that there are "fresh-water sharks" in the lake. Actually, they are just visitors from the faraway Caribbean.

Snook are the mainstay of sport fishing in Costa Rica. Large snook are plentiful along all parts of the Caribbean and Pacific coasts, as well as in rivers throughout the country.

All along the Río San Juan there are lesser rivers flowing into it from Costa Rica. At the confluence of the San Juan with the Colorado,

Sarapiquí, San Carlos, Infernito, Pocosol, Medio Queso and Frío rivers there are some excellent angling for tarpon and snook. None of these rivers is heavily fished and all require a bit of enterprise to reach. But those who make the effort are usually well rewarded.

The Río Frío

An exception to this rule of relative inaccessi-bility is the Río Frío, which passes right through "downtown" Los Chiles – an approximate three-hour drive, on paved roads, from San José.

The Río Frío is full of tarpon, snook, white drum, gar and other exotic species. Some

ROLLING FOR AIR

Tarpon are one of the few fish that are capable of taking in air directly through the mouth rather than by filtering water through their gills. This ability is necessary because these big active fish need more oxygen than they can get from the waters that they sometimes inhabit.

This method of direct breathing accounts for the phenomenon known as "rolling," when they come to the surface and flop on their side while gulping air. This unusual adaptation also makes it possible for tarpon to swim freely between saltwater and freshwater and even in oxygen-depleted water.

LEFT: gone fishing; searching for the catch of the day.
RIGHT: a proud fisherman with his freshly caught *mahi-mahi* (dolphin fish), off the Nicoya coast.

people fish right from the municipal landing in Los Chiles; others with boats launch them there and venture north or south. For those who don't have a boat, it is possible to rent a *panga* (barge), driven by a knowledgeable local person who also acts as a guide. These *pangas* can be found at the municipal landing.

Some tarpon, as they swim up the Río San Juan, apparently take diversions far into the side rivers. This is the case with the Río Frío. Thirty minutes by boat south of Los Chiles is the convergence of the Río Frío and the Río Sabogal. Here tarpon up to 45 kg (100 lbs) seem to be present at all times.

Every morning and every evening the giant fish, too big to be in a narrow river, leap high into the air, re-entering the water with a thundering splash. It is a sight every fishing enthusiast would love to see. It can also be one of the most frustrating experiences imaginable, because there are days when these fish just won't take a lure. However, just the sight is well worth the trip – and there's always a good chance of hooking into one of them.

More river fish

The Río Frío, as well as most of the other rivers of Costa Rica, is full of a fish often overlooked by anglers. The *machacha,* a silvery speedster,

is an unusual fish in that it is primarily a vegetarian. *Machacha* can often be found under the overhang of *chilemate* trees waiting for ripe fruit to fall into the water. Costa Ricans fish for them using pieces of banana or tomato, but *machacha* will also take small lures or flies running, changing directions, diving and leaping into the air. They can grow up to 9 kg (20 lbs) and 1–2 kg (2–5 pounders) are common and offer great sport. Their flesh is bony but tasty.

Up a few of the rivers that feed into the San Juan, particularly the Sarapiquí, you can find the *bobo*, a difficult but rewarding quarry. These fish, which weigh up to 14 kg (30 lbs), feed in shallow, fast-moving water. They are relatives of the saltwater mullet and are pure vegetarians. But they can be taken on small spinners and they offer great sport as they fight hard through the rapids.

In these Atlantic-slope rivers you can also find other exotic species including the *mojarra*, a strong, sharp-toothed, brightly colored pan fish resembling a perch on steroids, and related to the sun fish.

Sea angling

For most people, fishing off the Pacific coast of Costa Rica means angling for sailfish, marlin and tuna. All along the Pacific coast there are sport fishing operations springing up and all are finding success.

Operators in the Gulf of Papagayo were the first, and the area was often shown to have the most productive sailfishing in the world. Sails here are not the scrawny Atlantic variety. They are hefty, healthy Pacific sailfish averaging over 45 kg (100 lbs). Fought on a 7-kg (15-lb) line or less, they offer fantastic sport and a spectacular show full of graceful jumps. Laws require that all sails (except record catches) are released and this is generally respected by fishermen.

In recent years, marlin have been discovered along most of the Pacific coast. Offshore, dolphin, tuna, and rainbow runner are plentiful. Offshore reefs also offer great fishing for snapper, including the prized *cubbera*.

Often overlooked are the fishing possibilities straight from the Pacific beaches. Every beach on the Pacific coast offers the chance to take various types of jack and drum, as well as trophy-sized snook from the surf. Mouths of rivers and streams often attract congregations of snook. Casting from rocks often locates snapper and rooster fish.

Roosters abound on Costa Rica's Pacific coast. The colorful, wide-bodied and powerful fish with the long, spiky dorsal fin that gives it its name, is particularly plentiful in the water surrounding the rocks in Puntarenas or the nearby Pacific port of Caldera. Once hooked, the rooster fish raises its "comb" and speeds away across the surface, offering a unique show and fight.

LICENSED TO FISH

You can buy a fishing license from Deportes Keko, Ca 20 and Av 4–6 in San José (tel: 223 4142).

of a rhinoceros and if it gets there it will almost certainly cut the line on underbrush.

The *guapote* is a spectacular fish. A breeding male has large bulbous protrusions above the eyes that "light up", displaying many colors on its flank. *Guapote* in Lake Arenal, the main place where they are fished, weigh up to 9 kg (20 lbs) or more, although a 7-kg (15-lb) fish is about as much as most can handle. The *guapote pinto*, or painted guapote, can be found in rivers that flow into the San Juan.   ❑

The *guapote*

The star of Costa Rica's few lakes is the *guapote*. Some people call this fish the "rainbow bass," although taxonomically it has nothing to do with bass. The main similarity to bass is in the way it is fished: casting or flipping plugs or spinner baits.

Once hooked, the resemblance is soon forgotten. The *guapote* is to a bass what a diesel is to a model train; it is not a light tackle fish. Once hooked, it heads for cover with the force

LEFT: unfamiliar faces in the fish market.
ABOVE: fishing for trout and *machín* in the breathtaking mountains north of San Isidro del General,

TROUT AND MACHÍN

Wild trout have never done well in Costa Rica (although farmed trout do very well). Despite numerous attempts to stock them in high mountain streams, they have never really thrived. Trout fishing is possible in the breathtaking mountains between San José and San Isidro del General, such as the Río Savegre in the San Gerardo de Dota valley area, and, even if the fish are somewhat small, the scenery alone makes a day spent here worthwhile.

If you cannot find any trout then a good substitute is the *machín*, a fish which is found in rivers where trout would be expected. It puts up a vigorous fight, very similar to that of a trout.

TICO COOKING

When you can try Painted Rooster and Married Man on the menu in Costa Rica's

sodas, why spend time at fast-food or international restaurants?

While it is possible in Costa Rica to order anything from sushi to *huevos rancheros* (Mexican-style eggs), part of the joy of traveling is sampling local cuisine.

The Ticos' basic diet is simple, low in fat and rich in proteins and carbohydrates. Fruits, fresh vegetables, beef and abundant salads are the

Salsa Lizano. Most often these contain cornflour, salt, garlic, black pepper, onion, coriander, paprika and a small amount of hot chili. "English sauce," the native version of Worcestershire sauce, is also used, albeit sparingly, by most cooks. Jalapeño peppers, from the mountain towns of Zarcero and Cervantes, are very

trademarks of Costa Rican cooking. *Picadillos* are found in every Tico home: diced potatoes, *chayotes* (water squash or vegetable pears) or string beans are mixed with finely chopped meat, tomatoes, onions, cilantro (fresh coriander), bell peppers and whatever the cook feels may add flavor to the pot. Leftover *picadillos*, fried with rice, are served for breakfast, usually with hot *tortillas* (a kind of pancake), and are called *amanecido*.

Costa Ricans season their food with a mixture of dry spices called *condimentos mixtos* (mixed seasoning), which is readily available at the markets. There are many different brands of liquid sauces as well, the most famous being

good and not as hot as the Mexican varieties. In fact, most Costa Ricans do not like very spicy food, although tabasco and chili sauce are always on the table in inexpensive restaurants.

Gallo pinto and casado

The classic Costa Rican dish of *gallo pinto* (literally, painted rooster) is rice and black or red beans mixed with seasonings including onion, cilantro, garlic and finely chopped bell pepper. While predominantly a breakfast dish in the city, rural Costa Ricans eat *gallo pinto* three times daily, accompanied by homemade corn *tortillas*. For breakfast they order it with scrambled or fried eggs and sour cream, or *natilla*.

For lunch, businesspeople, professionals, students and farmers alike usually have a *casado* (meaning husband)– a hearty combination including rice, beans, cabbage salad, fried plantains and chicken, fish or beef. An example of Tico macho humor, the name *casado* derives from the ordinary daily fare a man supposedly receives after he is married.

More Tico favorites

Another typical dish is *olla de carne* (literally, meat), a hearty stew that includes a small amount of beef and many vegetables common to the region: often *ñampi* and *camote* (both relatives of the sweet potato), *chayote* (water squash), carrots and potatoes. It is usually served with white rice – something Ticos feel no meal is complete without. This dish can be traced back to Cervantes' novel *Don Quixote*.

The *olla podrida* is the great-grandparent of the soup the people in Costa Rica love the most. What gives the distinct flavor to the Costa Rican version is the mixture of vegetables cooked in it: yucca, green plantain, sweet potato, *tannia*, *tacacos*, taro, pumpkin, carrot, *cho-cho*, onion, cabbage and whatever else comes to hand.

Another interesting soup that is available at neighborhood restaurants throught the country is *sopa negra,* made with black beans, onions, cilantro and hard-boiled eggs.

For lunch or dinner, *arroz con pollo* (rice with chicken) or *arroz con mariscos* (rice with seafood) are filling, inexpensive meals served in *sodas* and hotel restaurants.

Other local favorites include *lengua* (cow's tongue), and *mondongo* (cow's stomach lining). While tongue is tender and often deliciously prepared, *mondongo* has a strong taste and is not appreciated by most foreigners.

The ubiquitous accompaniment to most meals is plantains – a sweet relative of the banana. It must be cooked before eating and is usually cut into strips and fried in oil or lard (called *manteca*).

Bocas and *bebidas*

Some bars still serve *bocas* ("mouthfuls") with drinks in the same tradition as Spanish *tapas*.

PRECEDING PAGES: an astonishing tropical harvest.
LEFT: the bustling San José restaurant scene.
RIGHT: succulent *gambas* (shrimps).

Traditionally they were complimentary but these days are increasingly sold separately.

Favorite *bocas* include *ceviche* (raw fish marinated in lemon juice), *carne en salsa* (meat stewed in a tomato sauce), fried cassava, and fried chicken. Beer, rum and *guaro* (a sugarcane alcoholic drink) are favorite local tipples.

Special occasions

On weekends, Costa Ricans love to eat two versions of *chicharrones* – either deep-fried pig skin (including the layer of fat just below the skin) or tender chunks of lean pork that has been simmered slowly. *Chicharrones* are

COSTA RICAN NOUVELLE CUISINE

The concept of Costa Rican nouvelle cuisine may sound like a contradiction in terms, but increasing exportation of food has stirred new interest in the country's vegetables and fruits. New recipes and traditional ones alike have been imaginatively rewritten.

Pejibaye soup, a delicate orange creamy broth, features at banquets. The common, but never ordinary, mashed black beans *(frijoles)*, well-seasoned with onions, sweet peppers and cilantro, are now served at formal dinners as *hors d'oeuvres*. Posh restaurants offer native cooking nights, starring such delicacies as plantain soufflé and pork-filled cassava pastries.

served with *tortillas* and wedges of lemon.

At Christmas, everyone eats *tamales*, which are made with *masa*, a corn dough, stuffed with different fillings, then wrapped in banana leaves and steamed. The dish is of Aztec origin and is eaten throughout Central America. It is very rarely the same in any two countries. In Costa Rica, *tamales* are traditionally filled with tender bits of pork, rice, carrots, olives, and sometimes dried plums.

Easter fare

Since colonial times, the Easter meal has been an important and traditional celebration. The

Catholic Church's prohibition on eating red meat during Lent explains why fish, pastries and sweets are popular for the Easter celebration. Since the 19th century, *bacalao con papas* (salt cod and potatoes) has been traditionally prepared for Easter. Huge quantities of salt cod are imported from Europe especially for this occasion.

Just before Easter week, particularly in and around the Cartago area, a type of fruit similar to the pumpkin, but oval and quite large, is sold in the streets. These are *chiverres*, and a preserve made with them, called *cabellito de angel* (angel's hair), is eaten during Easter throughout the Central Valley.

Costa Rican *ceviche* is an Easter speciality, but is available all year round at any neighborhood *cevichería*. It is prepared by marinating small cubes of fresh white fish or shellfish in a sauce made with lime juice, olive oil, fresh cilantro, onions and bell peppers, for at least 12 hours. Most Costa Rican cooks believe in keeping the lime juice to a minimum and using cilantro freely to perfume the fish. It is similar to the Mexican dish of the same name, and both show the influence of the Aztecs. *Patacones*, crisp green plantain sliced and topped with black mashed beans, are a necessary accompaniment to fresh *ceviche*.

Fresh *palmito* (palm hearts) are also traditionally eaten during Lent, but can be bought any time pickled in vinegar. *Palmitos* and rice is an elegant, festive dish served with grated cheese on top. *Flor de itabo* is the flower of a plant often used in the fences of the coffee farms. The plants have a very white bunch of lily-like flowers, which are also eaten for Easter, stewed in butter with eggs and tomato.

Regional cooking

Costa Rica may only be a small country, but it still maintains several clearly differentiated regional cuisines.

The foods of Limón are exotically tropical and flavorsome. The area offers a wide diversity of dishes influenced by African and West Indian cooking. The names of the ingredients *(haki, yokotaw, bami, calaloo)* have the beat of Calypso and reggae, as do the names of the dishes themselves *(tie-a-leave, dokunu, johnny cake)*. You will also find strong traces of Chinese cuisine, as there are many Chinese living in the area.

The trademark of the cooking of Limón is coconut. Coconut oil and milk are used generously in most recipes, including the traditional rice and beans. For this popular dish, rice is cooked in a pot filled with red beans, coconut milk and aromatic herbs. It is the regional variation of the traditional *gallo pinto*, but in Limón it is usually served on Sundays and on festive occasions. Another local dish is *rondon*, a spicy fish and vegetable stew.

From their African background the *Limonenses* have kept the original names of many ingredients; the use of tubers, such as the yam; and maintain the using of green leaves in soups and stews. Their African heritage also shows in their use of herbal teas made with an infinite variety of plants. From their ancestors' hard lives in the sugar plantations of the West Indies, the *Limonenses* have inherited many products that were included in the daily rations of the slaves: breadfruit, salt cod, mangoes, cassava, plantains and a great variety of tropical fruits. And from the demands and preferences of their British masters, they have retained several recipes for cakes, pastries and breads.

In Guanacaste, pre-Columbian traditions in cooking are very much alive. A larger variety of corn dishes are cooked there than in the rest of the country, including delicious pastries. *Tam-*

fast, eaten with hot *tortillas guanacastecas*, which are larger than the ones eaten in the rest of the country. African slave women were brought to the region during colonial times to work in the kitchens of the *haciendas*. They also left their mark on many exotic recipes still cooked in that province. *Ajiaco* and *bajo*, stews made with a mixture of meats and vegetables, maintain their African origins.

On the Pacific coast, Puntarenas presents recipes using ingredients from the sea, including *guiso de cambute* (conch stew) and dishes featuring different combinations of fresh shrimp, lobster and squid. ❑

ales, *chorreadas*, *tanelas* and many other regional delicacies can still be found throughout Guanacaste. Some beach hotels there are starting to include them on their menus.

Since cattle farming is one of Guanacaste's main resources, milk products are often very good. *Bagaces* (a hard, salted cheese, used grated and added to other recipes) has been, since the 19th century, an important part of the salary of the *peones* (farmhands). *Cuajadas* (fresh cheese balls) are usually served at break-

LEFT: *empanadas* (meat or vegetable patties) are a typical country fair food.
ABOVE: *gallo pinto,* the national dish.

THE CHOROTEGA LEGACY

Long before the white man arrived, the indigenous Chorotega tribe prepared a very thin unleavened cornmeal pancake called the *tortilla*. It is the main ingredient of Costa Rican *gallitos*, a type of hors d'oeuvre made by wrapping *tortillas* around mashed black beans, spicy meat, a spoonful of vegetable stew, pork chunks, or whatever else takes the chef's fancy.

The Chorotega also prepared *tamales*, rectangular pieces of corn dough stuffed with deer or turkey meat and a sauce made from tomatoes, pumpkin seeds and sweet peppers. The sauce, called *pipian*, is still prepared today in a very similar way.

FRUITS OF COSTA RICA

Whether piled high in the market, served up on a plate or whipped into a milkshake,
Costa Rica's rainbow of fruits is a delightful assault on all the senses

Fernández de Oviedo, a Spanish writer who came to Costa Rica in the l6th century, was probably the first European to chronicle the country's astounding variety of tropical fruits. Enthusiastic at every new discovery, he pronounced the pineapple the "best-looking, most wonderful lady in the vegetable world."

De Oviedo probably didn't get to taste all of Costa Rica's different fruits. There are simply too many, and they are available for every possible taste preference throughout the year. Get up early in the morning in San José and visit the Mercado Borbón, or the produce market off 10th Avenue, or the dozens of fruit stalls near the Coca Cola bus station. Or go to the open-air produce and fruit markets on Saturday morning, held in almost every town on the Central Plateau, to see and taste the season's harvest. Along the highways and main roads will be vendors of all kinds of fruit and fruit drinks. In this chapter, we take a look at Costa Rica's A–Z of fruits – from *anona* to *zapote*.

Anona

A strange-looking heart-shaped fruit, also called "the bullock's heart," the *anona* changes from green to a dark reddish-brown as it ripens. The sweet pulp is milk white and contains several large black seeds. After cutting it in half, eat it with a spoon, using the skin as a bowl. The *anona* is related to the custard-apple (*anona chirimoya*) found in the northern part of the country. It has a delicate sweetness and a delightful fragrance like rose-water. Mark Twain described it as "deliciousness itself".

Breadfruit

Breadfruit, like bananas, are grown in the Atlantic region of Costa Rica. This fruit of Polynesian origin was introduced to the West Indies by Captain Bligh, and the Jamaicans planted it in Limón. An attractive, ornamental tree with large leaves, the breadfruit is an ingredient in many Caribbean dishes.

Caimitos and other stars

The *caimito* or Costa Rican star apple looks just like a star when cut, similar in taste to the mangosteen (an exotic fruit found in Malaysia and Thailand). This glossy fruit varies in shade from purple to light green. The sweet flesh is usually eaten fresh, but in Limón you can still find it made into a mixture called "matrimony," prepared by scooping out the pulp and adding it to a glass of sour orange juice.

Carambolas, which also look like beautiful stars when cut in thin slices crosswise, are used as garnishes for desserts and for making juice. This shiny, five-sided pinkish-yellow fruit is about 5–8 cm (2–3 in) long.

Cashew fruit

An exotic cousin of the mango, the cashew fruit is best known for the kidney-shaped nut attached to its lower end. The fleshy portion, or apple, varying in color from brilliant yellow to flame-scarlet, is eaten fresh here. Its superb color and penetrating, almost pungent, aroma make this one of the most delectable of all tropical fruits. The flesh is soft, very juicy and zesty. It is also used to make a jam, a wine and a refreshing beverage similar to lemonade, which retains the special aroma and flavor of the unique fruit. In the late 1970s, the government decided to plant many areas with cashews, to be exported abroad. The venture was a failure, but the trees are still there.

There was a wonderful side effect, too: parakeets and parrots adore the fruit, and many species that were almost extinct are now increasing their numbers while dining on abundant cashew apples. Beware, if the seeds are not roasted before eating, they are poisonous.

beverages. Foreigners find the flavor somewhat suggestive of a combination of pineapple and mango, but *Ticos* consider that to be heresy.

Guava

A bestselling book about the acclaimed Colombian writer Gabriel García Marquez has the provocative title *The Guava's Perfume*. You will better understand how the title elicits the Latin American experience if you visit a home when guava jelly is being cooked. The entire house fills with the aroma of this wonderful fruit. But cooking is not obligatory; you can simply eat the guava raw.

Granadilla

The sweet *granadilla* (passion fruit) is a favorite all over Central America. This fruit is oval and orange to orange-brown. Within the hard, crisp skin, a bundle of seeds is surrounded by an almost liquid, translucent and wonderfully tasty pulp. Use a spoon to eat it.

Guanabana

Related to the *anona*, the *guanabana* is unrivaled for its use in sherbets and refreshing

LEFT: cashew apples; the gray part is the edible nut.
ABOVE: paw-paw near Turrialba. Squeeze a dash of lemon or lime juice on the flesh to give it a zing.

Another fruit, called in English "Costa Rican guava" *(cas)*, is yellow in color, round, and has soft white flesh. It is acidic, but highly valued for jelly-making and for drinks. If you see it on a menu, under *"naturales"*, try a freshly squeezed *jugo de cas* (*cas* juice).

Loquat

The loquat *(níspero)* is a small, oval-shaped fruit with a large stone, pale-yellow to orange in color. It is also called the Japanese medlar. The flesh, firm and meaty in some varieties, melting in others, is juicy and of a sprightly acid flavor. Although commonly eaten fresh, it can also be used in cooking.

Mango

Alajuela's Central Park is full of mango trees with their tempting fragrance, and that is why the town, second in importance only to San José, is called Mango City. Alajuela's mangoes are sweet, firm and delicate. The ripe mangos are sweeter and spicier, but smaller and softer than the unripe *mangas*. The aroma is spicy and alluring. Few other fruits have a historical background as developed as the mango, and few others are so inextricably connected with religious beliefs. Buddha himself is said to have been presented with a mango grove, so that he might find rest beneath its graceful shade.

fresh, as is its yellow-version cousin. Some refer to the yellow variety as the hogplum because hogs are very fond of them and fatten on the fruit that falls to the ground from wild trees in the forest.

The coco-plum *(icaco)*, on the other hand, is never eaten fresh, but its white flesh is made into a sweet preserve, called *miel de icaco*. Another cousin, the *ambarella (yuplón)*, was brought to Jamaica by Captain Bligh of *Bounty* fame. It came to Costa Rica in the hands of English-speaking Jamaican immigrants to the Port of Limón. It is eaten uncooked, with a little salt, or made into a preserve.

Besides eating them as dessert fruits, Costa Ricans make mangoes into chutney – that spicy sauce well-known to those who enjoy Indian food – as well as preserves, sauces and pies.

Mombín

The Spaniards said the *mombín* (or *jocote*) was a type of plum when they first saw it, but it really has nothing in common with the plum. This fruit is juicy and spicy, unlike any other. The *tronador* is the best variety. Street vendors sell brown paper bags full of *mombínes* from August through October, the color varying from dark green to bright red, depending on ripeness. The *mombín* is usually eaten

Nanzi

You'll recognize a nanzi *(nance)* by its fragrance. This small, round yellow fruit has been popular among Costa Ricans since pre-Columbian times, but foreigners tend to find its smell too strong. It is used for preserves, wines and jellies. *Nances en guaro* (nanzis in liqueur) are very good. Left to ferment in liqueur for nine months, they take on an amber-brown color. Nanzi sherbets are also very popular.

Paw-paw

Paw-paw (or papaya) grows almost everywhere in the country, and most tourists are particularly enamored of a drink called *papaya en leche*, a sort of papaya milkshake. There are two varieties: the huge local papaya and the smaller, sweeter Hawaiian version. Papaya is also excellent as a meat tenderizer.

Pejibaye

More a vegetable than a fruit, this was a treasured food of the aboriginal peoples. You will surely see it on the fruit stands, with its glossy orange skin and black stripes, resembling a large acorn. Cooked and peeled, its yellow pulp tastes very good when a little mayonnaise is added to it to soften its rather dry texture. It cannot be eaten fresh. *Pejibaye* soup is one of the most exceptional dishes of Costa Rican cuisine.

Rambutan

The most exotic sight in a fruit market in Costa Rica has to be the rambutan *(mamon chino)*. The bunches of red and orange fruits, sometimes called "hairy lychees", look like gooseberries covered in fleshy spines. To eat them, simply cut the leathery rind with a sharp knife and pull it back from the pulp.

Rose-apple and mountain-apple

The fragrance of the guava is only rivaled by that of the rose-apple *(manzana rosa)*, a beautiful round fruit, whitish green to apricot-yellow in color, and perfumed with the scent of the rose. The flesh is crisp, juicy and sweet. As a preserve or crystallized, it is delicious. If you eat it fresh, don't overdo it since the seeds are poisonous when eaten in large quantities.

A relative of the rose-apple, the *ohia* or mountain-apple *(manzana de agua)* is a beautiful oval fruit, white to crimson in color. Its flesh is apple-like: crisp, white, and juicy but not very flavourful. *Ohia* jam is exquisite.

Sapodilla

One of the best fruits of tropical America from the province of Guanacaste is the *sapodilla* or naseberry, here called *chicozapote* or *níspero*. It is a dessert fruit, rarely cooked or preserved in any way. The French botanist Descourtilz described it as having the "sweet perfumes of honey, jasmine and lily of the valley."

LEFT: a mountain of melons at Cartago.
RIGHT: the humble *pejibaye* has become an unlikely star of Costa Rican cuisine.

Zapote

A relative of the *sapodilla*, the *mammee-sapota* or marmalade-plum *(zapote)* kept Cortés and his army alive on their famous march from Mexico City to Honduras. The bright salmon-red color of the pulp catches the eyes of tourists walking the Avenida Central in San José. Street vendors, knowing the sales appeal of the beautiful color, cut the marmalade-plums in halves.

Beware, however, if you are not used to the very sweet fruits of the tropics – the flavor of the *zapote* may be rather cloying. Very ripe *zapotes* are used to make the most wonderful ice creams and sherbets. ❏

REFRESCOS

Refreshing fruit drinks such as *fresco de maracuyá* (passion-fruit) accompany every Costa Rican meal. One of the favorite and most nourishing is made from *moras* or blackberries. The berries are blended, strained and added to sugar water or milk. One of the more thirst-quenching drinks is made from *cas*, a type of guava.

A *tamarindo refresco* is similar in color and taste to apple juice. It is made from the seed pod of the tamarind tree. Tamarind seeds and pulp wrapped into balls the size of oranges are available at every market. The seeds are put into hot water to wash off the sticky tamarind and then are mixed with sugar and water.

COFFEE

When white coffee blossoms blanket the fields of the Central Valley, filling the air with a sweet jasmine-like fragrance, the Ticos call it "Costa Rican Snow"

You might well surmise that coffee is indigenous to Costa Rica, but it's not. The Spanish, French and Portuguese brought coffee beans to the New World from Ethiopia and Arabia. In the early 1800s, when seeds were first planted in Costa Rica, coffee plants were merely ornamental, grown to decorate

patios and courtyards with their glossy green leaves, seasonal white flowers and red berries. Costa Ricans had to be persuaded, even coerced, into growing them so the country might have a national export crop. Every *Tico* family was required by law to have at least a couple of bushes in the yard. The government awarded free plants to the poor and grants of land to anyone who was willing to plant coffee on it.

The Central Valley is the ideal place for the production of coffee. Its altitude, above 1,200 meters (4,000 ft); its temperatures, which average between 15°C and 28°C (59°F and 82°F); and its soil conditions are all perfect for coffee cultivation. Coffee estates quickly occupied much of the land, except for that needed to graze oxen. As the only Costa Rican export, the country's financial resources were organized to support it. By 1840, coffee had become big business, carried by oxcart through mountains to the Pacific port at Puntarenas, and from there by ship to Chile from where it was transported to Europe. By the mid-1800s Costa Rica's oligarchy of coffee barons had risen to positions of power and wealth, for the most part through processing and exporting the golden bean, rather than by actually growing it.

A mixed blessing

Costa Rica was fortunate in its early development of the coffee industry, but at times it has been a mixed blessing. The country incurred a heavy debt borrowing US$3 million from England to finance the Atlantic railroad so coffee could be exported from the Atlantic port of Limón. And when coffee hit bottom on the international market in 1900, the result was a severe shortage of basic foods in Costa Rica that year.

This dependency on an overseas market has left the Costa Ricans vulnerable on many occasions. Throughout the 20th century, coffee prices fluctuated wildly and the health of the nation's economy varied accordingly.

Traditionally, banana, citrus and poro trees were planted in the coffee fields to provide some

---

COFFEE TO EUROPE

In 1843, an English sea captain, William Le Lacheur, returning to England from the United States, stopped in at Costa Rica's Pacific port of Puntarenas in search of ballast for his empty ship. As it happened, 1843 was an exceptional year for coffee production and the farmers had more beans than they could sell.

They made a deal with Le Lacheur and loaded up the holds of his ship with coffee, allowing him to use the heavy sacks as ballast. He made the trip to England around the Cape, and two years later he returned to pay the coffee planters their profit. And thus began the Costa Rican-European coffee trade.

shade for the coffee plants. Later, coffee hybrids were developed that did not need shade and tree-less fields allowed more yield per acre. These varieties, however, were found to deplete the soil more rapidly and required fertilizer to enrich it, adding to the cost of production. Today, many coffee-growers have returned to the traditional shade-loving plants, pleasing environmentalists who advocate shade-grown coffee.

The coffee plant itself is grown in nurseries until it's a year old, at which time it is trans-planted to the field. Two years later it bears harvestable berries and, with care, will continue to bear fruit for the next 30 to 40 years.

November to January, during school vacation and Christmas holidays. Traditionally entire families in rural areas picked coffee together, some of the money earned going for Christmas presents and new outfits. But today, most coffee is picked by migrant workers from Panamá and Nicaragua.

Costa Rican coffee has been traditionally mixed with other coffees destined for world-wide export. But today, consumers demand the unadulterated stuff: 100 percent pure Costa Rican coffee. And the coffees from the highland regions around Poás, Barva de Heredia, Tres Ríos and Tarrazú are rated by many aficiona-dos among the best in the world. ❑

Since coffee grows best in a mountainous cli-mate, many of the hillsides in the Central Valley are covered with rows of the bright green bushes, reflecting the sun with their shiny, luxuriant leaves. Some of the fields seem almost vertical and it is difficult to see how pickers keep from tumbling down the slopes as they collect the berries. The answer lies in the ingenious solution of planting the trees directly behind one another so that the trunk of the downhill tree serves as a foothold for the pickers. Coffee is harvested from

LEFT: fast hands; Costa Rica has the greatest coffee productivity per acre in the world.
ABOVE: coffee pickers *circa* 1920.

CAFE BRITT

The best way to get a taste of Costa Rica's coffee culture is to take Cafe Britt's exceptional Coffee Tour. Located almost 1 km (²/₃ mile) north of Heredia in Barva (signposted from Heredia center), this theatrical, highly entertaining experience takes visitors through the entire coffee process, from growing the coffee cherry to correctly tasting the final product. Combining ele-ments of professional theater, a multimedia show, a farm visit, plant tour and tasting session, Cafe Britt whirls the visitor through the world of coffee in about two hours. You must reserve your tour in advance by telephoning 260-2748.

PLACES

A detailed guide to the entire country, with principal sites cross-referenced by number to the maps

Costa Rica may be a relatively small country, but don't think that means there's little to see or do here. Some of its beaches rival the best of the Caribbean for their crystal waters and white sand. Inland, lush forests and towering volcanoes attract walkers and nature lovers from all over the world. Indeed, national parks comprise a greater proportion of national territory than any other country in the world, amply justifying Costa Rica's reputation as the home of eco-tourism.

We begin the places section in the capital, San José, the small but bustling metropolis that acts as the international gateway to Costa Rica. It is not a beautiful city, but like most capitals it has a buzz. It's worth staying a day or so to visit some fascinating museums, from the underground Gold Museum to the Jade Museum atop a sky-scraper. It is also a good base for exploring the country, and there are some excellent lodges in the nearby mountains offering activities from horseback riding to whitewater rafting.

Next we focus on the Central Valley. This is the country's green and fertile heartland. It is an area of agricultural towns, coffee farms and many cultural treasures. From here it's a short hop to the beaches of the Central Pacific; these are some of the best in the country. Particularly famous is Manuel Antonio whose perfect white sands are the stuff of tropical dreams.

Many visitors regard the north as the true Costa Rica. This is almost a country in itself with the wonderful beaches of the Nicoya Peninsula, the great cattlelands of Guanacaste and the natural riches of Monteverde and the Sarapiquí. By night, Arenal Volcano, belching sulfurous smoke and oozing red lava, is an unforgettable sight.

By contrast, the Caribbean Coast presents Costa Rica's laid-back face: its tall palms, radiant sunshine and aquamarine waters beckoning visitors to share in its indolent lifestyle.

Our tour ends in the south, off the beaten track, amid a wild and wonderful region of vast tropical forests and Central America's highest peak. The Osa Peninsula and the Golfo Dulce are truly a world apart, often accessible only by boat, small plane or on foot. And in special picture features we'll tell you more about Costa Rica's volcanoes, its traditional handicrafts, its abundant flora, and its spectacular birdlife including its proudest natural treasure, the aptly and exotically named resplendent quetzal.

All the sites of interest are numbered on specially drawn maps to help you find your way around. Don't worry about getting lost – everyone does. But then, just getting there is half the fun of enjoying this remarkable country. ❑

PRECEDING PAGES: Atlantic coastline; *páramo*, an unusual ecosystem seen on the summit of Mount Chirripó; Basílica de Nuestra Señora de los Angeles in Cartago.
LEFT: a *campesino* ponders the origin and significance of this giant stone sphere.

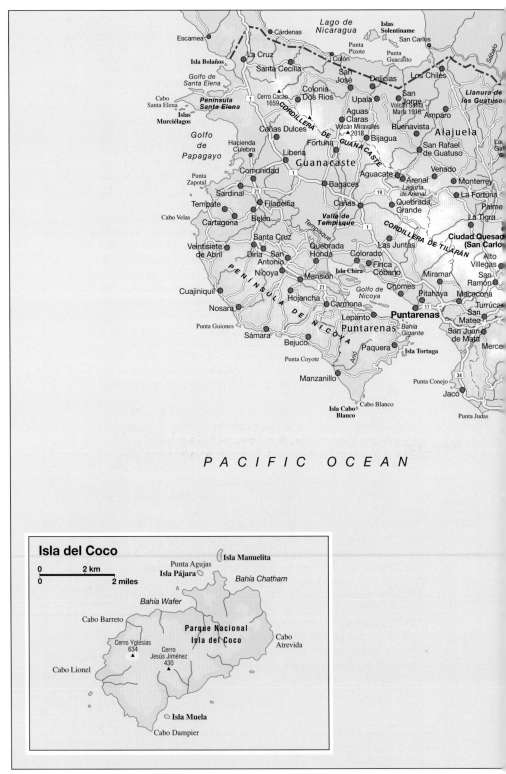

PACIFIC OCEAN

Lago de Nicaragua
Islas Solentiname
Cárdenas
San Carlos
Escamea
Punta Pizote
Punta Guacalito
Sábalo
Isla Bolaños
La Cruz
Colón
Los Chiles
Golfo de Santa Elena
Santa Cecilia
San José
Delicias
Cabo Santa Elena
Península Santa Elena
Colonia Dos Ríos
San Jorge
Llanura de los Guatuso
Cerro Cacao 1659
Upala
Volcán Santa María 1916
La Ga
Islas Murciélagos
Aguas Claras
Amparo
Cañas Dulces
Volcán Miravalles 2018
Buenavista
Alajuela
Golfo de Papagayo
Hacienda Culebra
Fortuna
Bijagua
San Rafael de Guatuso
Liberia
Guanacaste
Venado
Comunidad
Aguacate
Arenal
Monterrey
Punta Zapotal
Bagaces
Laguna de Arenal
La Fortuna
Sardinal
19
Palme
Tempate
Filadelfia
Cañas
Quebrada Grande
La Tigra
Cabo Velas
Belén
Valle de Tempisque
CORDILLERA DE TILARÁN
Ciudad Quesad (San Carlo
Cartagena
Santa Cruz
Quebrada Honda
Las Juntas
Alto Villegas
Veintisiete de Abril
Diriá
San Antonio
Colorado
Finca Cóbano
Miramar
San Ramón
Nicoya
Isla Chira
Macacona
Cuajiniquil
Mansión
Chomes
Pitahaya
Turrúca
Nosara
Hojancha
Golfo de Nicoya
17
San Mateo
Punta Guiones
Carmona
Lepanto
Puntarenas
San Juan de Mata
Sámara
Puntarenas
Bahía Gigante
Merce
Bejuco
Paquera
Isla Tortuga
Punta Coyote
Arío
Manzanillo
Punta Conejo
34
Jacó
Isla Cabo Blanco
Cabo Blanco
Punta Judas

PENÍNSULA DE NICOYA

CORDILLERA DE GUANACASTE

Tempisque

Isla del Coco

0 —— 2 km
0 —— 2 miles

Isla Manuelita
Punta Agujas
Isla Pájara
Bahía Chatham
Bahía Wafer
Cabo Barreto
Parque Nacional Isla del Coco
Cabo Atrevida
Cerro Yglésias 634
Cerro Jesús Jiménez 430
Cabo Lionel
Isla Muela
Cabo Dampier

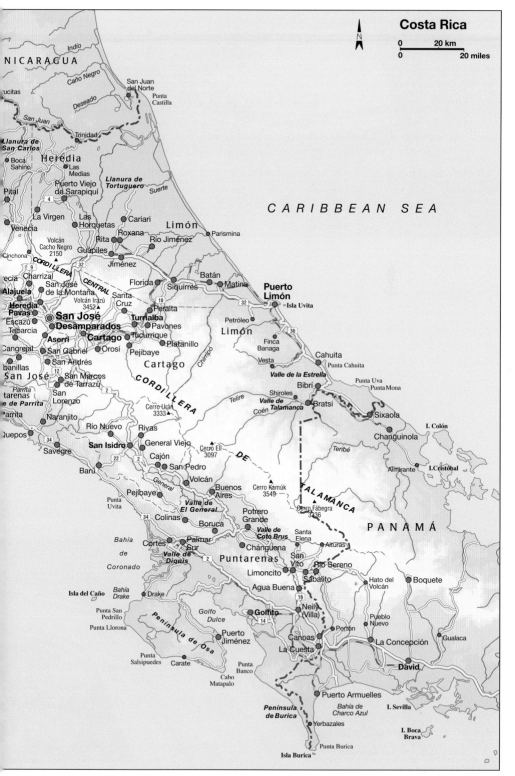

Costa Rica

NICARAGUA

CARIBBEAN SEA

PANAMÁ

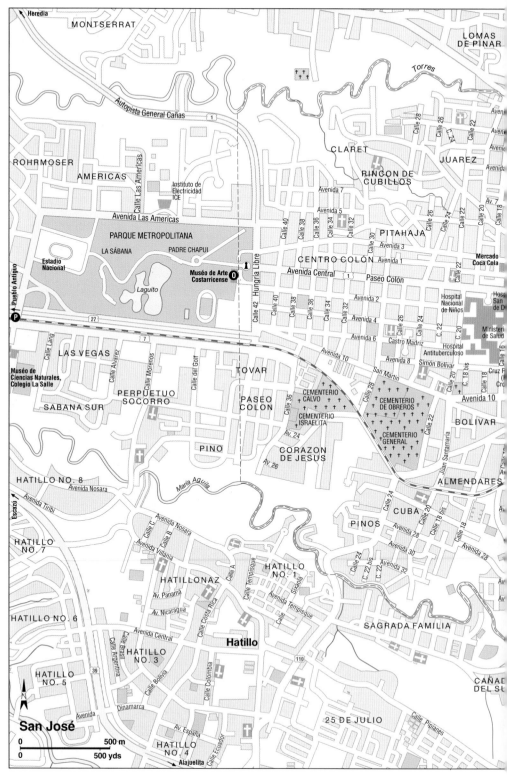

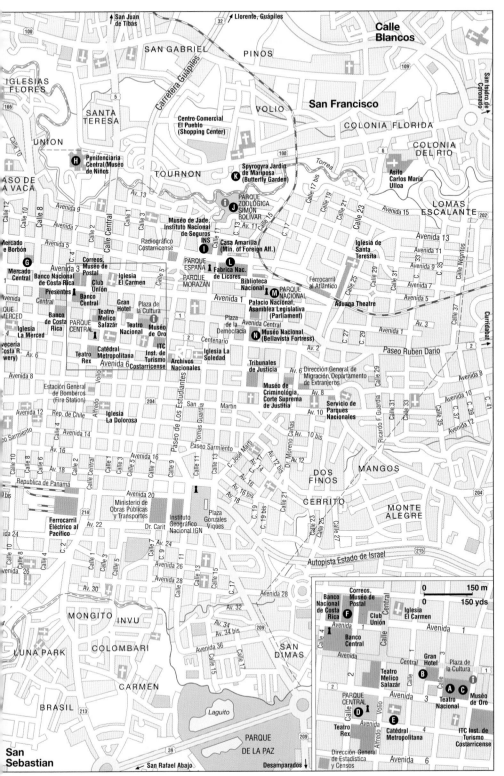

San Juan de Tibás
Llorente, Guápiles
32
100
Calle Blancos
SAN GABRIEL
PINOS
109
San Isidro de Coronado
IGLESIAS FLORES
166
Carretera Guápiles
VOLIO
San Francisco
COLONIA FLORIDA
SANTA TERESA
Centro Comercial El Pueblo (Shopping Center)
108
COLONIA DEL RIO
6
UNION
Calle 10
TOURNON
Torres
Asilo Carlos María Ulloa
LOMAS ESCALANTE
202
PASO DE LA VACA
Av. 13
Penitenciaría Central/Muséo de Niños
H
Spyrogyra Jardín de Mariposa (Butterfly Garden)
K
Calle 17 bis
Calle 19
Calle 21
Calle 23
Avenida 15
Avenida 13
Calle 12
Calle 10
Calle 8
Avenida 9
Calle 1
Calle 3
Muséo de Jade, Instituto Nacional de Seguros
PARQUE ZOOLÓGICA SIMÓN BOLIVAR
J
Av. 11
Calle 15
Iglesia de Santa Teresita
Calle 33
Calle 35
Avenida 11
Calle Negritos
Avenida 7
Calle 2
Calle Central
Radiográfico Costarricense
Calle 11
Casa Amarilla (Min. of Foreign Aff.)
INS
C. 17
Calle 25
Calle 29
Calle 31
Avenida 9
Avenida 7
Avenida 5
Ferrocarril al Atlántico
Mercado e Borbón
G
Av. 4
Correos, Museo de Postal
PARQUE ESPAÑA
Fabrica Nac. de Licores
Biblioteca Nacional
Calle 37
Currídabat
Mercado Central
Banco Nacional de Costa Rica
PARQUE MORAZÁN
PARQUE NACIONAL
M
Aduana Theatre
2
Avenida
QUE MERCED
Central
Presentes
Club Unión
Iglesia El Carmen
Avenida 1
Palacio Nacional, Asamblea Legislativa (Parliament)
Av. 3
C. 27
C. 29
Avenida 1
Banco Central
Gran Hotel
Plaza de la Cultura
Avenida Central
Paseo Ruben Dario
2
Iglesia La Merced
Banco de Costa Rica
PARQUE CENTRAL
Teatro Melico Salazár
Teatro Nacional
Museo de Oro
Plaza de la Democracia
Museo Nacional (Bellavista Fortress)
Av. 2
Catédral Metropolitana
ITC Inst. de Turismo Costarricense
Iglesia La Soledad
Tribunales de Justicia
Dirección General de Migración, Departamento de Extranjeros
Avenida 8
Teatro Rex
Avenida 6
Archivos Nacionales
Av. 6
Avenida 8
Estación General de Bomberos (Fire Station)
Paseo de los Estudiantes
San Martin
Museo de Criminología, Corte Suprema de Justicia
Av. 8
Av. 10
Servicio de Parques Nacionales
Rep. de Chile
204
Iglesia La Dolorosa
Tomás Guardia
Paseo Sarmiento
C. José Martí
Dr. Moreno Cañas
Av. 10 bis
MANGOS
204
Av. 16
Av. 14
Av. 12 bis
Av. 12
DOS FINOS
República de Panamá
Av. 18
Av. 16 bis
CERRITO
MONTE ALEGRE
215
Av. 20
Ministerio de Obras Públicas y Transportes
Instituto Geográfico Nacional IGN
Plaza Gonzales Viques
C. 19 bis
Calle 23
Calle 25
Calle 27
Ferrocarril Eléctrico al Pacífico
214
Av. 22
Dr. Carit
Autopista Estado de Israel
Av. 24
Av. 26
Av. 28
209
MONGITO INVU
Av. 30
Av. 32
Av. 34
Av. 34 bis
SAN DIMAS
209
LUNA PARK
COLOMBARI
Avenida 36
CARMEN
BRASIL
213
Laguito
PARQUE DE LA PAZ
209
San Sebastian
39
San Rafael Abajo
Desamparados

0   150 m
0   150 yds

Correos, Museo de Postal
F
Banco Nacional de Costa Rica
Club Unión
Iglesia El Carmen
Avenida
Banco Central
Gran Hotel
B
Plaza de la Cultura
Teatro Melico Salazár
A
C
Teatro Nacional
Museo de Oro
PARQUE CENTRAL
D
E
Teatro Rex
Catédral Metropolitana
ITC Inst. de Turismo Costarricense
Dirección General de Estadística y Censos
Avenida 6

SAN JOSÉ

*With modern high-rises ranked alongside tile-roofed,
faded colonial villas, Costa Rica's capital may seem a jumble
at first. Yet it possesses a certain* Tico *charm*

Map
on pages
130–131

The growth, some might say the flowering, of San José, began on that day, sometime during the first half of the 19th century, when Europe decided to have its daily cup of coffee.

By the 1850s, San José had been transformed from a humble village to a boom town. Everything had to be the best, the most modern, the most European. With every bag of coffee that was exported, there was a proportionate enrichment of the economic, social and cultural life of the *Josefinos*, as the people of San José are called. And as the city became wealthy, so its inhabitants became more refined, more sophisticated, and more worldly.

The golden age

By the end of the 19th century, San José was booming from the profits of its coffee exports. It was the third city in the world to have public electric lighting; one of the first to have public telephones; the first in Central America, perhaps in all of Latin America, to initiate free and compulsory public education to all of its citizens; and the first to allow girls to attend high school. Admittedly, the roads were unpaved, but most upper-class homes had had pianos.

Through much of the first part of the 20th century, San José continued to prosper and build: a national library, schools, banks, parks and plazas, ministries, numerous hotels, theaters, a sumptuous post office, bookstores, hospitals, churches, a magnificent Palace of Justice, and an international airport.

And then, in 1956, Costa Rica's population passed the 1 million mark. The international focus of influence had shifted and the people ceased coveting things European and became heavily influenced by North American standards and sensibilities.

The modern city

Cars and trucks began to appear where there had only been the gentle horse and buggy, ox carts, pedestrians and bicycles. The population doubled over the following two decades.

By the mid-1970s, the air in San José had become noticeably dirty and the once civilized, narrow streets had become overwhelmed with a relentless rush of cars and people, all seemingly in a big hurry to get somewhere. Graceful, ornate old buildings were torn down and replaced with harsh, ugly copies of North American modern architecture. San José, the civilized 19th-century city, could not adapt its physical limitations to meet the demands of its consumerist 20th-century people. And today, in the early 21st century, this conflict has engendered a city that, by most standards, is traffic-clogged and unattractive.

PRECEDING PAGES: a section of ceiling in the National Theater. **LEFT:** political exposure at a tender age. **BELOW:** the National Youth Symphonic Orchestra.

TIP

Theft is a problem in San José. The best way to have a hassle-free day is not to take anything with you that can be snatched. Wear a money belt and leave your passport and other valuables at your hotel.

Oases of calm

Fortunately, amid the miasma of diesel fumes, and the hordes of people, there are still some islands of repose where you can rest and refresh yourself as you search to find the heart of this city. The National Theater is probably the most beautiful building in the country and its coffee shop is a favorite place; quiet, elegant, yet alive. And to relax, sipping a *refresco natural* on the veranda of the Grand Hotel, while listening to marimba bands and the burble of 20 different languages as other people rush around the plaza, should not be missed.

The National Museum and the Gold Museum are worth seeking out, along with the world-class Jade Museum; there are souvenir shops, good theaters, many good restaurants, an abundance of cabarets and nightclubs, and a few interesting art galleries. There are also some extraordinary remnants of old San José, hints of what a handsome, delightful place this used to be, not so long ago.

Getting your bearings

Before you embark on the following tour of the city, or indeed go looking for any address within San José, sit down with our map *(see pages 130–131)* and familiarize yourself with the way it is laid out. The city is organized on a grid system of numbered streets *(calles)*, which run north to south, and avenues *(avenidas)*, which run east to west. The northern avenues and eastern streets have odd numbers; the southern avenues and western streets have even numbers.

Confusingly, however, buildings are not numbered and, for the most part, only in downtown San José do any streets have names. Addresses are often given in the following format: Metropolitan Cathedral, Calle Central, Avenida 2–4, meaning that it is on the Calle Central between Avenida 2 and Avenida 4.

BELOW: a bustling downtown shopping street.

Alternatively and more commonly, addresses are given in terms of distance in meters (*metros*), north, south, east or west from known landmarks. It's as well to know, however, that *Ticos* often equate a city block with 100 meters (no matter how long or short it really is). The end result of all this is that *Ticos* and visitors alike can be seen wandering the city streets perpetually stopping one another to ask for directions. The good news is that people are generally happy to help and, if nothing else, it gives you a chance to talk to the locals.

The best time to walk in San José is on a Sunday morning, when there is less traffic on the streets. Or, during the week, go early, before the rush and roar of the city has yet to begin.

The heart of the city

The Plaza de la Cultura marks the heart of the city. The area around this large square is a popular meeting point for traders, artisans, street musicians, painters, actors, in fact just about anybody and everybody. The pride of the square is the **Teatro Nacional Ⓐ**, without doubt the finest building in San José, if not all Costa Rica. Its construction was financed by 19th-century coffee barons, who, embarrassed that there was no appropriate venue here for the world-renowned opera star, Adelina Patti to perform (she had snubbed San José on her 1890 tour of Central America), offered to pay a tax on every bag of coffee exported.

Modeled after the Paris Opera House and neoclassical in style, the theater was opened in 1897 with a production of *Faust*. It is on four levels, with a well-equipped stage system and a main audience seating floor that is adjustable to different heights. The floor plan is in the form of a horseshoe, and the acoustics are excellent. The detailing was done by Spanish and Italian artisans. Ironically,

ABOVE: mountains of fruit for sale at the Central Market.
BELOW: quiet Sunday morning on Paseo Colón.

City Buses

Buses are ubiquitous in San José. They go everywhere throughout the city and its surrounding areas. Some downtown streets are clogged with them: shiny new Mercedes models, freshly washed and festively painted with murals on their rear windows; sooty, rusty wrecks emitting thick black smoke; recycled school buses from the US, scrupulously cared for and graced with fanciful names to give them new life.

Whether new and slick or decrepit and smoky, the buses have a common trait. They are wonderful windows into Costa Rican life. Most everyone uses them: students on their way to classes; women in heels, dressy clothes and impeccable make-up on their way to work; country folk coming into town to do business of one kind or another; young mothers taking children to doctors' appointments at the social security hospital; men with briefcases and neat pants and shirts. They're all on the bus, heading this way or that.

And for a fistful of colones, you can climb aboard and join in the great comings and goings of life on the Central Valley. A bus ride in San José is not particularly comfortable, especially during peak hours, but there's no better or more enjoyable way to make quick and often delicious observations on *Tico* life and characteristics.

For one thing, chivalry is still alive. Or is it a simple sense of decency, of caring for others, a quiet courtesy? Young men will assist older men or women with children in tow up the steps, a seated passenger will offer to hold your packages while you stand, someone will always offer his or her seat to an older person or a pregnant woman. The bus driver will wait for someone making a last-minute dash. A young boy, known to the bus driver by name, boards on Paseo Colón and, for a few stops, becomes the bus's official door-opener. Then the boy tires of the game and, saying goodbye to the driver, leaps off at the next stop.

A wizened old *campesino* (peasant), returning from a trip to the city, takes a long time to board. He carries with him a heavy burlap bag, redolent of coffee beans and *pejibaye*.

A small girl in a rumpled pink dress enters the parked bus, waiting for its scheduled departure at the Coca Cola bus stop. She speaks to the driver, then stands at the front of the bus, singing a mournful song about love. When she finishes, she moves down the aisle with an open hand, into which we drop our small change.

Take at least one bus ride in San José. Board near the beginning of the line, when you can still get a seat, and watch the rush of humanity come aboard, pausing to place their fare in the driver's hand, pushing past the turnstile, greeting friends and neighbors as they make their way down the aisle, more passengers stop after stop, until it isn't possible to squeeze another body on.

It's a good idea to take a ride outside the city too. The best trip is the Periferica bus, which, as the name suggests, goes around the periphery of the city, and allows you a glimpse of some of San José's most desirable suburbs as well as some of the shabbier parts of town. ❑

LEFT: traveling "a la Tica" is a quick way to get an insight into local life.

Adelina Patti never did come to Costa Rica, but Costa Rica's top-quality National Symphony Orchestra performs here with illustrious international guest artists; their season begins in March. There are also daily tours where you can admire the marble, gold, bronze, tropical woods, crystal chandeliers, velvet drapes and statuary. The ceiling fresco is famous and features a bucolic scene of coffee and banana pickers *(see pages 128–29)*.

The **Cafe del Teatro Nacional** features changing art exhibits and is a very popular place, serving excellent salads, snacks, desserts and specialty coffees.

Adjacent to the National Theater is the **Gran Hotel Costa Rica ❸**, renowned as a meeting place for tourists who gather in its outdoor cafe where musicians often entertain with marimbas. Inside is a rather tacky 24-hour casino.

Beneath the Plaza de la Cultura is the capital's best museum, the **Museo de Oro ❻** (Gold Museum). On the east side of the square in cool, darkened, cavernous rooms, the collection features more than 2,000 brilliant pre-Columbian artifacts made by the indigenous peoples from the southwestern part of the country. Highlights include tiny half-man, half-bird figures, and erotic statuettes (open Tues–Sun 10am–4.30pm; entrance fee). The museum also contains the national coin collection and occasional exhibitions of modern art.

Before leaving the Plaza de la Cultura pay a visit to the Costa Rica Tourist Office (ICT) at the entrance to the Gold Museum for news of what's on in town.

More museums

A short walk west of the Plaza de la Cultura along Avenida 2 is the **Parque Central ❹** (Central Park), another great place for people-watching. *Ticos* complained when most of the park's trees were cut down in the 1980s, leaving only

Map on pages 130–131

TIP

On the Avenida Central side of the Plaza de la Cultura is a branch of Pop's Ice-Cream Parlor, generally agreed to be the best in Costa Rica. It is always crowded.

BELOW: the National Theater.

TIP

At the northern end of the Parque Central, look out for the neoclassical facade of the Teatro Popular Melico Salazar.

BELOW: the Central Market is one of the most colorful and dynamic places in the city.

a few royal palms, but at least it is now a safer place. The Gaudí-like kiosk in the center of the park was donated by the Somoza family of Nicaragua and sometimes hosts open-air concerts on weekends.

Directly in front of the park is the huge **Catedral Metropolitana** Ⓔ (Metropolitan Cathedral). It is of little architectural merit, but do notice the finely carved wood ceiling of the Chapel of the Holy Sacrament; also its walls, so carefully adorned with flower motifs that it almost looks as if they have been tiled. The cathedral provides a refuge of peace from the hot bustling city, and microphone-amplified midday Masses are well attended by local people.

Due north of Parque Central, along Calle 2, is the **Correos** Ⓕ (central post office) in a grand old building that also houses the **Museo de Postal** (Post Office Museum, open Mon–Fri 8am–5pm, Sat 8am–noon) and a pleasant cafe, as well as an ICT office. Three blocks west of the post office on Avenida 1 you'll find the **Mercado Central** Ⓖ (Central Market), the city's best market, dating from 1881. There are over 200 stalls selling everything from old kitchen utensils to saddle bags, fresh fish, coffee and spices by the kilo, to religious icons. The prices are some of the cheapest in the city. At the center of the hall are the snack stands, a good place to find real *Tico* food at real *Tico* prices. Keep your hand on your wallet as pickpockets operate here (and just love tourists), but don't be deterred from diving into this den to witness gritty *Tico* life at first hand (open Mon–Sat 6.30am–6.30pm).

If you have children in tow, you might at this point like to make a diversion a few blocks north to the old Penitenciaria Central (city jail), now the **Museo de Niños** Ⓗ (Children's Museum), which has lots of interesting interactive exhibits that are entertaining for adults, too. There is a good summary of *Ticos'* historical developments, with models of Amerindian huts, Caribbean wooden shacks and modern housing (open Tues–Fri 8am–3.30pm, Sat–Sun 9.30am– 4.30pm; entrance fee). It is in a rough part of town, however, so take a cab, rather than walking there.

On Avenida 7, on the north side of the Parque España, is the not-to-be-missed **Museo de Jade** Ⓘ (Jade Museum; open Mon–Fri 8.30am–3.30pm; entrance fee). It can be found on the 11th floor of the National Insurance Institute, better known as the INS **Building**, a useful landmark that also offers great views over the city. Alongside the museum's carefully crafted jade pieces *(see page 28)*, most of which are *colgantes* (amulets or pendants), are masterpieces of pre-Hispanic sculpture from all regions of the country.

Opposite the Jade Museum is one of the capital's most interesting old buildings, the **Edificio Metalico** (Metal Building school), shipped here in 1892 from Belgium to house 1,000 students. Next door to the museum under the shade of an ancient ceibo tree is the **Casa Amarilla** (Yellow House), the home of the Foreign Ministry, but constructed in 1816 as the Court of Justice. You can take a look inside its foyer.

Nature in the city

A block north of the Jade Museum is the **Parque Zoológico Simón Bolívar** Ⓙ (Simón Bolívar Zoo), with a small collection of African, Asian, and Costa

Rican animals. Although the zoo has received much-needed renovation in recent years, it is still a fairly sad place for the ill-housed animals, especially the larger ones. Geared primarily toward locals and school groups, nevertheless the park makes for a pleasant stroll especially on a weekday morning, when you may have it all to yourself (open daily 9am–4.30pm; entrance fee).

Immediately north, at the back of the park, is the enchanting **Spyrogyra Jardín de Mariposa ⓚ** (Spyrogyra Butterfly Garden). It's not far, as the butterfly flies, but the entrance is a long way off on foot, so you will need to take a cab from the zoo to get to this secret city garden. One of the main aims of Spyrogyra is to help rural women find alternative sources of income from laboring in the fields by exporting butterfly cocoons to Europe and the US instead (open daily 8am–4pm; entrance fee). In addition to the many colorful butterflies, there are gardens and hummingbirds to enjoy.

Arts, history and culture

Also close to the INS building is the **Fábrica Nacional de Licores ⓛ** (National Liquor Factory), also known as FANAL. Founded in 1856, the complex, which takes up a whole city block, has been turned into an arts and cultural center, somewhat confusingly also known as the Centro Nacional de la Cultura y la Ciencia or CENAC (National Center of Culture and Science). Pop into the pretty courtyard and amphitheater which lead to another part of the complex: the **Museum of Contemporary Art and Design**, with changing exhibitions of art, sculpture and photography. FANAL is open Tues–Sat; free except for some special exhibits; check the *Tico Times* for what's on. One block southeast of here is the **Parque Nacional ⓜ** (National Park). This is the largest of San José's

Map
on pages
130–131

ABOVE: crested iguana at the zoo.
BELOW: central post office *(Correos)* and Post Office Museum.

Map
on pages
130–131

parks, where lovers drape themselves over park benches and bureaucrats eat their lunches under the shade of the 50 or so native tree species. It's a very pleasant place by day, and well-lit by night, but probably not advisable to stroll in alone after dark. In the center of the park is a monument depicting victory in the war against the hated *filibustero*, William Walker *(see page 45)*.

Two blocks south of here, on Calle 17, is the **Museo Nacional ◐** (open Tues–Sun; entrance fee) housed in the old Bellavista fortress, which still bears the bullet marks from the 1948 Civil War. Constructed in 1870, the building served as a barracks until the abolition of the army in 1949. The collections provide an overview of Costa Rica's history and culture, and include displays on burial ceremonies, a treasury of gold pieces and rustic furniture from the colonial period. In the courtyard are cannons and some of the mysterious stone spheres found in the south of the country *(see pages 28 and 251)*. From the terrace of the building there are fine views down onto the city and the amphitheater-like Plaza de la Democracia, where open-air concerts are sometimes held. Artisans congregate to sell handicrafts and souvenirs in a roofed-over corridor of market stalls, and even if you don't find too much from Costa Rica there are generally bargains to be had in handmade clothes from Guatemala and El Salvador.

ABOVE: gold plate, Museo de Oro.
BELOW: potatoes make a change from rice and beans.
RIGHT: foxgloves.

Sabana Park and Pueblo Antiguo

The large grassy area of **Parque La Sabana** occupies what was Costa Rica's first international airport. The Spanish-style building has been converted into the **Museo de Arte Costarricense ◐** (Museum of Costa Rican Art). This features revolving exhibitions of works by the country's finest 19th- and 20th-century painters and sculptors as well as works by international artists (open Tues–Sun when there is an exhibition mounted; entrance fee). In the *Salón Dorado* (Golden Room, upper story), French artist Luis Ferrón has immortalized Costa Rican history in a striking-looking stucco and bronze mural.

Across from the southwest corner of the park is the Museum of Natural Sciences, also known as the **Museo La Salle**. The main attraction is a huge collection of stuffed animals. With pickled snakes, toads and fish; a stuffed swan suspended from the ceiling; and a scale model of a US space shuttle, the place has a faintly eccentric air (open daily, entrance fee).

Sabana Park is a popular weekend retreat for *Tico* families who come here to picnic, ride their bikes, skate, play and feed the ducks in the park's many lakes. Kite vendors also do a brisk trade on breezy days. Sporting facilities include soccer fields, tennis courts, a swimming pool (only occasionally open), and jogging trails. The park should be avoided after dark, however.

A short bus ride northwest of Sabana Park in the district of La Uruca is the **Pueblo Antiguo ◐** (literally "Old Village"), an idyllic re-creation of old Costa Rica set in the Parque de Diversiones. Actors demonstrate traditional craft skills and bygone agricultural techniques, and there are other shows plus restaurants serving local food (open Fri–Sun 9am–7pm; entrance fee). Sunday is the best day to visit, when a carnival is always enacted in an authentic setting. ❏

THE CENTRAL VALLEY

The heartland of Costa Rica is home to 60 percent of the nation's people. It is the center of government, agriculture and commerce, and has the oldest cities and many cultural treasures

Map on page 146

T he Central Valley *(Valle Central)*, or Central Plateau *(Meseta Central)*, as it is often called, is strictly speaking neither a valley nor a plateau since it contains both kinds of landscape. The Central Highlands might be a more apt name for this area, only 24 km by 64 km (15 miles by 40 miles), where two mountain ranges meet. You'll find rich, volcanic hills and river-filled valleys, with altitudes reaching up to 1,500 meters (4,500 ft).

The good life

The countryside is beautiful and variable. The climate is salubrious. The air is sweet and soft. The people are generally friendly, dignified and independent. Volcanoes, some still active and smoking, others dormant or extinct, rise up above the hills around the valley. Above them, a big sky is constantly changing – dark, charcoal rain clouds; intense, searing patches of blue; fluffy white cumulus; and occasional rainbows. All come and go in quick succession.

There are misty, almost enchanted places such as the Orosí Valley or dusty farm towns such as Santa Ana; adobe villages that sing of old Costa Rica, such as Barva; and crowded, noisy, relentlessly vital cities, such as San José or Cartago. And they're all easily accessible. Daytrips by bus or car, or with tour groups can easily be arranged.

Passing through the small, highland towns and villages, you see what in Central America is the unusual and impressive sight of people living in houses on plots of land that they themselves own and farm. Neighborhoods are often a hodgepodge of larger, fancy homes and smaller, humble ones. Housewives in aprons chat in front yards as they watch their babies. Children in school uniforms play together as they walk up the road for lunch at home. Produce from backyard fruit trees is for sale on little tables or stands in front of houses: soft-fruit preserves, homemade cheese and sour cream, oranges, candy-stuffed grapefruit, mangoes, tomatoes. Visitors are accepted with a mild, easy curiosity; no one seems especially surprised to have a *gringo* walk into the local *soda* and order *arroz con pollo* (chicken and rice).

San José, Alajuela, Cartago and Heredia are the largest and most important cities of the Central Valley. Radiating out from San José are towns and suburbs, each with its own flavor and identity: international Escazú; bland Rohrmoser; exclusive Los Yoses with its lovely old residences; San Pedro, home to many good restaurants, the University of Costa Rica, and one of the largest shopping malls in Central America. There are also four national parks to explore, several volcanoes to climb and Guayabo National Monument, the country's most important archeological site.

PRECEDING PAGES: grazing in the hills above Heredia. **LEFT:** Central Valley coffee plantation. **BELOW:** the parish church is the focus of every Costa Rican village.

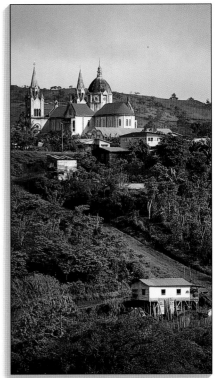

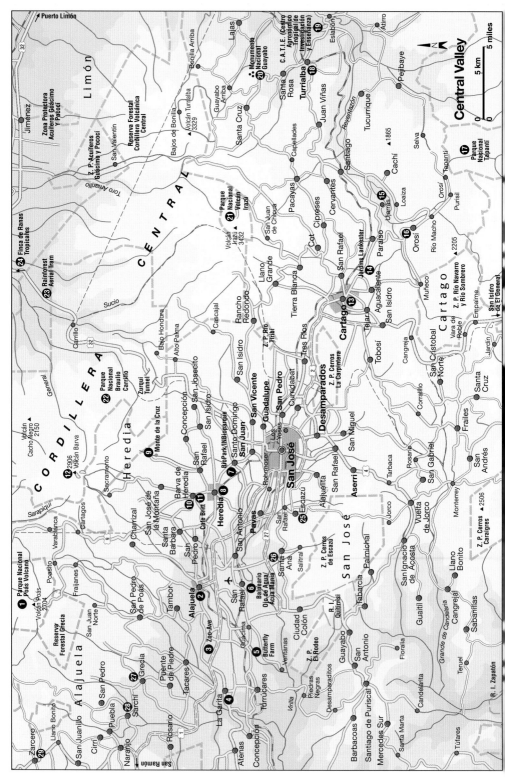

Central Valley

Though most travelers visit the Central Valley between December and March to escape the winter chill of North America and Europe, these months are Costa Rica's dry season, its "summer." Frequent travelers to the area know that it is the rainy season in Costa Rica, with its afternoon downpours and dramatic displays of lightning, when the Central Valley is at its magnificent best: lush and colorful. Best of all, the air and San José itself are cleansed by a daily bath.

Map on page 146

Poás Volcano National Park

The most developed of all the parks is **Parque Nacional Volcán Poás ❶**, a popular attraction. It is only 37 km (25 miles) from San José on good roads leading through the city of Alajuela. Poás can become crowded and cloudy, so it's best to visit early in the day when views are better and before the throngs arrive. The cool freshness of the air as you ascend the mountain is invigorating, but it can get chilly and rainy, so dress appropriately.

A map of the nature trails is available at the Visitors' Center, where there is an insect exhibition and a cafe. From a lookout point above the crater, there is an overview of the volcano, which in 1989 shot ash a mile into the air. The main crater, which is 1.5 km (1 mile) wide and 300 meters (1,000 ft) deep, is one of the largest in the world. Poás rarely has violent eruptions and is one of the more accessible active volcanoes on the continent. It is active in 40-year cycles and is currently producing acid-like rain and sulfurous gases. It is therefore not advisable to stay for more than 20 minutes near the active crater. Just a 20-minute hike away is another crater, which is filled with a jewel-colored lake.

ABOVE: mangoes in Alajuela.
BELOW: a streambed in Braulio Carrillo National Park.

Well-maintained trails lead through a landscape rich with wildflowers and a multitude of mosses, bromeliads and ferns. The resplendent quetzal *(see page 206)* can be seen here at certain times of the year.

Descend from the park to one of the nearby restaurants and enjoy the local specialty of *fresas en leche*, strawberry milkshake, or stop at one of the roadside stands to buy strawberry preserves and cookies made by local women. Alternatively, continue to the nearby La Paz Waterfall Gardens and set off on 4 km (2 miles) of trails past hummingbird and orchid gardens and the largest butterfly observatory in the world en route to five impressive waterfalls. To spend more time in the mountain air consider an overnight stay at La Providencia Ecological Reserve or cozy Poás Volcano Lodge.

Alajuela and environs

As you descend by some 200 meters (660 ft) into **Alajuela ❷** (pop. 160,000) it becomes noticeably warmer. To relax, you can join the old-timers in the central park, amid an orchard of mango and other mature trees. Here the colorful Festival of Mangoes takes place every July for nine days.

Alajuela is the birthplace of Juan Santamaría, the young Costa Rican whose courage was responsible for the routing of William Walker and his *filibusteros* from Costa Rica in 1856 *(see page 45)*. **The Museo Juan Santamaría** in the former jail, one block from the central park, tells his story (open Tues–Sun 10am–6pm; free).

From Alajuela take the old highway toward the Pacific – La Garita. En route is **Zoo-Ave** , which has more than 80 species of Costa Rican birds, as well as monkeys, deer, crocodiles and giant tortoises (open daily 9am–5pm; entrance fee). **La Garita** ❹ is expansive and green, filled with lovely homes and gardens, fields of shiny green coffee bushes and plant nurseries *(viveros)*. La Fiesta del Máiz restaurant, open on weekends, is an interesting experience, and features the near-endless variety of tasty dishes that *Ticos* make from corn.

The most spectacular of all Costa Rica's butterflies is the Blue Morpho, a veritable giant that grows up to 13–20 cm (5–8 inches) long.

A few kilometers southeast near Guacima is **The Butterfly Farm** ❺, a breeding farm for more than 500 different kinds of exotic butterflies, which are exported by the tens of thousands to waiting markets in Europe. The Butterfly Farm is full of interest with its waterfall, extensive tropical plantings and the endless color variations of the butterflies themselves (open daily 8.30am–5pm; tours 8.30am, 11am, 1pm and 3pm; entrance fee). The Blue Crowned Motmot Restaurant, on the same site, is recommended.

Water holes

If it's a warm day and you feel like cooling down and splashing around, then stop on the way back to San José (6 km/4 miles before town) at the **Balneario Ojo de Agua** ❻ (open daily 8am–4pm; entrance fee). Thousands of gallons of water pump out of this natural spring every hour of the day and around it has been created swimming pools and a boating lake. The wet season is the best time to go, when the spring is in full flood. At weekends, however, Ojo de Agua is very busy with locals. The water isn't just used for recreational purposes, it is also pumped to Puntarenas *(see page 181)* to use as a major part of its water supply.

BELOW:
Volcán Poás in an active phase; signs warn visitors not to linger too long near the summit.

Coffee country

A day trip to the province of Heredia, the center of Costa Rica's coffee production, quickly takes you away from the heat and clatter of San José. Just 24 km (15 miles) from the city, you can walk in an evergreen forest or cloud forest reserve rivaling those of much more remote and inaccessible areas.

Map on page 146

En route to Heredia from San José is Santo Domingo, which retains an historical charm with low, white stucco houses trimmed in traditional royal-blue paint. Just to the southwest of the town center is **BioPark/INBioparque ❼**, a 5.5-hectare (13½-acre) coffee estate turned naturalist center that provides an entertaining introduction to Costa Rica's biodiversity. Trails lead through three representative eco-systems, passing a serpentarium, an ant farm and tarantula and frog exhibits. There are guided tours by naturalists, excellent videos on biodiversity, exhibition halls that give an overview of the national parks' system, a pleasant restaurant, a lakeside cafe and an excellent shop with gifts for naturalists aged nine to 90 (open daily 7.30am–4pm; entrance fee; tel: 244 4730).

Heredia ❽ (pop. 75,000) lies 9 km (6 miles) north of San José, and is known as *La Ciudad de los Flores* (The City of Flowers). The city was first settled in 1706 by Spaniards. Many fully stocked stores suggest that this coffee-rich area is affluent, and, indeed, by Costa Rican standards, it is. **The National University** is located in Heredia; it turns out the nation's teachers and has one of the best veterinarian schools in Latin America. The old town center, with its colonial Casa de Cultura, pitted fort and lovely church, is a pleasant place to stroll. The **Inmaculada Concepción**, constructed in 1796, is adorned with bells brought from Cuzco, Peru and its "seismic baroque" construction has enabled it to survive many earth tremors.

ABOVE: the lovely church of Sarchi.
BELOW: after church on Sunday; spectators at a soccer match.

The newer section of Heredia looks like many modern Developing World cities, with dangling wires, and electrical signs hanging across the streets advertising the global spread of North American brands.

Alpine scenery

TIP

After a hike in the Bosque del Río, pay a visit to the Hotel Chalet Tirol, where top-quality French cooking refreshes weary walkers.

Take the road to **San Rafael** and begin the ascent into the mountains. Villas above the town are architecturally alpine, often down to Tyrolean paintings on the shutters. Driving through here, you get the feeling of having suddenly entered into an Austrian watercolor landscape. Wealthy *Ticos* of earlier generations were educated in Europe and returned to their country with a great appreciation for the architecture of Northern Europe, which is evident in this cool, mountain area. Now, many young *Ticos* go to North American universities, and with this shift in academic background, cultural affinities are changing.

Above San Rafael the temperature drops dramatically. Six km (4 miles) above the town, in wonderfully fresh mountain air, Hotel and Villas La Condesa offers horseback riding in the surrounding hills, hiking, a swimming pool, luxury rooms, and a conference center (tel: 267 6000). Next you will pass a sign to El Castillo Country Club (some facilities available to non-members for a fee). The road beyond El Castillo continues to **Monte de la Cruz ❾** where a small shrine sits in a private cloud forest-reserve. For Sunday hikers from San Rafael, far below, this is a favorite destination.

Proceed downhill to the fork and turn back uphill to El Tirol. Costa Ricans like to stroll the roads, especially on Sundays, the traditional day for visiting with family; bus services are reduced on Sundays, further necessitating walking. *Tico* drivers are used to sharing the roads with pedestrians, but some foreigners

BELOW: the coffee crop, all picked by hand, earns Costa Rica over US$200 million in exports each year.

in rental cars can find such driving conditions unnerving. Before El Castillo, look for a sign indicating **Bosque de la Hoja**. Here, you can hike along a lovely road bordered by graceful trees, for a mile or so, to the Heredia Water Works, and from there, walk to other unpopulated areas that are perfect for hiking.

Tell the guard at El Tirol gatehouse that you are going to **Hotel Chalet Tirol** and drive through a residential area of weekend cottages and retirement homes set in alpine fields. A good road leads through a cypress forest where sun filters warmly through branches and dapples meadow wildflowers.

Hotel Chalet Tirol sits in the middle of a cloud forest reserve bordering Braulio Carrillo National Park. A fern-choked trail winding under orchid and bromeliad-laden old trees allows visitors to hike several hours through the cloud reserve to the border of the national park. A grove of A-frame wooden cottages awaits those who choose to spend the night.

As you descend, the warmth of the valley below is welcome. The road to San José de la Montaña is lined with flowers grown for export in wonderfully fresh, cool mountain air.

Barva and environs

In **Barva de Heredia ❿**, founded in 1561, colonial-era adobe houses surrounding the central park are being restored, giving the entire area the atmosphere of a colonial town. If you stand on the steps in front of the adobe **Basílica de Barva**, which dates back to 1767, and look out over the red tile-roofed adobe houses to the mountains beyond, you will get a sense of what the Central Valley probably looked like in the 18th century. The Basílica de Barva was built on an ancient Amerindian burial ground. Close by is the small grotto of the **Virgin of Lourdes** (1913).

Map on page 146

In the hills just outside Barva is the lively and entertaining Aventura de Café tour at the **Cafe Britt** ⓫ coffee farm, which takes you from raw bean to hot, steaming final product, using a multimedia, theatrical approach (open May–Nov daily 11am; Dec–Apr daily 9am, 11am and 3pm; entrance fee; transport to and from San José available.) Ask to taste the ripe, red fruit that surrounds the coffee bean. It is surprisingly sweet and good, though beware eating too many at once as they act as a mild laxative.

Artisans from Barva produce wonderful baskets: shopping baskets, baskets used by coffee pickers, and fruit and bread baskets. You will see them on sale by the roadsides.

In **Santa Lucía de Barva**, 4 km (2½ miles) north of Heredia, the **Museum of Popular Culture** has renovated the charming and graceful González house, a 19th-century home, built just around the time that coffee cultivation was beginning to change Costa Rican life forever (open daily; entrance fee).

Barva Volcano

There is a road to **Volcán Barva** ⓬ that runs just above the town of Barva de Heredia, and then through San José de la Montaña and on toward Sacramento. The volcano is on the western side of Braulio Carrillo National Park; the

ABOVE: Spanish fort, Heredia.
BELOW: Lankester Gardens.

approach road is in terrible condition and cars without four-wheel drive must be left 4 km (2½ miles) from the park entrance. From here it's an enjoyable hike through pasture land and cloud forest dripping with moss and epiphytes to the crater lake. An alternative one-hour hike will take you to **Laguna Barva** (2,900 meters/9,514 ft), a green lake in an extinct crater rimmed with trees.

If you are still feeling energetic, there is the smaller Laguna Copey to explore, another 40-minute walk away. You may be rewarded by sighting a quetzal there – but don't bank on it. Wherever you hike on Volcán Barva, bring raingear, a compass and waterproof shoes or boots – even in the dry season – and be sure to keep to the designated paths. The roads in this area criss-cross one another and are not at all well-marked. Even *Josefinos* taking Sunday drives have to stop passersby and ask for directions.

Cartago and south

Cartago ⑬ (pop. 110,000) is 23 km (14 miles) south of San José. It was the capital of Costa Rica until 1823, when it lost its status to San José. Its illustrious colonial past is obscured, however, since repeated earthquakes and eruptions of Irazú Volcano have destroyed most of the colonial buildings. Throughout their history, Cartagans have attempted to build a temple to Saint James the Apostle, patron saint of Spain. The first church, begun in 1562, was finished in 1570, and was one of only two in the entire country. When it was destroyed, a stronger building was erected in 1580 on the same site. This, too, was leveled by the trembling earth. Subsequent churches met the same fate and when Cartago's massive cathedral, begun early in the 20th century, was toppled by the 1910 earthquake, all efforts to rebuild were abandoned. The roofless cathedral walls

Vásquez de Coronado wrote to the Spanish king of Cartago: "I have never seen a more beautiful valley, and I have laid out a city between [its] two rivers."

BELOW: flowering bougainvillea in front of the 17th-century ruins of Costa Rica's oldest church at Ujarrás.

Map on page 146

with their empty Gothic windows still stand. The site, called **Las Ruinas** (The Ruins), is now a garden with a small pond and is a popular and romantic spot.

Cartago, once the center of Costa Rican culture, is still her religious center. The enormous **Basílica de Nuestra Señora de los Angeles** (Basilica of Our Lady of the Angels), a Byzantine structure that dominates the landscape for miles, was built in honor of Costa Rica's patron saint, *La Negrita*.

From Cartago it is a short trip to the **Jardines Lankester ⓮** in Paraíso de Cartago. It is said that Paraíso (Paradise) was named by weary Spaniards moving inland from the Atlantic coast who found its cooler weather and lack of malarial mosquitoes paradisical. English botanist Charles Lankester, sent to Costa Rica by a British company to work on coffee planting, arrived in 1900 at the age of 21. The coffee venture failed, but he decided to stay and bought 15 hectares (37 acres) of land to preserve local flora, especially orchids and bromeliads, and to regenerate a natural forest. Today, Lankester Gardens is run by the University of Costa Rica. Hundreds of species of orchids attract orchid fanciers from all over the world, particularly in the peak flowering months of February through April (open daily 8.30am–3.30pm; entrance fee). The garden is also a great bird-watching spot.

The Sanchiri Lodge, not far from Lankester Gardens, is a good place to stop for a light snack. The open dining room offers guests stunning views across the Orosí valley.

Ujarrás

South of Cartago the landscape becomes green, misty and almost magical, especially during the verdant rainy season. At **Ujarrás ⓯**, on a beautiful site, are the ruins of Costa Rica's oldest church, Nuestra Señora de la Limpia, dating from the 17th century.

The first place of worship constructed in this region was not the church, but a shrine in honor of La Virgen del Rescate de Ujarrás, who, in 1565, appeared to an Amerindian fishing on the banks of the Reventazón River. The apparition came from inside a small tree. The man carried the trunk to the center of Ujarrás, but by the time he got there, it had become so heavy that even a dozen men could not lift it. The phenomenon was interpreted by the Franciscan fathers as a sign that the Virgin wanted them to construct a shrine on that spot to be used by both the indigenous population and the Spanish, and so it was constructed.

A hundred years later, in 1666, so the story goes, a band of pirates led by the notorious Mansfield and Henry Morgan landed on the Atlantic coast of Costa Rica with the intention of sacking the country. The Spanish governor, Juan López de la Flor, assembled all available fighting men and sent everyone else to the mission to pray. The pirates came inland as far as Turrialba and then, mysteriously, abruptly turned back. Some say the pirates were tricked by de la Flor, who had posted the few men and guns he had at strategic points in the hills and then leaked the word that there was an ambush awaiting the pirates. A few gunshots from different points convinced the pirates to retreat. Other accounts say their retreat was a miracle

BELOW: raging torrents flood the spillway of the dam at Cachí *(see p154).*

worked by the Virgin. The grateful townspeople built the church of Ujarrás to commemorate the miracle, though it was destroyed 100 years later by an earthquake. Its remains stand among gardens and trees draped with Spanish moss.

The Orosí River Valley

TIP

Near Orosí is La Casona del Cafetal, a restaurant set in the *hacienda* of a large coffee plantation. After lunch here you can rent a boat for a ride on its lake.

A few kilometers beyond Orosí, the **Cachí Hydroelectric Dam** channels waters from a reservoir on the Reventazón and Orosí rivers into an immense spillway. The concrete-dam structure contrasts sharply with the lush natural terrain surrounding it, as does the power of the rushing water with the peace of the river.

Just up the road toward Orosí, some 5 km (3 miles) north of the Hotel Río Palomo restaurant, on the bank of the river, is **La Casa del Soñador** (the House of the Dreamer), a simple two-story cane structure surrounded by primitive wood sculpture. Here Macedonio Quesada, a famous Costa Rican primitivist artist lived and worked until his death in 1995. His work can be seen in galleries around San José, but it is best viewed in this charming cane building where his sons now work, producing melancholy *campesino* (peasant) and religious figures from coffee wood. Visitors are welcome.

The town of **Orosí** ⓰ is untouched by the earthquakes that have leveled the colonial structures of Cartago, and it retains the look of an earlier Costa Rica. Make your first stop Orosí Turismo, in the center, where you can pick up useful information on the town. Visit the colonial church of San José de Orosí (the oldest church in use in Costa Rica) and the former Franciscan monastery, now the **Museo de Arte Religioso** (Museum of Religious Art), just north of the church, which features artifacts from the colonial era (open Tues–Sun; entrance fee). Take a walk around town and have a snack at one of the *sodas*.

BELOW: the Basilica of Our Lady of the Angels is one of the country's most sacred sites.

LA NEGRITA

The origins of Cartago's Basilica of Our Lady of the Angels are rooted in the miraculous. In 1635, a young girl walking through the forest that once grew on the site of the basilica discovered a dark-skinned statue of the Virgin Mary. A priest carried the statue, called La Negrita, to the parish church, but it mysteriously returned, twice, to its location in the forest.

In 1926, the Catholic Church built a basilica on the spot to house the statue. Today, in the shrine room, cases full of abandoned crutches, plaster casts and votive offerings (some made of gold) representing various parts of the body testify to the cures effected by La Negrita, Costa Rica's patron saint. Water from the spring behind the church is also said to have healing powers and the faithful fill their bottles from there.

On the patron saint's feast day, August 2, thousands of pilgrims gather at the basilica. Many walk the 22 km (14 miles) from San José; devoted penitents making the last part of the journey on their knees. Some walk from as far afield as Panamá and Nicaragua. On that day, the image of the black virgin is carried to another church in Cartago and then, in a solemn procession, through the city and back to its shrine in the basilica.

Just above the valley there is a lookout site *(mirador)* and park, maintained by the ICT (Costan Rican Institute of Tourism). Its large area of sloping, well-trimmed lawns provides spectacular views over the Reventazón River with Cachí to the left and Orosí to the right. It makes a perfect spot for a picnic and a pleasant walk.

Map on page 146

Tapantí National Park

The upper part of the **Orosí Valley** has enormous rainfall, rendering it unsuited for agriculture: thus it still has magnificent virgin rainforest. **Parque Nacional Tapantí ⑰** protects the rivers that supply San José with water and electricity. It also offers great birdwatching, fishing and river swimming. Birdwatchers will want to get an early start and arrive in Tapantí when the park opens at 7am. The drive from San José is especially beautiful at dawn. Past the coffee plant, turn right and drive for 10 km (6 miles) over poor roads.

Trails are well-marked in the lower part of the refuge. Oropendulas – black, raven-sized birds with golden tail feathers and stout ivory-colored bills – nest in colonies within the park. Clusters of 30 or more pendulous nests hang from branches high in the trees. Two eggs are laid by the oropendula females, but parasitic giant cowbirds steal a spot in the nest for their own eggs, letting oropendula females raise their chicks. An exchange is affected, however, as the baby cowbirds, which feed on botflies, keep the baby oropendulas free from these parasites. Visitors usually hear oropendulas before seeing them. The males let out a gurgling, liquid-like song, then bow and flap their wings to the females in unusual courtship displays.

The creek running parallel to Oropendula Trail is filled with smooth, warm

ABOVE: Orosí's church.
BELOW: the House of the Dreamer, near Orosí.

boulders and invites hikers to cool their feet in the water, and perhaps lie back for a mid-morning snooze in the sun. However, it is always advisable to take raingear and warm clothes on the trails.

Turrialba

Turrialba ⓲ is a busy town, its streets and parks bustling with people of all ages, talking, yelling, buying, selling. The open fruit and vegetable market that lines the sidewalk along the river features some of the freshest and best-looking produce available in Costa Rica, most of it grown in the hills above town. Turrialba's reputation as a whitewater river-rafting center is growing, and rafters and kayakers from all over the world are discovering the Reventazón and Pacuare rivers *(see pages 98–99).*

Just a few miles beyond the town of Turrialba on the highway is CATIE, the **Centro Agronómico Tropical de Investigación y Enseñanza** ⓳ (Center for Tropical Agronomy Research and Teaching). On this 800-hectare (2,000-acre) research plantation, scientists are experimenting with the introduction of more than 5,000 varieties of 335 species of crops with economic potential. More than 2,500 varieties of coffee and 450 varieties of cacao, as well as many varieties of bananas and pejibaye palms, are part of the seed bank of CATIE.

Work is being done here on the critical problems of deforestation, overgrazing and the sensitive ecology of the river basins. Guides demonstrate the cultivation, processing and care of palms, coffee, cacao and orchids. (If you are not with a group, call ahead to arrange a tour, tel: 558 2460.)

Visitors to CATIE and the surrounding areas usually stay at the Hotel Wagelia or at the basic Hotel Interamericano. About 5 km (3 miles) out of town on the

ABOVE: Turrialba is becoming a popular rafting center.
BELOW: the symbiosis of water buffalo and egret.

road toward Siquirres is the very luxurious Casa Turire, a lavish plantation-style hotel in the grounds of a sugar cane, coffee, and macadamia nut plantation. In the mountains above the valley, not far away, is the Turrialtico, which has handsome rooms with lovely views of Volcán Irazú.

Map
on page
146

Guayabo National Monument

The **Monumento Nacional Guayabo** ❷⓪ is the site of a large pre-Columbian center on the slope of Volcán Turrialba, 18 km (11 miles) from Turrialba. Archeologists are still unclear as to whether this was purely a ceremonial site or a combination administrative/ceremonial center. The ancient stone ruins and the remains of stone roads radiating out to surrounding areas date from 1000 BC to AD 1400, when the site was abandoned for some as yet unknown reason, but speculation suggests disease or starvation.

Visitors can take a self-guided tour through the excavated area, which contains a complex system of stone aqueducts, building foundations, and roadways amid a setting of guava trees, wild impatiens and clusters of oropendula nests. Stone-lined graves, now empty, served as the first indication to archeologists that a cultural site was nearby. In addition, there are several large petrographs, the significance of which remains a mystery.

About 20 km (12 miles) north of Guayabo, on the slope of Turrialba volcano, is Volcán Turrialba Lodge, with comfortable wooden cabins and wood-burning stoves to ward off the evening chill. Hikes and horseback rides to the volcano's extinct crater are exhilarating in the clear mountain air (tel: 273 4335).

On the way back to Cartago stop for rest and refreshment in the village of Cervantes at La Posada de la Luna (tel: 534 8330).

Around Guayabo grow the best pejibaye in the country. Look out for houses selling the fruit, which must be cooked, since you cannot eat them raw.

BELOW: volcanic farmlands on the Meseta Central.

Braulio Carrillo Park
and Volcán Irazú Park
both suffer from secu-
rity problems. Don't
leave anything of value
in a parked car, and if
you intend hiking,
check first with the
park authorities as to
the security situation.

BELOW: relaxing at
a lookout point over
the beautiful Orosí
Valley.

Irazú Volcano National Park

Easily accessible from Cartago is **Parque Nacional Volcán Irazú ㉑**. From
the 3,800-meter (11,000-ft) summit, it is possible on a clear day to see both the
Atlantic and the Pacific. Irazú, Costa Rica's highest volcano, also known as El
Coloso, broke a 30-year period of silence with a single, noisy eruption on
December 8, 1994. It previously erupted on March 19, 1963, the day of the
arrival of President John F. Kennedy in Costa Rica.

For two years Irazú continued to shower ash over much of the Central Valley.
People carried umbrellas to protect themselves. Ash piled up on the Reventazón River, causing it to flood and destroy 300 homes. Roofs caved in from the
weight of the ash and San José's air was temporarily turned black.

A visit to Irazú is a relatively easy half-day tour from San José. Visitors can
go to the top ridge, walk along the rim of the main crater and look across an
other-worldly landscape consisting of a brilliant green lake and black-and-gray
slopes, punctuated with plumes of white steam jetting into the air, escaping
from fissures in the rock. There are also wonderful hiking and birding trails in
the Prusia sector of the park.

Braulio Carrillo National Park

Only 45 minutes from downtown San José is **Parque Nacional Braulio
Carrillo ㉒**. Take the highway to Limón and turn off before the Zurquí tunnel
at signs to the park. Or alternatively, you can take the entrance 17 km (11 miles)
beyond the tunnel at the La Botella Trail, where the grade is not so steep and
strenuous. The trails are often muddy and snakes are sometimes sighted; be
sure to wear sturdy boots and mosquito repellent.

Occupying 445 sq. km (170 sq. miles) of mostly primary forest, Braulio Carrillo National Park was founded in 1978 thanks to pressure exerted by environmentalists who feared that the opening of a highway between San José and Guápiles would provide loggers and developers with access to rapidly vanishing virgin forest; deforestation had followed the opening of many other roads throughout the country. A compromise was reached: the road would go through, but the 32,000 hectares (80,000 acres) of virgin forest surrounding the highway would be preserved as a national park. The park thus embodies some ideals of enlightened progress.

Braulio Carrillo contains five distinctly separate forest habitats, dominated by the wet tropical forest. Hundreds of varieties of orchids and ferns, and a majority of the bird species native to Costa Rica are found here. In order to understand the life cycles, to spot the camouflaged wildlife and avoid missing spectacular vistas, it is essential to arrange for a guide through the National Parks Service or an eco-tourism agency. A circular trail begins behind the kiosk. The lingering impression of Braulio Carrillo is of vastness: huge canyons, misty mountains and the ubiquitous broad-leaf plant, the Poor Man's Umbrella, covering the hillsides.

Rainforests made easy

For a bird's-eye view of the forest canopy adjacent to Braulio Carrillo, take a ride on the **Rainforest Aerial Tram ㉓**, a 90-minute, 1.3-km (1-mile) trip through the forest's treetops, 35 meters (100 ft) above the forest floor. The "tram" allows visitors to experience the forest canopy up close: to breathe the steamy air, to catch the unforgettable tropical smell of damp, mossy tree trunks

Map on page 146

ABOVE: Costa Rica's national orchid.
BELOW: all aboard for the Rainforest Aerial Tram.

and, if you are very lucky, to spot the elusive wildlife. It is located about 5 km (3 miles) north of Río Sucio on the road to Puerto Limón, about 50 minutes from San José (open daily, reservations recommended, tel: 257-5961; entrance fee includes tram ride, video and a short hike).

Amphibian-lovers won't want to miss the **Tropical Frog Farm** ㉔, 6 km (4 miles) past the Aerial Tram. On display are more than 200 tiny, colorful poison-dart frogs – easy to miss in the wild – along with their larger, nocturnal cousins, the endearing red-eyed leaf frogs that have become an almost ubiquitous mascot throughout Costa Rica. The frog farm is a protected habitat, and also has original frog art for sale (entrance fee).

San José suburbs

On the west side of San José are the suburbs of Pavas, Rohrmoser, Escazú and Santa Ana. The rather colorless, modern suburbs of **Rohrmoser** and **Pavas** are chiefly of interest to certain travelers due to the presence of the Embassy of the United States of America. Owing to this, many diplomatic personnel live along the wide, nearly treeless streets of Rohrmoser, in modern houses protected by wrought-iron grillework. **Escazú** ㉕ was originally a crossroads of trails between Amerindian villages. Because water was abundant there, the Amerindians found it a good place to spend the night on their journeys, and gave it the name Escazú, which in their language means "resting place."

Spanish settlers were also attracted to Escazú: they settled in the hills and began farming. It was during these early days that Escazú became known as the city of the witches and today there remains a tradition of metaphysical and mystical arts practiced clandestinely in the village.

TIP

The San José suburb of San Pedro is one of the capital's liveliest areas thanks to the presence of the university. It features several good restaurants, bars and nightspots.

BELOW: Escazú and the Central Valley from the air.

Escazú is an interesting if sometimes chaotic blend of old Costa Rica and a modern, international community, with a large contingent of North Americans. It is sometimes jokingly referred to as "Gringolandia." The town center has adobe buildings; an attractive, Ravenna-style church; and, of course, a soccer field. Just outside of town are enclaves of fancy homes owned by North Americans, Europeans and wealthy locals, drawn to Escazú by the agreeable climate and superlative views. Unfortunately, the town's main road is now clogged with traffic and lined with fast-food chains and clothing stores.

In the hills to the east of the town, in an area called **Bello Horizonte**, are many fine old residences with lovely gardens. It is worth a drive through the hills of Bello Horizonte to visit **Biesanz Woodworks**, the studio/workshop of Barry Biesanz, an accomplished artist who works with Costa Rican hardwoods. Wooden bowls and boxes, remarkable for their grace and fluidity, are on display in his new, *hacienda*-style showroom, which is surrounded by an interesting herb garden with an ornamental pond.

San Rafael de Escazú is a newer section of town along the highway to Santa Ana. It has several shiny commercial centers where the town's glamorous inhabitants do their shopping, with international stores, supermarkets, a dazzling array of trendy restaurants and glitzy interior-design shops.

On the old road to Santa Ana, across from the new Los Laureles shopping center, there is a large walled compound with lights, guards, and surveillance paraphernalia. It isn't a high-security penitentiary: it's the residence of the United States Ambassador to Costa Rica. Halfway to Santa Ana on the old highway is the luxurious Alta Hotel.

Map
on page
146

ABOVE: Central Valley adobe house.
BELOW: Escazú celebrates its heritage of witches.

Santa Ana

Although condominiums, luxury villas and shopping centers are rapidly urbanizing the town, a rural atmosphere still survives in **Santa Ana** ㉖, a town once famous for its onions, which hang braided on the lintels and eaves of rustic restaurants along the road. On the west side of town there are still a few stands selling pottery, baskets and locally grown onions.

Above Santa Ana is a reminder of its recent agricultural past. The **Historical Museum of Agriculture** has displays of 19th-century farm implements, along with a traditional sugar mill and live animals (open Mon–Fri 8am–4pm, Sat–Sun 9am–5pm, entrance fee; tel: 282 8434).

Rancho del Macho is high in the hills above Santa Ana. Sit under the stars, overlooking the city lights, and enjoy the balmy breezes; sip a cold beer and partake of delicious grilled onions and barbecued chicken and beef. To get to Rancho del Macho continue on the old highway through the town of Santa Ana, past the huge red cross, and continue straight for about half a kilometer until you see the Rancho del Macho sign indicating you should turn left. From here just follow the signs up the hill.

For a taste of modern luxury, the Hotel Alta, halfway between Escazú and Santa Ana on the old road, has an excellent restaurant and sometimes exhibits local artists' work.

If you are in search of more ordinary pursuits, look for **Multiplaza**, one of the largest shopping malls in all of Central America. It is located just off the freeway on the way to Santa Ana, across the road from El Camino Real Hotel.

Ciudad Colón can be reached by backroads from Santa Ana, through rolling hills, or by way of the freeway. It's best known perhaps to those who have come to inspect the **University for Peace**, which is on a well-marked road not far out of town. The University for Peace, sponsored by the United Nations to study the ways of peace, and to offer a counter to the teachings of war colleges that predominate in many other countries, offers graduate courses to students from all over the world. There are hiking and birding trails throughout the property, as well as popular picnic areas beside a lake populated by geese and ducks.

Returning to Santa Ana via back roads, you will come to **La Cabriola**, a popular weekend restaurant and picnic site where horses can be hired. The food at La Cabriola is nothing special, but the gently rolling hills above it are beautiful and perfect for horseback-riding.

Near Escazú, at the village of San Antonio de Escazú, an annual ox-cart festival, Día de los Boyeros, *is held in March. It attracts around 100 painted antique carts and the great oxen that pull them, plus thousands of visitors.*

Sarchí and surrounding villages

For a half-day excursion of craft shopping and sightseeing around typical Central Valley villages, head north through Alajuela toward Sarchí, stopping en route at **Grecia** ㉗. This tidy little place has been voted the cleanest town in Latin America. It is definitely worth taking a stroll around and is well known for its unusual dark-red, all-metal church. Just a few minutes' walk away is the popular World of Snakes, which has more than 150 snakes from all over the world (open daily 8am–4pm; guided tours; tel: 494 3700).

The approach to the mountain town of **Sarchí** ㉘ is unmistakable. Distinctive and colorful Sarchí decorative designs can be seen on bus stops, bars and bakeries, restaurants and houses.

BELOW: Grecia's metal church was imported from Belgium in 1897.

Sarchí is a crafts center heavily geared toward the tourist trade where you can see artisans painting traditional ox-cart designs *(see pages 164–165)* and creating household furnishings out of tropical hardwoods. Around 1910, as legend has it, a *campesino* (peasant) was crossing the Beneficio la Luisa when it occurred to him to decorate his ox-cart wheels with colorful mandala-like designs inspired by ancient Moorish decoration.

Surprisingly, the art form caught on. Originally, each district in Costa Rica had its own special design and locals could tell just by looking at the cart where the driver lived. It was also said that each cart had its own distinctive "*chirrido*," or song of the wheels, by which people could identify who was passing by, without the listener even glancing upward.

As late as 1960, the most typical mode of transportation was the ox-cart since it was the only vehicle that could transport agricultural products through the rugged Costa Rican terrain. The father of former president Oscar Arias Sánchez made his original fortune hauling coffee by ox-cart to Puntarenas. The painted carts are still in use today in villages as close to the capital as San Antonio de Escazú.

There are pleasant little roadside stalls on the outskirts of Sarchí selling homemade candied fruits, honey and fudge. In comparison to the large commercialized furniture shops that predominate in Sarchí, a visit to these small stands is very friendly and personal, as though stepping into a Costa Rican home for a chat.

About 15 km (9 miles) up the road is the town of **Zarcero** ㉙. Should you arrive on a day when the highland clouds are swirling through the town or when a drizzling fog is bathing everything in soft, diffused light, you might feel that you have just walked into a fantasy dreamland.

Unique in Costa Rica, and possibly the world, is the **Parque Central** in Zarcero, a museum of topiary. Evangelisto Blanco, the park gardener, has clipped and pruned cypress bushes and hedges into a whimsical garden of amazing creatures: birds, rabbits, oxen, bulbous elephants with lightbulbs for eyes, a bull ring complete with spectators, matador and charging bull, a cross-bearing Christ, a man wearing a top hat, and a cat with tail flying, riding a motorcycle along the top of a hedge.

Evangelisto has been sculpting the hedges alone for over 40 years, 7 days a week, including holidays. The energetic compulsion of Evangelisto's work has been compared to the creations of Antonio Gaudí, in Barcelona in Spain, and of Simón Rodía, who created the Watts Towers in Los Angeles. Unable to afford marble or stone, Evangelisto works with the plants as his medium of self-expression creating extraordinary sculpted shrubs.

About 8 km (5 miles) after the turn off for Sarchí, along the Pan-American Highway, is the exit for the 200-year-old colonial town of **Palmares**. This lovely area used to be a tobacco-growing center. Unaffected by the vicissitudes of modern tourism, it is a model town through which to stroll and view typical *Tico* life. ❏

Map on page 146

BELOW: taking a break from planting new coffee bushes.

POTTERS, SCULPTORS AND GOLDSMITHS

The Amerindians of Costa Rica left behind gold, pottery and stone artifacts. Most of their traditions were destroyed by the conquistadores

Because Costa Rica was a cultural and commercial meeting point for ancient civilizations in the Americas, native Costa Ricans absorbed and modified known techniques in ceramics, gold and jade work, weaving and stone carving. Early inhabitants, especially in the pre-Columbian port of Nicoya (in the province of Guanacaste), traded with travelers from as far away as Ecuador and Mexico. They also developed their own style of decorating pottery: beasts that are half-bird, half-man and people with exaggerated genitals, suggesting a fertility-rite culture. Examples of the pottery, which was widely traded, can be found throughout Central America.

Visitors to the Museum of Gold, the Jade Museum and the National Museum can see early pieces and learn more of their history and uses.

CRAFTSMEN AND ARTISTS

While the Spanish never found the gold deposits that inspired them to name the land "Rich Coast," early Costa Ricans worked with both gold and jade (not found in the country) to make statuettes and other decorative pieces. Although these traditions – along with stone work and the southern Pacific tradition of making fine white cloth – have been all but lost, pottery and the more modern craft of ox-cart decoration have been revived by the tourist dollar. For pottery, visit Guatil and Nicoya, for other crafts try Sarchí.

Other examples of Costa Rica's crafts, less compromised by modern tourism, are found in the wild south of the country; *molas* (hand-sewn appliqué) pieces are produced around Drake Bay, and grotesque balsawood masks are made by the Boruca people.

▷ **"HOUSE OF THE DREAMER"**
Self-taught sculptor Macedonio Quesada, who died in 1997, whittled charming statues depicting Costa Rican life. His two sons continue the tradition, sculpting in coffee wood in the Orosí Valley. Some of the pieces are for sale.

▽ **COTTAGE INDUSTRY**
Costa Rica's clay-rich soils provide excellent material for pottery, most of which is shaped without the aid of a potter's wheel. Many Guanacaste families have outdoor ovens for baking pots.

◁ **EARLY STONE WORK THE HARD WAY**
Early Costa Ricans used granite andesite and sedimentary stone to fashion stone figures with wooden tools. It is thought that they may have split the rocks by inserting wooden dowels into cracks and soaking them with water. The expanding wooden dowel would then have cracked the stone.

ORNAMENTED OX-CARTS

Used exclusively to transport coffee and other agricultural products until well into the 20th century, wooden ox-carts are unmistakably Costa Rican, and symbolize the self-reliance of the small farmer (much like covered wagons do in the US).

Ideally suited for the country's mountainous conditions and rutted dirt roads, ox-carts are still common in many parts of the country. The carts, which come in all sizes (including a miniature about the size of a toy car), are made in Sarchí, the wooden crafts capital of the country. There, master carvers began painting the carts in the early part of the 20th century. Originally adorned with bright colors and geometric patterns, these days ox-carts are being decorated with jungle scenes, wild animals, flowers and other non-traditional designs.

Visitors to Sarchí can have a go at painting the carts themselves with fine-tipped brushes, or alternatively they can leave it to the experts and order a custom-painted cart; these are often used as decorations at hotels and the country estates of the wealthy.

◁ **BRILLIANT BIRDS, MAGNIFICENT MEN**
Reproductions of pre-Columbian gold figures make excellent gifts.

▷ **LIVING TRADITIONS**
Boruca Amerindians make their woven goods and carved gourds according to traditional designs.

◁ **PAINTED POTS APLENTY**
Although the Chorotega culture no longer exists, their descendants use water-based paints to decorate inexpensive pottery with whimsical animals and other pre-Columbian images.

▷ **SONG OF THE WHEELS**
Neighbors can recognize the distinctive sound of each other's ox-cart in motion.

THE CENTRAL PACIFIC

*The Central Pacific beaches are among the best in Costa Rica,
and Manuel Antonio National Park is the stuff of tropical dreams.
And there is a host of natural wonders to see en route.*

Map
on page
170

W hen the chaos of San José becomes just a bit too much, take a day trip to the Pacific coast and get away from it all at the beach. The nearest is Jacó, one of the country's most lively and popular seaside destinations, a little less than two hours away. Some of the country's finest beaches, at Manuel Antonio National Park, are just an hour's drive south of Jacó, but if you don't want to drive, there are inexpensive flights from San José to Quepos (adjacent to Manuel Antonio). Buy tickets well in advance during the dry season.

The road to the coast

If you go by car, and want to take the fast route to the coast (as opposed to the old scenic route, *see page 174*), turn off the highway toward Atenas, past the Juan Santamaría International Airport, then head through La Garita de Alajuela. One of the first lowland towns that you'll approach is Orotina. The road to Orotina winds through coffee plantations built on precariously steep slopes. Driving along the ledges of these mountains, the views are often of rich green farmland and undulating valleys; and looking up at the almost horizontal estates, you may find it difficult to imagine how coffee can possibly be harvested here.

As you approach the **Río Tárcoles bridge ❶**, you'll notice tourists clustered at the railings, cameras and binoculars aimed down. The fascination here is **crocodiles** – gray, primordial behemoths, some as long as 7 meters (20 ft) basking on the muddy banks or stealthily patrolling the brown river, with only snouts and crenellated spines showing above the waterline. Most reptilians in Costa Rica are the smaller cayman species. This is the easiest place to spot these larger American crocodiles or *crocodylus acutus*. There can be as many as 20 of them lurking here at the river's mouth.

The **Carara Biological Reserve ❷** borders the highway between Playa Jacó and Puntarenas just past the bridge. Carara lies in a transitional zone between humid and dry forest, and sustains wildlife from mountainous terrain, primary and secondary forests, lagoons and marshlands of the Tárcoles River. The vegetation in Carara covers a similarly broad range: from shady evergreens to clustering epiphytes and strangling vines. Among the birds most commonly spotted here are vultures, toucans and guans, ducks and macaws. Squirrel, howler, white-faced and spider monkeys are often seen, and, much more rarely, wildcats such as margays, jaguarundis, ocelots and jaguars. There are also sloths, coatis and agoutis, as well as a variety of reptiles and lovely, blue morpho butterflies. Guides, available by advance request (contact the National Parks Service), are invaluable in interpreting the ecological complexity of this reserve.

PRECEDING PAGES: Manuel Antonio National Park. **LEFT:** a cascade waters the plants. **BELOW:** scarlet macaw at Carara Biological Reserve.

More than 200 pairs of scarlet macaws are the great glory of Carara. These enormous red, yellow and blue parrots mate for life and live for over 30 years. The macaw nests in December, and by January the young are strong but still in their nests. They make easy prey at this point for thieves who sell them on the black market. Ornithologists estimate that there are now 1,500–2,000 scarlet macaws in Costa Rica, almost double the number there were 10 years ago, thanks to conservation programs. Public-education campaigns to discourage people from buying macaw chicks have also had some effect in lowering the number of scarlet macaws in captivity, although it is impossible to estimate how many macaws are kept as pets.

Like most birds, macaws are easiest to spot during dawn or dusk. In the evenings, when the lowlands cool, pairs of macaws fly down from their daytime feeding areas in the mountains. At sunset, park your car near the bridge over the Tárcoles River along the highway outside of the park entrance and listen for their raucous squawking as they fly to their roosting areas in the nearby coastal mangroves. Also watch for shorebirds and waders that frequent the estuary. Roseate spoonbills, with their startling pink plumage, are spectacular at sunset. Crocodiles looking like inanimate logs bask on the river banks, apparently comatose, but are waiting for such a prize as one of the spoonbills.

The beaches

If you are anticipating the white powder beaches washed by gentle, clear waters of tourist brochures, then the beaches of the Central Pacific could be something of a disappointment (Jacó is a dirty gray). The lure of these places is their proximity to San José, their big waves for surfers and their lively atmosphere,

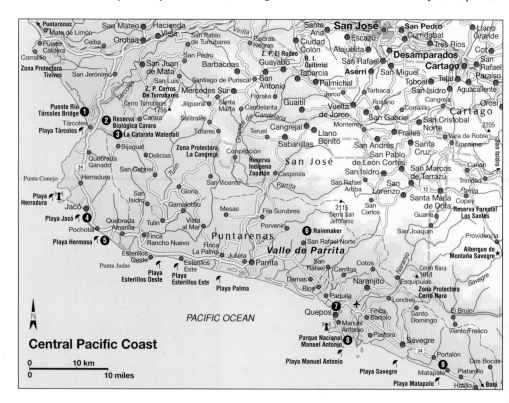

Central Pacific Coast

0   10 km
0   10 miles

PACIFIC OCEAN

Map on page 170

not their picture-postcard perfection. Still, with a bit of exploration off the main road, and once away from the density and hustle of the central beach scene, you will find some clean and appealing beaches and secluded coves.

Playa Herradura lies 5 minutes north of Jacó, its waves are gentle, and there is shade and trees for stringing hammocks; **Playa Esterillos** is a huge 11-km (7-mile) stretch of mostly deserted beach, about 10 km (6 miles) south of Jacó, but beware strong riptides; avoid Playa Tárcoles, which is polluted.

Crocodile tours run along the Tárcoles River, but don't use or encourage irresponsible operators who get their clients to feed the crocs with pieces of meat. Once a crocodile associates a person with food, then it is one dangerous animal.

Several kilometers from the Jacó-San José highway, 17 km (10½ miles) before Jacó Beach, is **La Catarata Waterfall ❸**, a 200-meter (650-ft) high falls. Be warned, though, the hour-long hike to La Catarata is strenuous. Hikers must be in good physical shape and should bring plenty of water with them. Alternatively, horseback-riding tours to the waterfall can be arranged from the **Complejo Ecológico La Catarata** at the top of the falls (tel: 661 8263). Nearby, **Hotel Villa Lapas** offers hikes along suspension bridges, a canopy tour and comfortable rooms in an all-inclusive resort hotel (tel: 637 0232).

Jacó Beach

Jacó Beach ❹ has a raucous, party-time, beach town ambiance, with hammocks slung between coconut palms, and plenty of cold beer. *Cabinas* are inexpensive to rent and readily available; they are usually clean and often situated right on the beach. In addition, there are several hotels, with swimming pools, bars, air conditioning and tour packages to other points of interest in this coastal

ABOVE: T-shirt bird motif.
BELOW: iguanas are a common sight all over Costa Rica.

province. Perhaps the hotel pool is the best place to swim in Jacó since the water is not very clean and there are dangerous undercurrents. Jacó has no shortage of amusements: horses, bikes, scooters and kayaks are available for rent. Chuck's Surf Shop rents surfboards, offers lessons and provides free information on surfing conditions. For dancing, try Disco La Central; for billiards and darts, visit The Onyx, above the Subway sandwich shop. The funky Beatle Bar is a popular, sports-oriented bar until 9pm, when the working girls move in.

A haven of elegance amid the honky-tonk Jacó atmosphere is Hotel Poseidon, in the center of town on a quiet side street. The restaurant serves sophisticated fare with a modern Pacific Rim take. At the far southern end of the beach, Hotel Club del Mar offers another enclave of sophistication, comfort and tranquility.

Along the coast some 3 km (2 miles) from Playa Jacó is **Playa Hermosa ❺**, one of the best surfing spots on the coast with very strong beach breaks. It is an easily accessible place where there is also a variety of wading birds to observe: great white herons and snowy egrets; and great blue, little blue, tricolor and little green herons. You may also see jacanas, walking on lily pads on their huge yellow feet; and black-bellied whistling ducks.

Head east on the coastal highway for around 40 km (24 miles) to the small plantation town of **Parrita**, dominated by an enormous African oil-palm development, which was established in 1985 by United Brands Fruit Company. Oil palms do very well here. Unfortunately, palm oil is much higher than other oils in saturated fats, and thus is declining in popularity. Palm-oil workers live next to the highway, in plantation villages of two-story, brightly painted homes, set in a "U" around what is the focal point of every *Tico* village: the soccer field.

Around 10 km (6 miles) east of Parrita is the tiny village of Pocares from where you should turn inland and continue for around 6–7 km (4 miles) to reach **Rainmaker ❻**, an exciting eco-project. Rainmaker was the first suspended walkway project in Central America and allows visitors to explore the rainforest canopy with the minimum of environmental disturbance. Boardwalks link six suspension bridges; one bridge spans 90 meters (300 ft) and at the highest point of the trail you will be a dizzying 25 stories above the jungle floor. Recently, a species of frog, feared extinct, reappeared in this reserve. Visits must be booked in advance with operators in Quepos and Manuel Antonio *(see below)*.

BELOW: driving in Costa Rica is rarely without interest.

Manuel Antonio National Park

Once an important banana-shipping port, **Quepos ❼** is now something of a dormitory town to its famous neighbor, Manuel Antonio, 7 km (4 miles) away. There is a regular bus service, some good accommodations, restaurants, shops, and nightlife, and the flavor of an old-time Costa Rican fishing and banana town. Its beaches are polluted, however. Regardless of where you stay, reservations are essential during the vacation season at both Manuel Antonio and Quepos.

The first mission in Costa Rica was established near here, in 1570. It was abandoned in 1751 and its ruins are located up the Naranjo River; the cemetery is still visible, as are remnants of the fruit orchard, which has regenerated from the original stumps. Just north of the church, pop into La Botánica, which sells cinnamon, glossy vanilla beans, bags of peppercorns, herbal teas, and fragrant spice mixtures.

Parque Nacional Manuel Antonio ❽ is composed of three long strands of magnificent white sand, fringed by jungle on one side, and by the Pacific on the other. The beaches are clean and wide. Above them are tall cliffs covered in thick jungle vegetation. In fact, this park is one of the few places in the country where the primary forest comes down to the water's edge in places, sometimes allowing bathers to swim in the shade. In order to protect the eco-system of the park, rangers allow a maximum of 600 visitors on weekdays and 800 on weekends. Avoid weekends when the beaches can seem crowded; early morning is the best time to visit when tourist groups are fewer and animal sightings easiest. There are always licensed naturalist guides available at the entrance to the park.

Playa Espadilla Norte is the first of the beaches, very beautiful, but also dangerous because of its unpredictable riptides. Accessible across a sand spit, which may be submerged at high tide, are **Playa Espadilla Sur** and **Playa Manuel Antonio**. Both provide safe swimming.

There is plenty to do in the national park. On the the beaches you can sunbathe, surf, swim, snorkel or perhaps rent horses from Equus Stables and go on a jungle trail outside the park. Sunset Sails offers 4-hour cruises on either a 16-meter (54-ft) or a more intimate 11-meter (37-ft) sailboat. Snorkeling and dolphin-watching are the main attractions (tel: 771 0001). There are trails for hiking and wildlife sighting – various species of monkeys can be seen, including capuchin, spider and white-faced monkeys, as well as tiny squirrel monkeys (called *titis* in Spanish). Birdlife includes many seabirds such as boobies, frigate birds, pelicans and terns. Snakes and iguanas are often seen and, if you are

TIP

Beware of over-tame monkeys in search of a free lunch at Manuel Antonio. Don't feed them as you not only create a begging colony, but risk catching diseases should they bite you.

BELOW: one of the advantages of flying to Manuel Antonio is the bird's-eye view.

Map on page 170

Map on page 170

ABOVE AND BELOW: beachside and poolside at the Costa Verde Hotel in Quepos.
RIGHT: pavoncillo flower.

sharp-eyed, sloths. Within the park are primary forest, swamps and tropical woodlands, all containing hundreds of species of plants. Other options in areas outside the national park include mountain biking, white-water river rafting or sea kayaking tours, available from Ríos Tropicales. For excellent assistance and information on the area, as well as books and papers in English and local handicrafts, go to **La Buena Nota** at the north end of the village of Manuel Antonio near the beach.

Just outside the park to the north, in the hills that rise up from the beach, there is a garish profusion of signs advertising an ever-growing number of hotels, international restaurants and *cabinas*. With rare exceptions, most accommodations on the ocean side of the road are built on the cliffs above the beach and offer views of the ocean rather than direct access to beaches.

You can get to Manuel Antonio by car, bus or plane. The road has recently been paved all the way to Quepos, and new bridges have replaced the rickety old wooden ones. You pass through some beautiful countryside, although the flat coastal section runs through endless green corridors of palm plantations, which soon becomes monotonous. It's about a three-hour trip by car, some four hours by bus and 20 minutes by plane. SANSA and NatureAir fly daily to Quepos. A final word about Quepos/Manuel Antonio: theft is on the increase. Be attentive: don't leave your belongings unattended on the beach and keep valuables in your hotel's safe.

The old highway to the Pacific

The road less-traveled to Manuel Antonio heads west of San José, through Ciudad Colón and Puriscal. It was once *the* highway to the Pacific coast. Today, most traffic heads through Orotina, leaving the old route for those interested in a much more relaxed drive, through unspoiled mountain terrain.

About 6 km (4 miles) west of **Ciudad Colón**, the old highway passes through the Guayabo reserve of the Quitirrisí Amerindians, who sell woven vine baskets and other handmade goods at roadside stands.

Santiago de Puriscal, a vital farming town with a once-beautiful church, damaged by an earthquake but still standing, is the last outpost of city life before reaching Quepos, on the Pacific coast. Soon after Puriscal the road is unpaved and winds its way through stunning mountains and valleys, carpeted with coffee, sugar cane and banana plantations, and rows of orange groves, populated only by small farms and settlements. This is untouched Costa Rica. Aside from one bumpy stretch just outside of Puriscal, the gravel road is generally in good shape, and there is little traffic. After the village of La Gloria the road quickly descends to sea level, south to Parrita, and onward to Quepos and Manuel Antonio.

Matapalo ❾ is a beach town 25 km (16 miles) south of Manuel Antonio on the Costanera Sur road (15 km/ 9 miles north of Dominical). The beach is long and quiet, the surf is big. To north and south respectively are **Playa Savegre** and **Playa Barú**, with seldom-visited but beautiful beaches. Visit both of these at low tide. ❑

The North

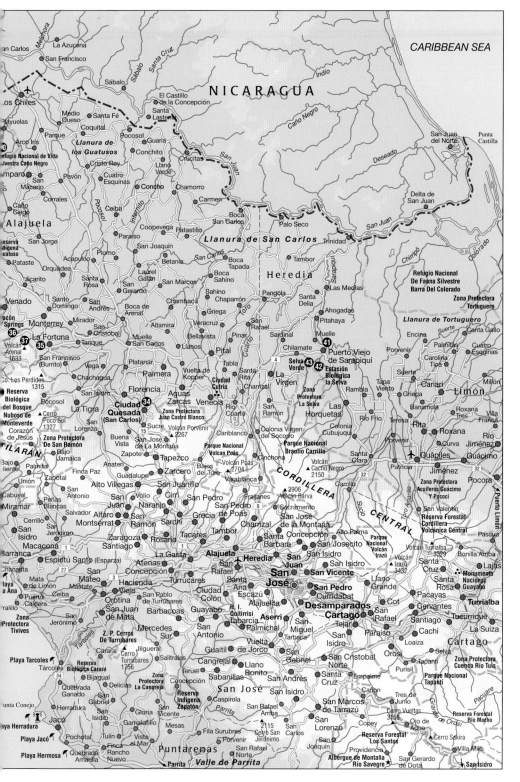

CARIBBEAN SEA

NICARAGUA

an Carlos
La Azucena
San Francisco
Los Chiles
Playuelas
Arco Iris
efugio Nacional de Vida
lvestra Caño Negro
mparo
San
Macario
Caño
Ciego
Alajuela
serva
dígena
uatuso
Pataste
Jicarito
Venado
acón
Springs
Monterrey
36
37 La Fortuna
35
Volcán
Arenal
1633
San Francisco
(Burrito)
o. Los Perdidos
1315
Reserva
Biológica
del Bosque
Nuboso de
Monteverde
Corazón
de Jesús
Zona Protectora
De San Ramón
ILARÁN
Bajo
liente
Palmital
Unión
Cabuyal
Miramar
Cerrillo
San
Isidro
Macacona
arranca
Barranca
Espíritu Santo (Esparza)
hacarita
laya
Mata
de Limón
a Ana
Puerto
Caldera
ralillo
Zona
Protectora
Tivives
Playa Tarcoles
Tárcoles
Reserva
Biológica Carara
unta Conejo
Herradura
aya Herradura
Jacó
Playa Jacó
Playa Hermosa
Quebrada
Amarilla

Medio
Queso
Santa Fé
Coquital
Parque
Pocosol
Llanura de
los Guatusos
Cristo Rey
Pavón
Cuatro
Esquinas
Corrales
Ceiba
Coopevega
Paraíso
San Jorge
Plomo
Orquedea
Santa
Rosa
Santo
Domingo
San Andrés
San
Gerardo
Boca de
Arenal
Mirador
San
Cristóbal
Tanque
Muelle
San Carlos
Vega
Platanar
Chachágua
Palmera
San Isidro
Florencia
Aguas
Zarcas
La Tigra
Ciudad
Quesada
(San Carlos)
34
Sucre
Volcán Porvenir
2267
Pocosol
San
Lorenzo
Buena
Vista
San José
de La Montaña
Zapote
Bajo
Jamaica
Tapezco
Anateri
Finca Paz
Guadalupe
Zarcero
Alto Villegas
San
Antonio
San
Juanillo
San
Juan
Volio
Cirri
San Pedro
Naranjo
Salvador
Alfaro
San
Ramón
Sardhi
Grecia
Sarchi
Tacares
San Pedro
de Poás
Zaragoza
Rosario
Tambor
Charrizal
Santiago
La Garita
Atenas
Concepción
San
Mateo
Hacienda
Vieja
Turrúcares
Mastate
San Pablo
de Turrúbares
Orotina
Ciudad
Colón
San Juan
de Mata
Barbacoas
Guayabo
Mercedes
Sur
San
Jerónimo
Cárara
Jilgueral
Z. P. Cerros
De Turrúbares
Cerro
Turrúbares
1756
Delicias
San
Antonio
Guaitil
Zona
Protectora
La Cangreja
Bijagual
Quebrada
Ganado
San
Gabriel
Gloria
San
Isidro
Mesas
Teruel
Llano
Bonito
Sabanillas
Reserva
Indígena
Zapatón
Caspirola
Pochotal
Tulín
Gamalotillo
Vista
al Mar
Finca
Rancho
Nuevo
Puntarenas

La Azucena
San Francisco
El Castillo
de la Concepción
Santa
Lastenia
Guaria
Crúcitas
Conchito
Llano
Verde
Concho
Chamorro
Carmen
Boca
San Carlos
Patastillo
Llanura de San Carlos
San Carlos
San Joaquín
Boca
Tapada
Betania
Laurel
Galán
San Marcos
Boca
Sahino
Sahino
Chambacú
Chaparrón
Altamira
Veracruz
Bellavista
Pinar
Pital
Tabla
Llanos
Vuelta
de Kopper
Ciudad
Cutris
Santa
Rita
Charrizal
Venecia
Río
Cuarto
San
Ramón
Bajos
del Toro
Varablanca
Volcán Poás
2704
Parque Nacional
Volcan Poás
Prajanes
2906
Volcán Barva
San Pedro
de Poás
Socramento
San José
de la Montaña
Charrizal
Santa
Barbara
Alto Palma
San Concepción
San Isidro
San Josecito
Alajuela
Heredia
San
Juan
San Isidro
San
Rafael
Santa
Ana
San
José
San Vicente
Escazú
Alajuelita
R.I.
Quitirrisi
Tabarcia
Aserri
San Pedro
Curridabat
Desamparados
Cartago
San
Miguel
Tarbaca
Palmichal
Tejar
Vuelta
de Jorco
San
Gabriel
San
Andrés
San Marcos
de Tarrazú
Empalme
Cañón
Concepción
Santa
Cruz
San Rafael
Arriba
San Isidro
San
Carlos
San
Lorenzo
Copey
Tres de
Junio
San
Joaquín
San Rafael
Norte
Parrita
Valle de Parrita
Providencia
Albergue de Montaña
Río Savegre
2115

Sábalo
Santa Cruz
Indio
Guaria
Conchito
San Juan
Boca
San Carlos
Palo Seco
Trinidad
San Juan
Delta de
San Juan
San Juan
del Norte
Punta
Castilla
Caño Negro
Tambor
Heredia
Santa
Delia
Pangola
Las Medias
Ahogadas
Pitahaya
Sardinal
Muelle
Chilamate
Santa Gallo
San
Rafael
La
Virgen
41 Puerto Viejo
de Sarapiquí
Selva
Verde
43
42
Estación
Biológica
la Selva
Zona
Protectora
La Selva
Las
Horquetas
Rambla
Río Frío
Santa
Clara
Colonia Virgen
del Socorro
Cinchona
Volcán
Cacho Negro
2150
Río Frío
Colonia
Cubujuqui
Parque Nacional
Braulio Carrillo
Porvenir
Cariblanco
Volcán
Barva
Carrillo
32
Zona Protectora
Acuíferos Guácimo
Y Pococi
San Valentín
Volcán
Irazú
Parque
Nacional
Volcán
Irazú
Volcán Turrialba
3329
Volcán
3432
Monumento
Nacional
Guayabo
Bonilla Arriba
Lajas
Santa
Cruz
Santa
Rosa
Pacayas
Cot
San
Rafael
Santiago
Cachí
Paraíso
Cervantes
Turrialba
Tucurrique
La Suiza
Cartago
Orosi
Tapanti
Loaiza
Selva
Purisil
Zona Protectora
Cuenca Río Tuis
Parque Nacional
Tapantí
Pacuare
Ojo de
Agua
Cerro
Vueltas
3156
Reserva Forestal
Los Santos
Reserva Forestal
Río Macho
Cerro Sakira
Villa Mills
San Gerardo
de Dota
San Isidro

Caño Negro
Chimpo
Colorado
Refugio Nacional
De Fauna Silvestre
Barra Del Colorado
Zona Protectora
Tortuguero
Llanura de Tortuguero
suerte
Encina
Porvenir
Palmitas
Carolina
Tica
Suerte
Tapa
Viento
Griega
Cuatro
Esquinas
Cariari
Limón
Roxana
Tres
Villa
Franca
Banamola
Rita
Roxana
Río
Jiménez
Curva
Guápiles
Jiménez
Guácimo
Pocora
32
Puerto Limón
Reserva Forestal
Cordillera
Volcánica Central
Pascua
Patricia
Teresa
Porvenir
CORDILLERA
CENTRAL
Sucio
Río
Sucio

THE NORTHWEST

Almost all of Costa Rica's natural attractions are represented in this large and rewarding region: miles of beaches and acres of tropical forests, interspersed with cattle ranges and cowboy towns.

Map on pages 178–79

San José

he northwest of the country is split into two provinces. The larger part is **Guanacaste** – a huge tract stretching endlessly toward the horizon. This is Central America's Big Country, where vast grasslands are punctuated by huge spreading guanacaste trees and bony, white Brahman cattle. During the rainy season, the landscape is a sea of green but in the dry season, the savannahs become sun-baked lakes of gold. Though traditionally cattle country, Guanacaste is nowadays also known for its wide beaches, many of which have been developed as part of major resort complexes. The international airport outside Liberia brings sun-starved tourists directly to their beach destinations.

Puntarenas province, which straddles the Gulf of Nicoya and takes in the South Nicoya Peninsula, is also becoming a vacation paradise of broad sandy beaches, turquoise waters, shady palm trees and some controversially large hotel resort developments. Also just within this region (though it actually belongs to Alajuela province) is the very popular **Monteverde Cloud Forest**.

PRECEDING PAGES: the tabebria tree. **LEFT:** getting down and dirty. **BELOW:** Guanacaste cowboy.

The *Guanacastecos*

The *Guanacastecos*, as the residents of this province are called, are an independent people. Many are descended from the Chorotega Amerindians with skin the color of tortoise shell, eyes a warm brown, black wavy hair and an easy, friendly grace.

In 1787, the Captaincy General of Costa Rica, which then governed the country from Guatemala, decided that Guanacaste should be part of Nicaragua. There it stayed until 1821 when the Captaincy General was dissolved and the people of Guanacaste were asked to decide their own national identity. Opinions were divided: the Northerners around Liberia wanted to be a part of Nicaragua and the Southerners on the Nicoyan peninsula wanted to revert to Costa Rica. A vote was held and the majority elected to be a part of Costa Rica.

Puntarenas

Many people think that **Puntarenas** ❶ (pop. 100,000) is simply a place to pass through so that you can get somewhere else: you pass through Puntarenas en route to the islands of the Gulf of Nicoya, or to the car ferries that go to the southern part of the Nicoya Peninsula.

Puntarenas used to be the country's main port, bustling with longshoremen, sailors on leave, prostitutes and merchants from San José who traveled by train to escape the city and conduct their import/export businesses. But the growth of the port of Limón and the more recent opening of the deep-water port at nearby **Puerto Caldera** have made Puntarenas somewhat of an anachronism.

Stretched along a narrow spit of sand – *punta de arenas*, or point of sand – Puntarenas is still worth exploring, though. You can even arrive here aboard a vintage diesel train, courtesy of the Tico Train Tour, which travels on weekends, leaving San José's old Pacific railroad station at 6am and arriving in Puntarenas at 11am. The train leaves Puntarenas for the return trip at 3.30pm, so there is just enough time for a stroll along the Paseo de los Turistas and a beach-front lunch (reserve ahead, tel: 233 3300).

Today, fishing is the main industry of Puntarenas. The tourism industry is small, though there are some recently spruced-up large hotels. There's also the new Puntarenas Marine Park at the east end of town with 28 large aquariums showcasing the marine life of the Gulf of Nicoya (open Tues–Sun 8am–4pm; entrance fee; tel: 661 5275). With its views of the long, arching coastline, the beach along the gulf is beautiful, and the sunsets over Nicoya are spectacular. Though the ocean waters were until quite recently badly polluted, they have now been cleaned up, and Puntarenas town beach now flies the Bandera Azul (blue flag), denoting an eco-friendly, clean beach inspected by government officials. The estuary and rivers, however, should be avoided.

Downtown

The crowded center of Puntarenas, three blocks back from the beach, bustles in the morning as the townfolk conduct business, often getting around town on bicycles. Everyone seems in a hurry, perhaps to accomplish what they need to before the onset of the afternoon heat. Though, like San José, an architectural victim of excessive concrete, Puntarenas still retains many of its older buildings: plank structures with latticework below the roof to permit the breeze. The

Take a trip into the glorious waters of the Gulf of Nicoya aboard the luxurious, 70-foot (21 meters) Manta Ray *catamaran, which sails from the Calypso dock in Puntarenas.*

BELOW: beach goers at Puntarenas.

wooden buildings are painted in such color combinations as bright turquoise and red, and together with the few remaining mansions of the merchants and the Church, they convey the flavor of a Puntarenas in its prime.

Visit the museum in the **Casa de Cultura** (House of Culture), formerly the city's jail, where exhibits feature the area's history, geography, natural history and indigenous crafts (open Mon–Sat, closed noon–1pm; free), plus the **Museo Histórico Marino** (open Tues–Sun), for a look at the city's seafaring history.

Evening is perhaps the best time to catch Puntarenas. Enjoy a late afternoon *refresco* at one of the *sodas* (cafes) on the **Paseo de Turistas** and watch the sun sink below the mountains of Nicoya across the bay. The *sodas* offer a chance to try some native Costa Rican drinks. This is perhaps the only place in the country to get *maté*, a type of milkshake with a lingering, nostalgic aftertaste. Try a cold, creamy *pinolillo* made with toasted, ground corn, or a "Churchill," a very sweet, cold fruit drink that includes condensed milk.

Seafood restaurants and hotels line the oceanfront. Most are air-conditioned or adjusted to catch the ocean breezes. The hotels along the estuary also offer free mooring and facilities to cruising sailboats. The Yacht Club here is extensive, well protected, professionally managed, and one of the very first stops a trans-oceanic yacht makes on the first leg of a trip from the West Coast of the US to more distant ports of call.

Just to the south, down the coast from Puntarenas, is **Playa Doña Ana**. Here the Tourist Institute (ICT) has developed a beach resort with bar, restaurant, showers and parking, on a cove well situated between two spectacular rock headlands. Costa Rica's second-largest surfing wave is just offshore and there are fantastic facilities for surfers, including rentals and repairs.

Map on pages 178–179

Above: crushed-ice fruit drinks stand.
Below: paddling a kayak in the Gulf of Nicoya.

If you like a game of golf or enjoy horseback riding, there are resorts on the Nicoya Peninsula that specialize in both activities.

The Gulf of Nicoya

Car ferries, as well as a smaller passenger-only *lancha* (launch), cross from Puntarenas to Paquera on the **Nicoya Peninsula**. The two-hour trip across the gulf passes by 40 or so islands, including **Isla San Lucas** ❷, Costa Rica's former prison island. The prison was closed in 1991 and the island deserted, except for the guards posted there to prevent vandalism. There are no restrictions preventing visits to the island, however, and visitors who are so inclined can view disturbing reminders of the life prisoners endured here.

Calypso Tours offers a cruise on its 21-meter (70-ft) catamaran and visits to the islands in the Gulf of Nicoya. It crosses the waters of the Gulf and visits **Isla Tortuga** ❸ (Turtle Island), where, in an idyllic setting of white sand and turquoise waters, you can enjoy what is perhaps the best seafood buffet in the country, as well as folk music and entertainment. There is also adequate time for swimming and sunbathing. Calypso, one of the oldest tour operators in Costa Rica, also offers other excellent tours, including fishing trips (tel: 256 2727).

The South Nicoya Peninsula

The ferry ride across the Gulf of Nicoya brings you to a different world. It is one of seasonally dry grasslands, gigantic spreading trees, rolling cattle ranches, memorable bays and beautiful beaches.

From the ferry landing at Paquera, Tambor is just a short drive, and Montezuma is about an hour away. Buses wait to meet the Paquera ferry to head south to Montezuma, but there are no such direct services from Playa Naranjo. If you are driving south from Paquera, the roads are largely unpaved, with few road signs, but the local people are used to giving visitors directions.

BELOW: tumbling waters at Catarata de Cangreja, near El Rincón de la Vieja.

The drive along the peninsula, although rough, is rewarding. It traverses miles of pastureland, through small towns and villages, past people on horseback and dwellings of every description – and every now and again reveals views of the blue bays of the Pacific.

Some 7 km (4½ miles) south of the town of Paquera lies the **Refugio Nacional de Vida Silvestre Curú** (Curú National Wildlife Refuge). Although small, the park encompasses five habitats and offers sanctuary to a surprisingly large and diverse number of plants, animals (including the white-faced monkey) and over 220 species of birds. It has three beautiful beaches, ideal for swimming and diving. There are modest accommodations available, along with horseback tours and sea kayaking to nearby islands. The hiking is also excellent. The refuge is private property, owned by the Schutt family; it's a good idea to call in advance to arrange accommodations and tours (tel: 641 0004 or 710 8236).

Bahía Ballena

A large, wide bay, **Bahía Ballena** ❺, which means Whale Bay, is a place of surprising beauty and tranquility. The waters are gentle and warm, with large flocks of pelicans diving for fish. January is an especially good time for sighting whales. The bay shelters two beaches, **Playa Pochote** and **Playa Tambor**. In the 1990s, however, its tranquil face was irrevocably and controversially transformed by the construction of the enormous Hotel Barceló Playa Tambor. The project inspired a passionate debate about what kind of tourism is best for Costa Rica: mammoth projects such as this, or small businesses that reflect the character of their communities. In the end, big business won. In the village of **Tambor**, inexpensive lodgings and good local-style meals can be found, and you

BELOW: a Costa Rican bullfight, where only the *toreros* get hurt.

might just get a sense of life as it was before the arrival of big-time tourism. Continuing southeast to the town of Cóbano the road leads to Montezuma.

Montezuma

Montezuma ❻, in many ways, feels like the end of the line. The partially paved road rolls down a hill and ends abruptly in front of a row of funky hotels, trendy new restaurants and bars, and *cantinas* (snack bars) on the beachfront. Here, young North American and European travelers outnumber the local people, who have accepted them with seeming good grace. Places fill up quickly everywhere in Montezuma during the dry season, so reserve well ahead.

Lodging and dining in Montezuma ranges from basic to luxurious, and the beach-going is exceptional. To the north of town there are wide, sandy beaches, with beautiful clear water, some with great shelling. A scenic footpath leads to a dramatic waterfall and river. To the south are beaches with surf crashing against volcanic rock – and, just a short hike away up a river, another waterfall with a pool for swimming. The first couple of rocky bays north of Montezuma have strong currents, but Playa Grande is safe for swimming.

Bikes and boogie boards can be rented at agencies in town, and horses through the Finca Los Caballos, outside of town, as well as through in-town tour operators. But most visitors to Montezuma seem to spend their time swimming, sunning or simply hanging out in this laid-back place that seems expressly designed for the youthful, low-budget traveler. Perhaps the most romantic restaurant in all of Costa Rica is tucked away on a rocky cove, a few minutes' walk south of town. Playa de los Artistas specializes in seafood served alfresco at driftwood tables illuminated at night by lanterns and starlight (closed Sun; tel: 642 0920).

BELOW: young *Guanacastecos* get in the saddle at a very early age.

Cabo Blanco

It is almost 11 km (7 miles) from Montezuma to the **Cabo Blanco Absolute Wildlife Reserve ❼** (open Wed–Sun until 4pm) along a little-used, unpaved road that runs parallel to the beach. There's a cluster of small *cabina*-hotels in the town of Cabuya. The reserve, established in 1963 through the inspiration and tireless efforts of Swedish immigrant Nils Olaf Wessberg, is Costa Rica's oldest protected wildlife region. Sadly, Wessberg was murdered while trying to establish a similar reserve in the Osa Peninsula, and he is fondly recalled as an important pioneer of the parks system in Costa Rica.

Originally, Cabo Blanco allowed no public access: all life there was to be protected, without any interference from humans. Today, however, approximately one-third of the reserve is open to visitors. It encompasses a wet, tropical forest on the tip of the peninsula and is one of the most scenic spots along the whole Pacific coast. There is a large population of marine and shore birds as well as mammals. In addition, there is a ranger station with restrooms and picnic tables, well-maintained trails and a lovely remote beach, where you may swim but not snorkel.

Strict rules guide the behavior of all visitors, starting with registration and a briefing at the reserve's administration center. To drive to the reserve you must cross two small streams, for which a four-wheel drive vehicle is recommended. The reserve is closed on Monday and Tuesday to reduce the impact of tourism.

Beyond Cabo Blanco, the road is rough and unpaved. During the rainy season it is muddy and some of the rivers and creeks without bridges are only passable in a four-wheel drive vehicle. During the dry season things don't get any more comfortable as a fine, brown dust coats travelers and plants along the roadway.

Surfers and nature-lovers have recently discovered Malpais and Santa Teresa, two beaches about 6 km (4 miles) north of Cabo Blanco. A clutter of hotels and restaurants has sprung up almost overnight to cater to an international, young surfing crowd. There are also a few luxury retreats here.

The Interamericana northbound

From San José the Interamericana Highway, route C1, cuts northwest straight through the heart of Guanacaste, via its capital, Liberia, and northward to Nicaragua.

At **Cañas** you first get the sense that immense Guanacaste is more like a separate country, caught somewhere between Costa Rica and Nicaragua, than it is a province of Costa Rica. Cañas, which was named for the fields of white-flowered wild cane that covered the countryside, is a cowboy town, with a frontier feeling, not unlike a village in Mexico. There is a fine hermitage a few kilometers north, just before the highway crosses the Corobicí River.

Four kilometers (2½ miles) north of Cañas on the highway is **Hotel Hacienda La Pacífica ❽**. This private reserve with comfortable cabins, beautiful pool and grounds has extensive trails that run parallel to the Corobicí River, which provides excellent vantage points for bird-watching. Over 220 different species have been identified here. One of them is the boat-

Map on pages 178–79

ABOVE: spiky agave in Cabo Blanco.
BELOW: waiting for the tide to turn in the Nicoya Peninsula.

billed heron, an exotic-looking bird with a wide, ungainly bill, the use of which has never been scientifically explained. **Las Pumas**, near La Pacífica, provides a shelter for some of Costa Rica's large cats that, for various reasons, are not able to live in the wild (open daily 8am–5pm; donations requested).

Founded 20 years ago by a Swiss animal-lover, Las Pumas provides a haven for rescued wild cats and other animals. Since the death of its founder, it has been run by the non-profit Hagnauer Foundation; donations are welcome.

Safaris Corobicí offers guided "floats" down the Corobicí on its 6-meter (17-ft) Avon rafts, a wonderful opportunity to observe the river habitat, especially the birds – laughing falcons, herons, trogons, wood storks, mot-mots, parrots, osprey, and, of course, egrets. Howler and white-faced monkeys all make their homes along the shores of the Corobicí. Plan for an early-morning trip to enjoy the best birding (tel: 669 6191).

Palo Verde National Park

Parque Nacional Palo Verde  is one of Central America's largest protected wildlife areas, situated near the mouth of the Tempisque River. To get there take the road from Bagaces to the west, off the Interamericana highway. Four-wheel drive is recommended, especially during the rainy season. If you are traveling independently, note that the southern entrance to the park, from Cañas, may be closed; be sure to call the National Parks Service office (tel: 200 0125) to find out which routes are open and which are the most navigable. Alternatively, book a tour with one of the many operators who visit here.

Palo Verde encompasses lakes, swamps, woodlands, grasslands and forest and is a major sanctuary for migrating waterfowl in Central America. Tidal fluctuations and seasonally overflowing rivers attract 300 species of terrestrial and waterbirds, including herons, whistling ducks, ibises and the immense Jabirú stork. Large mammals and reptiles are also abundant and can easily be

BELOW: father and son at a rodeo near Liberia.

seen during the dry season when they gather at waterholes. Coatimundis, armadillos, iguanas and crocodiles measuring up to 5 meters (15 ft) long are not uncommon here.

Map on pages 178–79

Only 25 years ago, currents and sediment run-off from Guanacaste formed a sand bar, which then became stabilized as an island in the middle of the Tempisque River near the head of the Gulf of Nicoya. Today, it is known as **Isla de Pájaros** ⑩. From the park a boat and guide can be chartered to this island; alternatively, you can ask to go along with the park rangers on their visits to Pájaros. This quiet place provides the isolation that is favored by many water birds. While the white ibis and a species of egret are the only birds that regularly nest here, roseate spoonbills, wood storks and anhingas also occasionally make their homes on Isla de Pájaros.

Liberia

The capital city of Guanacaste province, **Liberia** ⑪ was established over 200 years ago. It is also known as *Ciudad Blanca*, the White City. Original residents carried white volcanic earth and gravel from the nearby slopes of Rincón de la Vieja and Miravalles volcanoes to construct traditional white adobe homes. In the *Puertas del Sol* – "Doorways of the Sun" – style, these houses were designed to let both morning and afternoon sunlight into north-facing corner houses.

ABOVE: Sunday-best cowboy tack.
BELOW: bubbling mud pots at Rincón de la Vieja.

Many of these lovely old adobe homes can still be seen, off the city's narrow streets, just south of the park. Some of them are being restored, and the owners may welcome visitors inside to see the work in progress. Many of the houses have classical courtyards and grand rooms with high ceilings and 19th-century murals. The kitchens, to the rear of the house, open onto courtyards, where corn and other grains were once dried.

Early morning is an ideal time to take a walk through the center of Liberia. Visit **Agonía Church**, (located at the end of the main street) an adobe structure built in 1852 and one of the oldest Catholic churches in the country. Talk with the helpful people at the Tourist Information Center, located in the **Casa de Cultura** (Culture House), which is also home to the small **Museo de Sabanero** (Cowboy Museum; very irregular hours; free). Liberia is rapidly modernizing and even has a multiplex cinema now on the outskirts of town.

Rincón de la Vieja National Park

Continuing upcountry from the city of Liberia is the **Parque Nacional Rincón de La Vieja** ⑫ with four complete ecosystems contained within its 14,000 hectares (35,000 acres). The name, which applies to both the park and the volcano it protects, derives from the legend of an old woman who once lived on its slopes. Her house was referred to as "the old woman's corner" – hence Rincón de la Vieja.

Access is via a chalk-white road to the Las Pailas sector, or via a bumpy road via San Jorge to the Santa María sector, but the adventurous will find it virtually untouched. Hiking is excellent, along well-marked trails. Rainfall can be heavy so bring waterproof gear. April and May are the best times to visit.

At the junction of the Interamericana Highway just outside Liberia is the Bramadero restaurant. It is rich with the smell of leather tack and beef cooking in the kitchen. Dark-tanned cowboys sit at heavy wooden tables drinking beer.

BELOW: four-wheel drive vehicles are a good option if you can afford it.

The "official access road" to the park station at Rincón de la Vieja winds 27 km (17 miles) east out of Liberia. Appearing strangely snow-covered, it traverses an area of chalky earth that gives Liberia its nickname of the White City. At the ranger station at the end of the road you can climb to a look-out point for a view down the slopes of the volcano, across grassy plains, and all the way to the ocean. The station offers a good campsite next to the ruins of an old sugar-cane processing plant. It is about a two-hour walk from there to the hot springs, which offer a place to soak weary bones.

The most extraordinary area, located at the foot of the volcano, is **Las Pailas** or the Kitchen Stoves. Here, 8 hectares (20 acres) of hot springs, boiling mud pots, sulfur lakes and vapor geysers that color the surrounding rocks red, green and vivid yellow, offer a bizarre geological phenomenon unique to Costa Rica. It is said that the mud from the so-called Sala de Belleza (Beauty Salon) boiling pots makes an excellent facial beauty mask. Visitors must exercise extreme caution, however, since breaking through the brittle ground surface of the area can result in severe burns; it is much wiser to go with a guide.

Lodging is available at a number of inns. Closest to the Las Pailas entrance is the Albergue Rincón de la Vieja. To get there, go north from Liberia 5 km (3 miles), and turn right onto the gravel road that leads to the village of Curubandé. From there go approximately 2 km (1 mile) to the entrance to Hacienda Guachipelín, enter through the gate and continue until you see a sign saying "Albergue."

To the Nicaraguan border

A good base from which to explore the area north to the border is the **Hotel Hacienda Los Inocentes**, a former ranch, dating back to 1890, now a travelers' lodge, off the Interamericana Highway on the road to Santa Cecilia. This scenic byway is bordered by streams with waterfalls and acres of saplings being used in reforestation programs. Well-trained horses are available for visitors and the guides will match one to a guest's riding ability. Along streambeds, through forests and fields at the base of Orosí Volcano, the guides point out monkeys and sloths, iguanas, and rare birds – enriching your experience considerably.

At the end of a day in this region, consider making a short trip east to the village of Santa Cecilia to watch the sun set over **Lake Nicaragua**, or as the Nicaraguans have named it "the Sweet Sea". You may be fortunate enough to see freshwater sharks.

During the civil war in Nicaragua, many of the local young men from this area were drawn into the battle, either for or against the US-backed Contra forces who were trying to overthrow the ruling Sandinistas. Near here, in the northern addition to Santa Rosa National Park, a clandestine CIA airstrip was constructed to bring in supplies to aid the Contra effort, in violation of Costa Rica's neutrality laws. Built with the blessing of ex-president Alberto Monge, it was torn up under the administration of Oscar Arias in 1986. The Reagan administration took great umbrage and drastically decreased US aid money for Costa Rica *(see page 195).*

Map on pages 178–79

A rise in the bumpy road about 8 km (5 miles) beyond the center of Santa Cecilia brings the vast inland sea that is Lake Nicaragua into view. William Walker *(see page 45)* planned to conquer Nicaragua and to use the Nicaraguans as a labor force to build canals from Lake Nicaragua to the Pacific. He envisioned a waterway to transport goods by boat across the isthmus from the Pacific to the Atlantic. Wealthy investors in the United States backed this plan. But the defeat of Walker in Costa Rica, and later in Nicaragua and Honduras, put an end to the venture.

A trip to the bay at **Puerto Soley**, the northernmost Pacific beach of Costa Rica, passes through the small town of La Cruz, a stopping place for those traveling north through Central America, and for migrant laborers from Nicaragua crossing back and forth, seeking work in Costa Rica. From La Cruz there are wonderful views of the valley and Salinas Bay below. Winding down the hill, you'll pass a ranch established by Somoza, the ex-dictator of Nicaragua, before reaching Puerto Soley, a windswept beach with a new villa complex. Nearby, two large luxury hotels have recently been built. The wind is so strong here that the windsurfing conditions rival Lake Arenal and kitesurfing has also become popular.

Isla Bolaños

In the bay, the National Wildlife Refuge of **Isla Bolaños** ⓭ thrusts its rocky ledges 81 meters (267 ft) above the surface of the sea. An almost vertical island, it is the only nesting site in Costa Rica for the frigate bird and one of very few for the brown pelican. You can visit Isla Bolaños by arranging with local hotels for a boat: the 25-minute ride in his fishing boat gives a magnificent view of the

BELOW: a park ranger cycling to work on Playa Nancite, famous for turtle nesting, from August–December.

TIP

In Parque Nacional
Santa Rosa there are
fine views from the
look-out point at the
Monumento a los
Héroes – a large
concrete arch that
commemorates those
who fell in battle at
Santa Rosa in 1856.

shore. Permits to set foot on the island are issued by the National Park Service in San José or Santa Rosa (tel: 666 5051). However, visitors are not officially allowed between December and March so as to protect the nesting seabirds. The frigate birds make nests in the dense thickets of woody vines on cliffs 40 meters (131 ft) above the sea. It's not just for the isolation and protection of the remote island that they nest here: because of their wide wingspan and small bodies, they find it difficult to take off from a standing or running start like other birds, and therefore have to throw themselves into the air from a high ledge to catch the updrafts. In the dry season, when the frigate birds mate, you can see the males puffing out brilliant scarlet sacs on their throats in order to attract the females.

It is an enjoyable walk around Isla Bolaños and the return to Puerto Soley, over transparent blue water, watching the magenta sun setting behind shimmering evening clouds, makes the perfect end to the day.

Guanacaste National Park

Parque Nacional Guanacaste ⓮ was created in 1989 with foreign funds donated to Costa Rica's Neotropica and National Park foundations in order to protect the migratory paths of animals living in the adjacent protected area of Santa Rosa National Park *(see opposite)*.

Guanacaste Park encompasses a wide band of largely deforested land that extends from the Orosí and Cacao volcanos to the Pacific Coast. Dry tropical forest dominates this vast land, but habitats ranging from mangrove swamps and beaches to rain and cloud forest are also within the park's boundaries.

Over the past several hundred years, complex patterns of cutting, grazing, burn-

BELOW: poolside
perfection at El
Ocotal Resort.

ing and farming have dissected Guanacaste into a complex mosaic of life zones.

Dan Janzen, the visionary ecologist whose life work is the preservation and reforestation of Guanacaste, feels that this park will ultimately be restored to its original state. "Dry forests have been destroyed," Janzen says, "but they are tough, able to withstand six months of drought a year and are very regenerable." With the acquisition of Guanacaste National Park, the large tracts of land necessary for successful forest regeneration are now protected and under national park management. The park sustains large populations of many animal species that are able to find refuge during summer droughts and migrate freely between "islands" of forested areas.

Animals eat and disperse seeds from the trees, and have created these forest islands. Rainforest insects, important for pollinating dry forest plants, are attracted from nearby mountain slopes. In 20 years, significant canopy forest will have developed. And, in 200 or 300 years, full-grown tropical dry forests may again dominate Guanacaste.

Map on pages 178–79

Santa Rosa National Park

Parque Nacional Santa Rosa ⓯ encompasses virtually all of the environmental habitats of the region. A nearly infinite system of trails takes visitors through zones of deciduous tropical hardwoods to arid mountains with deserts of cactus and thorny shrubs, and along rivers lined with forests to mangrove-swamp estuaries near the beach. Two of its beaches, Nancite and Naranjo, are important turtle nesting sites. Elsewhere, many mammals, including monkeys and peccaries (wild pigs), plus over 20 species of bats, live in the park.

ABOVE: pestle and mortar, La Casona. **BELOW:** a Guaitil potter at work

During more than 20 years of scientific work at Santa Rosa, Dan Janzen has taught two generations of local people an intelligent appreciation of the forest. Through his work, residents of Guanacaste now have experience and expertise in firefighting, maintaining horses and managing cattle, identifying plants and dealing with "biotic challenges" like ticks, diseases, thirst and wounds. Jobs as research assistants, guides and reserve caretakers provide many with skills and a stable, long-term source of income.

Along Santa Rosa's **Naked Indian Path**, as with many of the park's trails, you pass through forest that, during the dry season, loses many of its leaves, making wildlife viewing easier for the naturalist. Huge multi-colored iguanas are commonly seen in the trees bordering the trail. Hiking toward Duende Creek and the bat cave, look for them sunning on tree branches.

Santa Rosa's significance as the location of the historic battle against William Walker *(see page 45)* was a primary factor in the government's decision to make it a national park. The final battle against Walker took place at the **La Casona** ("The Big House") *hacienda*. By coincidence, on the three occasions that Costa Rica has been invaded, it has been here that the invaders were eventually turned back.

Today, a different kind of battle is fought in Santa Rosa. The rangers at the station tell of their encounters with hunters. Though hunting is outlawed in the park, the law is virtually unenforceable due to the inadequate number of rangers. Armed hunters are frequently met by unarmed rangers who often must fight them to remove them from park boundaries. The low-paid rangers often risk their lives in these skirmishes. The long-running battle between rangers and poachers reached a terrible climax in May 2002, when a pair of disgruntled hunters set fire to La Casona, the historic farm estate, and burned it to the ground. The house, a landmark in Costa Rican history, has since been rebuilt and once again provides a window into the life of Costa Ricans during the colonial period (open 8am–4pm).

A trail leads from the house to a memorial to the heroes and martyrs of the battle. President Juan Rafael Mora's famous speech, in which he exhorted his countrymen to defend Costa Rica against William Walker, is preserved on an historic plaque.

Wartime secrets

The northern section of the park was expanded to include the ranch of former Nicaraguan dictator Somoza, who lived there so he could move easily and clandestinely back and forth across the border. The Costa Rican government was interested in expanding Santa Rosa Park to make possible a stable population for some of the park's species. It also felt that its best interests were not served by the presence of an ousted military dictator near its border.

So, in 1979, the **Murcíelago Hacienda**, owned by the Somoza family, was expropriated and made part of the national parks system. The *hacienda*, which lies on **Saint Elena Bay** with access to **Playa Blanca** and its untouched white-sand beach, is now a part of Santa Rosa Park. It can be reached from the entrance at the northern end of the park. A sign on the Interamericana High-

BELOW: a deserted Pacific Coast beach.

way past the main entrance to Santa Rosa indicates the way. A recent addition to the park is the land that was occupied by the formerly secret **Santa Elena Airstrip**, used by Oliver North and his cronies in their Iran-Contra activities *(see page 190).*

Map on pages 178–79

Santa Rosa National Park beaches

A rugged 13-km (8-mile) hiking trail, or four-wheel drive road during the dry season (inaccessible during the wet season), leads from the Santa Rosa ranger station to **Playa Naranjo**. White sand and clear water with excellent surf breaking near **Witch's Rock** *(see page 101)*, a monolith 2 km (1 mile) offshore, make Naranjo a popular but remote surfing destination. Boats can be chartered from Playas del Coco to Naranjo. Alternatively, there is camping at both playas Naranjo and Nancite.

The Santa Elena Airstrip was financed by a bogus Panamanian company set up by Oliver North. Its seizure by the Costa Rican government was a major source of friction between Costa Rica and the United States.

    Playa Nancite ⑯, one of Costa Rica's most pristine beaches, is northwest from Naranjo. Each month, usually on a waxing three-quarter moon, turtles come ashore here to nest. Tens of thousands may participate in the event, called an *arribada*, one of Costa Rica's grandest natural spectacles *(see pages 240–41)*. Exact times are unpredictable, as they are with most biological phenomena. Even though a full-scale *arribada* may not be taking place, solitary turtles can usually be seen nesting on Nancite and Naranjo beaches.

Playa Panamá to Playa Ocotal

Playas Panamá, Hermosa, Coco and Ocotal are beaches some 30–40 km (15–20 miles) from Liberia, at the end of winding roads, most of which are paved but pocked with mudholes and ruts during the rainy season.

BELOW: an idyllic beach scene on the Nicoya peninsula.

Playa Panamá ⑰, on a beautiful bay at the end of the road, is the site of a controversial Costa Rican Tourist Institute development called Papagayo, which had planned to bring a vast hotel complex – similar in style to the one that has transformed Cancún in Mexico – to the area. In the wake of fierce and long-running legal battles, however, the scale of the project has diminished somewhat and the full realization of a Cancún-style mega-resort is still a few years away. New hotels in this rapidly developing area are huge, all-inclusive package hotels.

Just south is **Playa Hermosa ⑱**, a sparkling cove with gentle surf. Cabinas Playa Hermosa, in a setting of beach almond trees, was one of the first hotels on the beach; it has recently been renovated.

The first view of the ocean coming from Liberia is of **Playas del Coco ⑲**, a honky-tonk little town of open-air bars, nightclubs, tiny restaurants, beach-front hotels, boardwalks and teenagers on vacation. The large cove and wide sandy beach bustle with activity. Skiffs filled with fish are brought ashore and off-loaded onto trucks parked on the sand. Radios playing in the beach-front seafood restaurants help to put people in the party mood with infectious Latin *salsa* and rock 'n' roll.

The north end of the beach is developing into a quieter, more sophisticated destination with newer, small hotels.

South of Coco Beach, at **Playa El Ocotal ⑳**, a luxury hotel rests serenely on a hilltop overlooking the pounding surf, sandy coves, rocky capes and islands of the Nicoya coast. El Ocotal Beach Resort commands incredible views. Its circular restaurant perched on the edge of the cliffs is open to the general public. There is a road to the quiet beach, near the entrance to the hotel, and

Hotel El Velero on Playa Hermosa is named for the sailboat which brought its French-Canadian owners all the way from Québec to Playa Hermosa. Its 12-meter (38-ft) sloop is available for cruises to secluded beaches, and for other trips.

BELOW: handsome craft at Playa Flamingo marina.

a shady cove provides good, sheltered swimming. Diving expeditions to local waters or as far away as Isla del Coco, can be arranged at El Ocotal or with Diving Safaris at Playa Hermosa (tel: 672 0012).

Continuing south there are other pleasant, less-visited beaches. It may seem as though it is an impossibly complicated maze of dirt and gravel roads, but remember that the ocean is to the west and the highway is to the east and you should never get too lost.

Punta Zapotal to Cabo Velas

From Comunidad, head south on the highway toward Belén. From there it is a short distance to **Playa Brasilito** and the **Flamingo Beach** area, which includes **Playa Potrero**. In the dry season, if you feel adventurous and have a four-wheel-drive car, you can negotiate the bumpy Monkey Trail shortcut that starts near Sardinal and emerges near **Playa Pan de Azúcar** (Sugar Loaf Beach). Ask the locals for directions.

Playa Conchal, once a deserted slice of beach composed of bottomless drifts of pink, orange, mauve and sunset-colored sea shells, lies just south of Flamingo. It is an ideal place to snorkel. To get there pass through Brasilito, a small town on a gray-sand beach with a few *cabinas* and a vintage, wooden hotel, and then head south to the end of the road.

Head back again to Brasilito, five minutes to the north, and you will come to **Playa Flamingo ㉑**, one of Costa Rica's more exclusive beaches, with its own marina and landing strip, or head up the hill to the **Hotel Colores del Pacífico**, a masterpiece of modern, minimalist architecture, clinging to a cliff overlooking Flamingo Bay (tel: 654 4769).

Map on pages 178–79

ABOVE: the taste of the tropics.
BELOW: shooting green turtles the ecological way.

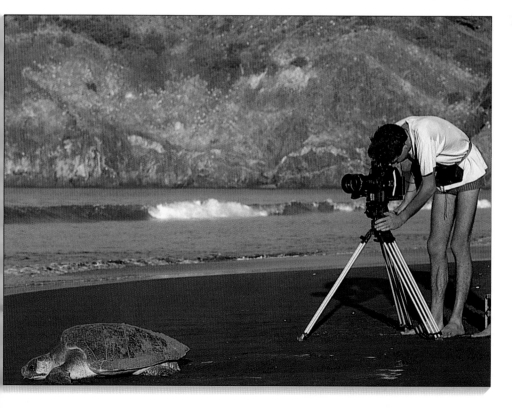

Development has proceeded apace on the beautiful beaches of Flamingo, which may owe its name to an early developer who mistook the pink-plumed roseate spoonbills who frequent the area for flamingoes.

Flamingo Marina Resort dominates a spectacular, white-sand beach, and looks out on rocks and islands dotting the horizon a few miles from shore. Wildlife, such as caimans, monkeys, and wading birds, once lived in the nearby estuary, but they departed, with the completion of the Flamingo Marina, the first fuel dock and full-service marina on the Pacific coast south of Acapulco. Presently, it provides service for transient yachts heading north or south and has dock space for 80 vessels, including a fleet of sportfishing charter boats.

To the north is **Playa Potrero**, a cove of coconut palms and calm water, which is an excellent place for a picnic and a dip in the ocean. A cluster of new hotels, from modestly comfortable to extravagantly luxurious, dot the beach. The views get better, although the roads get worse, as you continue north along this picturesque coastline toward **Playa Pan de Azúcar**.

When you arrive at Pan de Azucar, it is obviously the last resort. Stop in at the **Hotel Sugar Beach** for incredible views and enjoy a drink, lunch or a swim in the cove.

South of Cabo Velas

Go through Brasilito to Huacas and continue for 13 km (8 miles) south, where you will need to make a right turn for **Playa Grande ㉒** and **Playa Tamarindo ㉓**. Tamarindo is a national wildlife refuge, though you would scarcely realize it. The wildlife seems more concentrated in the town's many bars and clubs than it is in the nearby forest. The luxurious **Hotel El Jardín del Edén**, with pink-tiled roofs, is in the hills above the beach. The friendly, Swiss-owned Capitán Suizo on the beach is also luxurious. Relatively inexpensive lodging is available in the village of Tamarindo. Over the past five years, Tamarindo has experienced a major growth spurt, with commercial centers and condominium developments popping up everywhere. On the plus side, there is lots more to do in town, including dining at a plethora of international restaurants.

Tamarindo is a favorite surfers' haunt and has many surf shops, including the well-run Iguana Surf, where you can rent boards, kayaks and snorkeling equipment. Windsurfing is also becoming popular. Iguana Surf offers tours: one of its most popular is a 2-hour guided paddle through the estuary – a great way to see birds and wildlife.

Playa Grande is a 5-minute boat ride across an estuary, or it is a 1-hour drive over dirt roads. Like Tamarindo, it has excellent surf.

Playa Grande is also a major leatherback turtle nesting habitat, and the site of environmental conflicts between conservationists and developers. When ultimately resolved, they may well define Costa Rica's policies of ecotourism.

Las Baulas National Marine Park, which incorporates Playa Grande, was created in 1991 to protect the world's most important leatherback hatching area, and was expanded in 1995. It was estimated at that

BELOW: away from the beaches and resorts, everyday life trundles on at a slow pace.

time that there were only about 35,000 leatherbacks left in the world and approximately 900 of them came to Playa Grande to lay their eggs each year. Sadly, the population has subsequently fallen into a dramatic decline despite concerted efforts by the National Park Service and scientists to protect them. During the long nesting season from August to February, if you are lucky, you may see one or two turtles struggling up the beach to dig a nest. Visitors must join a guided group since beach access is strictly limited, and flash photography of the wildlife is completely forbidden.

On the beach at Playa Grande is **Hotel Las Tortugas**, a congenial, turtle-friendly hotel, with low-lighting at night for the turtle's well-being. Catch the Guanacastecan breezes from a comfortable hammock near the turtle-shaped swimming pool, chat with the garrulous owner of the hotel, Lewis Wilson, who was instrumental in establishing the marine park, or take a guided tour of the mangrove estuary on a pontoon boat whose motor is covered and nearly silent, ensuring a peaceful trip for riders and the birds they observe.

Playa Langosta, immediately south of Tamarindo beyond a rocky headland that is impassable at high tide, is also frequented by turtles, and by surfers who ride waves just in front of the estuary at the southern end. More sedate than its noisy neighbor, Playa Langosta is home to a few lovely B&Bs.

Head inland from Tamarindo for some 18 km (11 miles) and, at the junction of the 27 de Abril school, turn toward the coast and proceed for approximately 12 km (8 miles) to lovely **Junquillal Beach**. Junquillal is a paradisical, wide beach with high surf that gives you the sense of having found a secret place. But beware, all is not rosy in this Garden of Eden – there are rip currents and sharks to contend with.

Map on pages 178–79

TIP

For more on turtles, see the features on page 202 and pages 240–41.

BELOW: a glorious Nicoya sunset.

The Vampire Bats of Guanacaste

There are more than 100 kinds of bats in Costa Rica. They are everywhere, from the shrilling flutterings of millions that rise up from the deep caves of Barra Honda, to a quiet few hanging in the cool, darkened corners of La Casona in Santa Rosa Park. Most of them are benevolent, curious-looking animals, who feed on nectar, fruit and insects. But within Santa Rosa Park, in Guanacaste, inside a cave near Naked - Indian Path, lives a group of *Desmodex Rotundum*, or vampire bats.

Bats are beneficial, even necessary, as significant pollinators and disseminators of seeds, especially in deforested areas in Costa Rica. Researchers know them to be clean, docile – even friendly. Nectar bats are gregarious and hang from the ceilings of caves in tight clusters. In the evening, they feed on insects along roads or dry river beds.

At night, they search for nectar from white, night-blooming flowers, which they pollinate. Bats do much to control insect populations; it is estimated that a colony of 1 million bats can consume more than 4,500 kg (10,000 lbs) of insects a night.

Only three of the species drink blood. Hollywood and Victorian novelists have done their part in creating the myth of the vampire who lives on the blood of innocent humans. And there are certain other factors that contribute to the legends that surround this creature: the vampire bat has large thumbs that protrude from the wings, appendages used for stealthy crawling toward the prey. A flat, red, pig-like nose; large eyes; prominent front teeth; and relatively small and pointed ears make this one of the least appealing creatures of the night.

The caped and fanged, black-haired fictional figure from Transylvania no doubt rose up, fully formed, in the imagination of early movie makers who had heard of the nocturnal activities of these animals. For it is true that this species feeds mainly during the darkest hours, before the moon is out, quietly alighting upon a sleeping victim and making a painless incision with razor sharp teeth. Contrary to the myth, the blood of the victim is not sucked out, but rather lapped up, much as a cat drinks milk.

A bat does not drink its victim dry. Instead, rabies and other infections, introduced through the wounds, kill the prey. More than a million animals a year die this way. Humans are sometimes prey as well, and sleeping people have been infected by the bat with dreaded rabies.

Cattle ranchers are striking back against the vampire bat. Methods of extermination have included gassing their caves with toxic substances and dynamiting. Such methods, often born of an irrational aversion to the bat, do not specifically target the vampire variety. Unfortunately, anything and everything in the area is harmed or killed. A more precise, but equally extreme, system involves trapping the bats and coating them with poisons. When released, each bat will then fatally infect up to 20 others. ❑

LEFT: vampire bats inflict huge financial damage each year by infecting farm animals.

Inland to Santa Cruz

Map on pages 178–79

Heading inland from the coast at Paraíso, few populated areas disturb the unbroken beauty of the rolling hills and valleys. An occasional cluster of three or four houses indicates a village. Here chickens, ducks and the lone cyclist claim the road. The miles are marked by the infrequent passage of herds of noisy Brahman cows, turning traffic into a cattle drive, followed in their leisurely journey by *sabaneros* on horseback. These *Guanacasteco* cowboys don't direct the animals out of the road; they let the automobile wend its way through them. The cattle, with their sensitive faces, seem neither concerned nor curious.

Santa Cruz ㉔ (pop. 22,000) is a small, friendly town. In the central plaza, the modern church, built when the old one was destroyed by an earthquake in 1950, stands beside the original colonial clock tower. The central park is a quiet, shady place for sitting and viewing the life of a Guanacaste town.

Hungry visitors to Santa Cruz should not miss the experience of eating indigenous food at the **Coopetortilla**, 500 meters /76 yards west of the church. In a huge single-room building of tin and screen, an open wood fire is used to prepare the large, handmade *tortillas Guanacastecas*, rice and beans, and other local dishes. A sign says "*ambiente familiar*," or family atmosphere. For visitors wishing to spend the night in Santa Cruz, the Diriá (tel: 680 0080) provides air-conditioned rooms and a pool, and many *cabinas* are available around the town offering basic facilities.

One of the main visitor attractions in this part of Guanacaste is the small town of **Guaitil** ㉕, where you will find ceramic pots in the style of the pre-Columbian inhabitants of this part of Costa Rica. After the Conquest, pottery-

ABOVE: Guaitil pottery. **BELOW:** golden sands and mangroves at Tamarindo.

making died out here, possibly because the images adorning pots were considered pagan by the Catholic Church. The craft has been revived in recent years and today the popularity of these giant, luscious ceramic pots is obvious from their presence in the lobbies and dining rooms of many hotels in Guanacaste. It seems as though almost every house in the neighborhood of Guaitil has a kiln and pots for sale in the yard. The widest selection, however, will be found next to the soccer field in front of the church.

You may possibly see so-called pre-Columbian pottery for sale, though these pieces, if in fact they are pre-Columbian and not fakes, are taken from indigenous burial grounds and as historical artifacts are prohibited by the 1982 Patrimonial Law of National Archeology from being taken from Costa Rica. Their purchase also creates a market, which encourages desecration of burial sites.

If you don't already find that Nosara is the sort of place where you can totally unwind, try seeking out the Nosara Retreat, which specializes in physical and spiritual rejuvenation.

Nicoya

From Guaitil it is a scenic, 20-minute drive on a smoothly paved highway to the town of **Nicoya** ㉖, considered to be the cultural capital of Guanacaste. The pride of Nicoya is its central park and colonial church, now a museum (open 8am–noon, 2–6pm, closed Sun and Wed; entrance fee). Three hours off the Interamericana Highway toward the Pacific from Nicoya, and 7 hours from San José, on bad, bumpy roads, is the **Ostional National Wildlife Refuge** (*see box below and page 203*).

Playa Nosara

The beaches of Nosara and nearby Sámara are becoming increasingly popular destinations for North American and European vacationers. Playa Nosara is the

BELOW: against mighty odds, a baby turtle makes it to the ocean's edge.

THE ARRIBADA

Created to protect the endangered Olive Ridley turtle, the Ostional National Wildlife refuge is witness to the spectacular phenomenon known as the *arribada*, when tens of thousands of turtles come to the beach to lay their eggs. It is estimated that during these brief periods as many as 100,000 Olive Ridleys may come ashore to this isolated beach, and leave behind over ten million eggs. *Arribadas* generally occur at two to four-week intervals between the third quarter and full moon from April to December, peaking during July through September.

Presently, there is a controversial program of egg collecting in operation at Ostional, which gives the people of the nearby village the legal right to gather as many of the Olive Ridley turtle eggs as they can during the first 36 hours of every *arribada* in an attempt to prevent poaching.

If you wish to view the amazing sight of thousands of these creatures laboriously coming ashore to thump the sand with their flippers and dig their incubation holes to lay their eggs, then check in at the guard station on your journey down to the beach. And please remember to watch the activities as unobtrusively as possible.

most remote beach, and the only place to observe the local fishermen using ancient fishing techniques. **Nosara** itself is a small, nondescript inland town. The attractions here are Playa Pelada and Playa Guiones, two long white-sand beaches with excellent surfing waves and miles of beach bordered by forest and green sea grape edging the sand. The roads from Nicoya are nearly impassable during the rainy season, and many visitors fly here from San José.

Map on pages 178–79

Despite the difficulty getting here by road, the Nosara area is in the midst of a building boom. Private villas, small hotels and restaurants are being built by an international cast of characters, including a large contingent of nature-loving Swiss. A large part of Nosara is still protected as a reserve, and as a result it is more forested and richer in wildlife than other parts of the region. Coatimundis, armadillos, parrots, toucans and monkeys are plentiful. There is also excellent snorkeling, tide pool exploring and camping in the area.

Endangered eggs

At the far northern edge of Nosara, **Lagarta Lodge Biological Reserve** (tel: 682 0035) occupies an eagle's eyrie, high above its own private nature reserve with hiking trails and the **Ostional National Wildlife Refuge**, an important turtle-nesting site. Sadly, in season, you can still buy the eggs of endangered species of turtles, considered by many to be an aphrodisiac.

Some of the eggs have been excavated by adventurers, others have been purchased at *sodas* near the beach and are the booty of *hueveros* (egg-gatherers), who make an illegal business of raiding the turtles' nests. Others are part of a cache of eggs taken legally by those who are given permits by the government to take the eggs during the first 36 hours of an *arribada (see page 202)*.

ABOVE: statuesque white egret.
BELOW: another lazy day on the Nicoya peninsula.

TIP

Rip tides are a danger in Costa Rica and kill several visitors every year. Ask around first whether a beach is safe for swimming. If you are caught by a rip tide, don't panic and do not swim against it. Try to swim parallel to the shore, and eventually the breaking waves will carry you back in.

Playa Sámara and south

Playa Sámara ②, nearly an hour south of Nosara, has a beautiful white-sand beach and a good reef for snorkeling, which also protects the beach from direct waves. Swimming is safe in crystalline, shallow waters with minimal surf. Off season, there is a feeling of dramatic isolation. During the high season, Playa Sámara is popular with Costa Ricans and many *Ticos* have summer homes here.

Diving, snorkeling, fishing, bicycle and horse-back trips, and kayaking can be arranged by all the local hotels. On the south side of the beach is the exceptional Hotel Las Brisas del Pacífico, with a pool fronting the ocean and two delightful restaurants. To the north of the beach are smaller, basic *cabinas*, some camping sites and a few small hotels. There are regular flights to Sámara, which cut out the long and tiring drive. Driving is particularly difficult during the wet season, as you have to cross many shallow rivers between Nosara and Sámara.

A little way south of Sámara is **Playa Carrillo** ②, yet another near-flawless white-sand beach protected by an offshore reef. Beyond Carrillo are other extraordinary beaches: isolated, lonely places, sometimes with fresh water available, sometimes not. **Playa Caletas**, just a little way south of Carrillo on unpaved, almost non-existent roads, has large surf with offshore breezes. And further south still is **Punta Islita**. Located in the heart of a picturesque valley, Punta Islita Hotel has wonderful ocean views, a beautiful blue-tile infinity pool, and private porches with picture windows and hammocks.

Parque Nacional Barra Honda

BELOW: the aptly named elephant's ear plant.

About 21 km (13 miles) east of the town of Nicoya is **Barra Honda National Park** ③, a vast network of caves. Along the road to the new Taiwan Friendship Bridge that spans the Río Tempisque are national park signs showing the way to this seldom-visited place. On the flat ridgeline, 300 meters (1,000 ft) above the caves, is a *mirador* (look-out point) that can be reached via marked paths. Standing there along the high ridge, with the sounds of an enormous waterfall, amongst screeching tropical birds, howler monkeys and iguanas in the trees, looking out across the vast Nicoya peninsula, can be a humbling experience.

You don't have to be a dedicated spelunker to enjoy Barra Honda, though some of the caves are quite deep and require steep vertical drops to enter. With names such as *La Trampa* (The Trap), and *Terciopelo* (Fer-de-Lance viper), they may not sound inviting, but the formations are dazzling. One such formation, called The Organ, produces melodic tones when gently touched.

Ancient human remains, blind salamanders, vampire bats and strange birds share the world of darkness in the Barra Honda caves, which have escaped vandalism and exploitation because they lack an easily accessible horizontal entrance. Barrio Cubillo is the closest town to the park and is where you will find a community group led by Luis Alberto Díaz that provides cave tours. Basic lodging and good *campesina* food (try Las Delicias) are also available. In the dry season (Dec– Apr) it gets extremely hot, so be sure to bring a wide-brimmed hat and water.

Map on pages 178–79

The much-awaited Puente de la Amistad de Taiwan (Taiwan Friendship Bridge) opened in 2003. The ferry across the **Tempisque River** was the preferred passage back to the highway to San José, but the ferry service is no longer running.

It is another 185 km (115 miles) down the coast and up through the mountains back to San José. Along the highway, dozens of fruit stands offer an opportunity to load up on tropical fruit, honey and homemade candies before returning to the hustle and bustle of the capital.

Monteverde Cloud Forest

Atop the Continental Divide, some 180 km (110 miles) northwest of San José is the **Reserva Biológica del Bosque Nuboso de Monteverde** ③. Despite some recent road improvements, it is still a difficult place to get to and you should allow 4 hours' driving time from San José. Head for some 36 km (22 miles) past the turn off to Puntarenas, on the Interamericana Highway. After the turn off for Puntarenas, continue along the Interamericana to the Rancho Grande turning on the right. Follow this road through Sardinal. It's paved for the first 3 km (2 miles) or so, then becomes a gravel road, meeting up with the old, more pot-holed dirt road at Guacimal. Count on an hour to make the 37-km (21-mile) ascent from the main highway to Monteverde, allowing for scenic photo opportunities along the way.

Despite the ordeal to get here, every year tens of thousands of people visit the preserve. In order to protect the flora and fauna and the trails themselves, visitors are now limited to 100 at any given time – which means you may have to wait your turn. You should book at least one night's accommodation in

BELOW: with around 760 cm (300 inches) of rain per year, there are plenty of waterfalls in Monteverde.

The Resplendent Quetzal

The Resplendent Quetzal is rightly acclaimed as the most magnificent bird in the western hemisphere. Some 40 species inhabit the tropics worldwide and 10 are found in Costa Rica. It is one of the country's greatest natural treasures.

The pigeon-sized male owes his elegance to the intensity and brilliant contrasts of his colors, the sheen and glitter of his plumage, the beauty of his adornments and the great dignity of his posture. The rich crimson of his underparts contrasts with the shining, iridescent green of his head, chest and upper parts. His head is crowned with a narrow crest of upstanding feathers that extends from his small yellow bill to his nape. The pointed tips of the long, loose-barbed coverts of his wings project over the crimson of his sides in beautiful contrast. Most notable are his central tail coverts, which stretch far

beyond his tail and, like two slender green pendants, undulate gracefully when he flies.

As may be seen on many an ancient sculpture and modern painting, the long tail coverts were highly valued as personal adornments by the Aztec and Maya nobility. As Guatemala's national bird, the peaceful quetzal contrasts with the fierce predators and firebreathing monsters that other nations have chosen for their emblems. Guatemalans once believed that their symbol of liberty would die if deprived of freedom, but modern aviculturists have learned how to keep them alive in captivity – a hard negation of a beautiful myth.

The quetzal's song is eminently worthy of a bird so splendidly attired. Fuller and deeper than those of any other trogon, their songs are not distinctly separated but slurred and fused into a flow of soft and mellow sound that is unforgettably beautiful.

Monogamous pairs of quetzals nest in the holes of trees located in mountain forests or in nearby clearings. The hole, like that of a woodpecker, extends straight downwards from the opening at the top. Usually it is deep enough to conceal all of the sitting birds except the ends of the male's train. On the unlined bottom of the chamber, the female lays two light blue eggs. She incubates through the night and the middle of the day. The male takes a turn on the eggs in the morning and again in the afternoon. His train arches over his back and projects through the doorway, fluttering in the breeze. On an epiphyte-burdened trunk, the ends might be mistaken for two green fern fronds.

Sometimes, when his partner arrives to relieve him of his spell in the nest, he soars straight upward, right above the treetops, loudly shouting a phrase that sounds almost like "very-good very-good." At the summit of his ascent he circles, then dives into sheltering foliage. These "joy flights" seem to express the bird's great vitality.

Resplendent Quetzals are still abundant in the tracts of unspoiled mountain forests. So long as such forests are preserved, they are in no danger of becoming extinct, but if they are destroyed, then Central America will lose its most magnificent bird. ❑

LEFT: the quetzal with its favorite food, *aguacatillo*, a type of small avocado.

advance; to get the best out of the area a total of three days is recommended.

More visitors are attracted to Monteverde Cloud Forest than to any other forest reserve in Costa Rica, and usually for one purpose only: to sight the resplendent quetzal, the most colorful and spectacular bird in the tropics. Though listed as an endangered species throughout Central America, it is estimated that nearly 1,000 quetzals make their home in Monteverde. Be warned, however, it is a difficult bird to spot. With the exception of their almost luminous crimson breast, they are cloaked in radiant green plumage and easily disappear among the rich colors of the cloud forest. The best time to spot them is January to September and especially during the mating season, which runs from March through June.

Monteverde is much more than an opportunity to spot a quetzal, however. This misty verdant high-altitude cloud forest is home to a multitude of diverse creatures: 400 species of birds, 490 species of butterflies, 2,500 species of plants and 100 species of mammals. There are jaguars here, too, though they prove even more elusive than the quetzal. Pick up a checklist and map at the Visitors' Center. Guided tours are available. Before leaving the forest, visit the **Hummingbird Gallery**, across the road from the entrance. Owners Michael and Patricia Fogden, biologists and pre-eminent nature photographers, have spent two decades recording the fauna of Monteverde and their remarkable work is shown here.

Monteverde's Quaker community

The community of **Monteverde** ㉜ was established by a group of Quakers who, to escape the obligations of US military service, moved here from Alabama in 1951. To support themselves the Quakers began making cheese from milk brought to their primitive processing plant each morning by *Tico* dairy farmers.

Map on pages 178–79

ABOVE: Monteverde flora.
BELOW: sunrise mist rises above the forest canopy.

Today the Quakers produce tons of cheese daily: Monteverde cheese has become a proud Costa Rican specialty and can be found in markets throughout Central America. En route to the reserve, stop in at their cheese processing plant, **La Fábrica de Queso** (The Cheese Factory), for a tour (open Mon–Sat, Sun am; entrance fee), or watch the production through windows in the plant. Don't expect to see too many Quakers elsewhere in Monteverde, however. They keep themselves to themselves on their farms and generally avoid the commercialized town that Monteverde has now become.

Just north of here look in at CASEM (Comité de Artesanías Santa Elena-Monteverde), an arts and crafts cooperative founded by eight women in 1982. Today, more than 140 artisans contribute their work, which is on sale at less-than-downtown prices at the CASEM shop. Across the road is the popular coffee shop, Stella's Bakery, and Meg's Stables, which offers horseback-riding tours.

Other Monteverde attractions

Adjacent to Monteverde Cloud Forest preserve are two much smaller reserves. There is usually good wildlife viewing at the **Reserva Sendero Tranquilo** - (Quiet Path Reserve), which is open for guided tours only from December through August. You must book ahead by contacting the Hotel El Sapo Dorado (tel: 645 5010).

Opposite the Hotel Heliconia, on the road to Santa Elena, turn off left (heading west) to the **Monteverde Butterfly Garden** (El Jardín de las Mariposas), which exhibits all the butterfly species of the region (open daily 7am–4pm; entrance fee). Guided tours take you through the various stages of a butterfly's life and into a screened garden where hundreds of species flutter freely. The best

Mayan kings prized the iridescent green tail feathers of the quetzal more than gold itself. They also believed the bird could not live in captivity, and it was therefore the supreme symbol of freedom.

BELOW: a timid tapir, rarely seen in the wild.

Map on pages 178–79

time for a visit is when the sun is shining. There is also a leaf-cutter ant colony exhibition. Adjacent to the Butterfly Garden is the **Finca Ecológica**, which is a small private reserve with four loop trails. The longest only takes 2½ hours at a leisurely pace so is quite accessible to all visitors. Agoutis, coatis and sloths are often spotted, and porcupines and monkeys are also frequent visitors. The birdwatching is good, too – quetzals are seen here. The *finca* also offers popular night-time walks; tel: 645 5554 to reserve your place.

Another Monteverde attraction is **The Sky Walk**, a series of hanging bridges suspended Indiana Jones-style from platforms in the tree canopy. It's a wonderful way of getting a bird's-eye view of the forest. For the truly adventurous there is a wide choice of canopy tours that involve donning mountain-climbing harnesses and zipping through the trees suspended on strong cables.

Monteverde is also famous for its artistic community, with many resident wildlife painters, sculptors and textile artists. An international music festival is held every February to March. Both local musicians and international guest artists perform programs ranging from jazz to classical to Latino. Proceeds from the festival benefit local school music programs.

Santa Elena Reserve and around

Around 5 km (3 miles) northeast of Monteverde village is an outstanding local initiative, the **Reserva Santa Elena** ㉝, or Santa Elena Rainforest Reserve. It was created in 1992 as a local high-school project and includes several kilometers of well-kept paths. On clear days, you are treated to views of magnificent Arenal Volcano to the north. Tours are well-organized and cheaper than Monteverde, yet the flora and fauna (including quetzals, jaguars and howler monkeys) is every bit as impressive as that of its famous neighbor. There are four principal trails, all short enough to be done in a day. You also avoid the crowds here. The most exciting way of exploring the nearby forests is by joining a Canopy Tour (tel: 645 5390). You are winched up to the treetops by pulleys, then go from platform to platform on horizontal cables. Selvatura (tel: 645 5929) and SkyTrek (tel: 645 5238) both offer transportation from area hotels to their canopy tours bordering the reserve.

ABOVE: visitor and resident at Monteverde's Serpentario.
BELOW: false eyes ward off predators.

A little farther out, on the Atlantic slope, east of Monteverde Cloud Forest, is the **Children's Eternal Forest** (El Bosque Eterno de los Niños). Back in 1987, a group of Swedish schoolchildren raised and donated enough money to purchase 6 hectares (15 acres) of forest. Now, with support from young people from all over the world, they have bought over 22,000 hectares (54,000 acres). A small section of the forest is open to the public. Bordering the forest is the unspoiled and highly recommended **Ecolodge San Luis and Biological Station**. An integrated ecotourism and scientific research station run by tropical biologists, San Luis offers visitors many hands-on activities such as trails, farming, reforestation, cloud forest photography, birdwatching with expert guides, and Spanish language workshops plus the opportunity to experience Costa Rican rural life first-hand (tel: 645 5277). ❏

COSTA RICA'S WINGS OF WONDER

With more than 850 species of birds, Costa Rica is one of the world's foremost destinations for professional ornithologists and amateur birders

Despite its small size, Costa Rica has roughly the same number of birds as the whole of North America, and significantly more than Europe or Australia. This tremendous diversity is explained partly by the fact that the country is in the tropics, and partly by its position on one of the world's great bird migration routes, which links North and South America.

For most birders Costa Rica's resident species – rather than its migrants – are the ones that hold the most interest. The most sought-after sighting of all is undoubtedly the Resplendent Quetzal, a high-altitude fruit-eater that lives in the cloud forests of the Central Highlands. Quetzals are generally shy and quiet, and it takes patience to locate them. Toucans are much more vocal, while the scarlet macaw is garrulous and noisy, skimming over the treetops in fast-flying raucous pairs.

NECTAR FEEDERS

Costa Rica boasts about 50 species of tiny but pugnacious hummingbirds, which feed largely on a diet of sugary nectar and insects. They are often lured to artificial feeders and make an unmissable spectacle of color and whirring wings.

▷ **MID-AIR REFUELING**
A hummingbird, which can be surprisingly pugnacious for its size, feeds on a "hotlips" flower at Monteverde. Although hummingbirds live largely on nectar, they also catch insects to feed their young.

▽ **RESPLENDENT QUETZAL**
Rich and lustrous when seen in the open, the quetzal's iridescent green plumage provides effective camouflage against a background of leaves. The male's tail streamers are up to 1 meter (3 ft) long, and have to be folded around the body when the bird enters its nesting hole.

△ **OUTSIZE BEAK**
Although it looks unwieldy, a toucan's beak is very delicate. Internal air-spaces help to reduce its weight.

▷ **HANGING NESTS**
Montezuma oropendolas hang their long, bag-like nests from the branches of tall, isolated trees.

△ **WATCHING ON WATER**
Open waterways – such as the canals at Tortuguero – make good places to see birds when they set off at dawn to find food, or settle down to roost at dusk.

▽ **SUBMERSIBLE SWIMMER**
An anhinga or darter with its catch. Anhingas feed in lakes and coastal lagoons, and often swim with just their head and neck visible.

△ **INSECT-EATER**
The blue-crowned motmot lives in forests and coffee plantations, and spends most of its time watching for food from its perch. Its diet consists mainly of insects.

ENDANGERED SPECIES

Despite Costa Rica's efforts to protect its forests, habitat destruction has had a serious effect on some of its birds. The quetzal is particularly vulnerable because it depends on undisturbed cloud forest for survival. The three-wattled bellbird shares this habitat, and is equally threatened by its conversion to pasture. Great green macaws are the most threatened species of macaw. Conservation efforts on the Caribbean coast, where they exclusively live, include honoring farmers who maintain the *dipteryx* trees the macaws feed on. Numbers of green macaws have now stabilized at around 150 to 200. National parks and private reserves, such as Monteverde, are a lifeline to survival.

Even higher on the critical list is Costa Rica's biggest flying predator, the American harpy eagle. This giant monkey-eating bird is known to breed in the forests of the Osa Peninsula, but sightings of it have become extremely rare. A handful of species, such as the cattle egret and roadside hawk, have actually benefited from man-made changes to the environment, because they need open ground to feed.

THE NORTHEAST

Volcán Arenal is the star of the region, though the Sarapiquí River and the lodges of Rara Avis and La Selva are also popular with more environmentally conscious visitors

Map on pages 178–179

The region to the northeast of San José corresponds roughly to the area known as the Northern Zone. The landscape is lush and agricultural and, with the exception of Volcán Arenal, has traditionally only been the haunt of hardy independent travelers. These days, however, more and more visitors are discovering the magnificent rainforests of this region.

Around Ciudad Quesada (San Carlos)

At the foot of the Cordillera Central, **Ciudad Quesada** ③, often called by its former name San Carlos, is the gateway to the north and is the agricultural and commercial heart of the region. Its chief products are cattle, citrus and sugar cane. It's a pleasant, clean, bustling town of around 40,000 people and in the surrounding areas are several good places to stay.

Some 15 km (9 miles) north of Ciudad Quesada just beyond Planatar, and overlooking the Planatar River, is **La Garza**, a large working cattle and horse ranch, which has charming *cabinas* set among beautifully landscaped gardens and expanses of lawn. Guests are invited to go horseback riding, tubing, swimming or fishing for *guapote* on the river, and they can learn about the dairy, cattle and horse operations of the ranch.

The Tilajari Hotel Resort, near Muelle, around 22 km (14 miles) north of Ciudad Quesada, is a luxurious spread, set on several acres of rolling lawns overlooking the wide, muddy San Carlos River. It makes a good base for exploring this region, and offers tennis, swimming, racquetball, horseback riding and hiking in 300 hectares (750 acres) of rainforest. Further afield you can take fishing trips, and jungle river tours to Caño Negro Wildlife Reserve *(see page 220)*.

The Tilajari is also one of the lift-off points for an enchanting hot-air balloon ride over the **San Carlos Valley**. (Rides are also available at other sites; tel: 558 1000.) Standing in a traditional wicker balloon basket, under a multi-colored balloon in the quiet time just after dawn, you rise up, as if in a dream, over a forest preserve and look down into the tree tops at the howler monkeys and toucans who are just waking up. Moving on, over pasture lands, sugar cane and pineapple fields, over grazing cattle and horses, the sun rises and the countryside comes alive.

La Fortuna

From Muelle it's around 25 km (16 miles) west to **La Fortuna** ㉟ (also known as Fortuna de San Carlos). It's a busy, sun-baked village located near the base of Arenal Volcano, and functions as a gateway to the volcano with all sorts of tours and accommodation available.

PRECEDING PAGES: Volcán Arenal. **LEFT:** Sarapiquí waterfall. **BELOW:** white ibises.

Some 5 km (3 miles) east of La Fortuna is the turn-off to the **Río Fortuna Waterfalls**. They are accessible in an hour's easy horseback ride from La Fortuna through pastures and fields of ginger, corn, bananas and peppers. The ride requires a four-wheel drive vehicle. Once at the falls, a muddy hike down a slippery slope to the swimming area at the base of the falls makes the clear, fresh water all the sweeter.

Tabacón Hot Springs

Moving ever closer to the volcano, between La Fortuna and Lake Arenal, is the **Tabacón Hot Springs Resort and Spa** ❸. From here you can look directly up the small valley to the slopes of the volcano, and to cascades of glowing hot boulders. It appears dangerously close, yet the volcano also has a benign effect. Arenal heats Tabacón's therapeutic waters to a perfect temperature. Tiled slides, waterfalls and pools of varying temperatures are surrounded by tumbling warm-water creeks and lush gardens. You can even have a jacuzzi or a massage. Enjoy a meal in Tabacón's dining room and watch the erupting volcano from a quiet pool under the starry sky. And should you be there when the full moon waxes over Arenal, then that single experience is worth the trip to Costa Rica in itself.

Just west of La Fortuna, you can luxuriate in the warm mineral waters of the more affordable Baldi Termae. For about US$10, you can enjoy a bath and a view of the volcano (tel: 479 9651).

Down the highway, past the Tabacón Hot Springs Resort, is a dirt road going to the left and the **Arenal Observatory Lodge**, formerly a research facility for the Smithsonian Institution and Costa Rica's Universidad Nacional. It is the

BELOW:
an active Volcán
Arenal is an
unforgettable sight.

only lodge in the National Park, located on its own huge estate with primary and secondary forest, waterfalls, hiking and horseback trails. To get to the lodge follow the gravel road for 9 km (6 miles), crossing two rivers on the way. From here Arenal is only 1 km (⅔ mile) away and by night the air is rich with the sounds of howling monkeys and the glow of fireflies.

Map
on pages
178–79

Arenal Volcano

Until early July 1968, Arenal was a heavily wooded low hill, similar to many others in the area, near the village of La Fortuna. Then one morning the people there began feeling a few earth tremors. Suddenly, the forest started smoking and steaming. Women washing their clothes marveled at the sudden warm water which flowed in the creeks. Then, on July 29, all hell broke loose and **Volcán Arenal ㊲** exploded. Rolling clouds of gas and fountains of red-hot boulders and molten lava hit the countryside like a bomb. Official estimates put the death toll at 62, but local people claim that more than 80 people were killed. Over 5 sq. km (2 sq. miles) of land near the volcano was abruptly changed from pastoral farmland to a landscape out of Dante's *Inferno*.

Since then, Arenal has been continuously active. It is everyone's preconception of a volcano: conical, rising abruptly out of flatland vegetation. But do not attempt to climb it. The molten lava running down her western slope has a temperature of 926°C (1,699°F), not to mention an unpredictable spew of rocks, intense heat and poison gases. Sadly, every couple of years there is a visitor who disregards the warning signs and then the volcano claims another life.

The road west to **Nuevo Arenal** is dreadful and a four-wheel drive vehicle is recommended. This New Arenal is a town reborn from the old village of Are-

A sign at the base of Arenal Volcano reads "Volcano influence area. If you notice abnormal activity, run away from the area and report it to the nearest authority."

BELOW: beautifully landscaped grounds of the Tabacón Hot Springs Resort.

nal, which was flooded in 1973 to create the lake. Nuevo Arenal has a good number of friendly and inexpensive restaurants and small hotels – and a variety of pleasant accommodations are available along the road to Tilarán. A few kilometers east is the **Jardín Botánico Arenal** ❸ (open daily Nov–May 9am–5pm, closed Sun May–Oct; entrance fee), the work of Michael Le May, an indefatigable amateur horticulturist. It features over 1,000 native and exotic species and is a magnet to hummingbirds and butterflies. Late afternoon is the best time to visit, though visitor numbers are limited, so the gardens are never too busy.

Lake Arenal

ABOVE: cattle at
La Fortuna.
BELOW: naturalists
on a bridge over the
Sarapiquí near
Selva Verde.

Laguna de Arenal ❸ offers some of Costa Rica's most challenging freshwater fishing. The *guapote* is the favorite of fishermen there *(see page 105)*. Whether or not you choose to fish, charter a boat and guide to take you sightseeing on the lake. It is best to go in the early morning, when, for much of the year, the lake's surface is like glass and the volcano can be viewed as a crystalline reflection. A few local fishermen will probably be out on the lake, sitting on chairs perched on a pair of floating balsa logs, fishing for *guapote* with simple handlines.

From December through March, usually in the afternoons, northeasterly winds blow almost daily, and the lake is anything but calm and glassy. Between 40 and 50 knots of sustained breeze is not uncommon and whips Arenal into a sea of whitecaps. Latterly, it has become a favorite destination for experienced windsurfers attracted by these conditions. Tico Wind, in Nuevo Arenal, rents a full range of windsurfing equipment and also offers lessons. It is open from December 1 through mid-April.

The west end of the lake is the best for short board sailing and a number of windsurfing resorts have opened near **Tilarán** (pop. 7,750), an old-time Costa Rican town, whose name comes from the Chorotega words for "wind and rain." Another popular choice is the Hotel Tilawa, located 9 km (6 miles) north of Tilarán, with its well-equipped windsurfing school and easy access to the lake. Whether or not you are a windsurfer, it is a good place to spend the night as it is situated in the hills above the Guanacaste lowlands and is refreshingly cool. The countryside around the town is pastoral, the upland meadows spotted with dairy cattle. Villagers will arrange for boats and fishing guides on Lake Arenal.

It is perhaps predictable that such a myth-inspiring lake as Arenal would find a resident monster. A few years ago, some local fishermen were out on their raft early one evening and felt a strange rumbling in the water. Suddenly, right in front of them an enormous, hairy serpent with horns broke through the surface with a belching roar and a stench. Moments later it slid back into the depths, trailing a tail over 2 meters (6 ft) long. The fishermen scurried back to town and told the tale over and over. The story went around and, amplified by time and accounts of half-eaten horse carcasses found floating on the lake, the Monster of Lake Arenal is entrenched in local folklore.

Above Lake Arenal is placid Lake Coter and the Lake Coter Ecolodge, where you can hike miles of trails, ride horses over hills with views of Lake Arenal or zip along cables on a Canopy Tour through primary forest (tel: 440 6768).

Map on pages 178–79

Tourism is booming around the Arenal area and no one wants to be left out: in its own local leaflet, Tilarán proclaims itself as "the city of broad streets, fertile rains, and healthful winds in which friendship and progress is cultivated."

To Arenal via San Ramón

An alternative route to Arenal from San José is via **San Ramón**. It's a good idea to spend the night here as the guest of ex-Costa Rican President Rodrigo Carazo and his wife, Doña Estrella, at **Villa Blanca**, set on 154 hectares (380 acres) of cultivated land, surrounded by the beautiful **Los Angeles Cloud Forest**, also owned by the family. The reserve, which consists of 800 hectares (2,000 acres) of primary forest, has a 2-km (1-mile) trail paved in chicken wire to provide footing on slippery stretches.

From San Ramón continue north through San Lorenzo to La Tigra. On the gravel and dirt road between La Tigra and Chachagua is the **Hotel Bosques de Chachagua** cattle and horse ranch with 15 guest cabins. Elegant long-necked *Paso Criollo* horses are put through their paces by the Guanacastecan trainer. Guests with riding experience can take these powerful creatures on any of the ranch's many trails.

BELOW: having fun on the Sarapiquí.

North to Caño Negro

Head northeast from San Carlos, crossing the Río Planatar and on to Aguas Zarcas and the luxurious **Hotel El Tucano Occidental**. Here guests enjoy natural hot springs and deluxe accommodations, including an Olympic-size swimming pool, and jacuzzis fed with thermal waters. El Tucano has tennis courts, a mini-golf course and a natural steam sauna made of stone. The pools are also open to non-guests, for a small fee. North of Aguas Zarcas outside of Pital is **La Laguna del Lagarto**, a remote lodge that offers accommodations, hiking, horseback riding, canoeing, and boat trips up the Río San Carlos to the Nicaraguan border. This is an excellent birdwatching destination. A four-wheel drive vehicle is recommended to reach the lodge.

North of Arenal, toward the Nicaraguan border, is the magnificent and still seldom-visited **Refugio Nacional de Vida Silvestre Caño Negro ⑩** (Caño Negro Wildlife Reserve). It provides excellent birdwatching opportunities, including extremely large flocks of anhinga, roseate spoonbill, white ibis and Jabirú stork. The latter is the largest bird of the region and, in great danger of extinction. There are also several species of mammals here, including large cats. In the heart of this vast area is **Lago Caño Negro**. This lake covers around 800 hectares (2,000 acres) during the wet season, but almost dries up completely during the dry season.

Access to Caño Negro is from Los Chiles or Upala, on good roads northwest of Cañas. The best way to see its myriad species of bird and animal life, particularly during the wet season, is by boat, which can be hired in Los Chiles. In the dry season, horse rental is a good idea. Basic accommodations are available in Los Chiles and the village of Caño Negra now boasts two upscale hotels, one a fishing lodge and the other a luxurious Italian-owned hotel. Several tour agencies in La Fortuna, including Sunset Tours, offer day trips to Caño Negro.

The Sarapiquí region

The lush, tropical jungles along the **Sarapiquí River** region, on the Atlantic side of the Cordillera Central, are less than 100 km (60 miles) east of San José, yet once you are there it seems as though it is another continent. La Selva Biological Station, Selva Verde Lodge and Rara Avis, private reserves with lodging (*see below*), are all accessible via a paved circuitous highway which begins and ends in San José. The entire circuit, departing via Heredia and returning on the highway through Braulio Carrillo Park, requires approximately 5 hours of driving. A recommended stop along the route is Rancho Leona in La Virgen. Set right in the jungle, it offers good food, inexpensive lodging, and kayaking on the Sarapiquí River.

From San José drive to Heredia. Here the highway winds up the slope of Poás Volcano to Varablanca, where the short entry road to Poás intersects the main highway. If you depart early there will be more than adequate time for a visit to the volcano, before crossing the ridge and heading down through heavily forested mountain slopes, past a spectacular waterfall, to the lowland rainforest of the Atlantic seaboard.

An alternative route to Sarapiquí which is easier and just as scenic is to take the Braulio Carillo Highway east of San José, through Braulio Carillo National Park. Beware of driving after sunset, however, as thick night fog blankets this route

Puerto Viejo de Sarapiquí and Rara Avis

Puerto Viejo de Sarapiquí ④ is a small port town from which river boats depart for otherwise inaccessible settlements along these jungle waterways. Motor-driven dugout canoes laden with passengers and cargo depart regularly for the full-day trip up the

Rara Avis offers accommodations in treehouses, where guests with no fear of heights can spend the night on a platform 33 meters (100 ft) above the ground. The ascent, accompanied by a guide, is made with a rope and harness.

BELOW: the jungle trail to Rara Avis.

Sarapiquí to the **San Juan River**, on the Nicaraguan border, and then east to Barra del Colorado and the Atlantic.

Rara Avis is a pristine, 600-hectare (1,500-acre) rainforest reserve in the mountains above Las Horquetas. The main office and departure point for the reserve is in Las Horquetas, about 17 km (11 miles) south of Puerto Viejo de Sarapiquí. From here, whether you are continuing by horseback or tractor-drawn cart, travel to Rara Avis is difficult and can only be recommended for those who are both physically and mentally fit. The grueling 4-hour journey, over ruts, bogs, and rivers, is all part of the commitment to the adventure. On the road, the transition from cattle ranches to deep jungle illustrates the devastating effects of deforestation more dramatically than any textbook or film. The tractor and cart lurch along an eroded path, through cattle ranches littered with fallen and unused timber. Even cattle are few and far between. The open land is hot, dry, dusty and inhospitable. The soil is baked crisp by the tropical sun.

Deforested land ends at El Plástico Lodge, the last stop before the final 6-km (4-mile) trip to Waterfall Lodge, high in the forest. This former prison colony gets its incongruous name from the plastic sheets under which the inmates slept. From El Plástico, the road plunges into a dark, cool cathedral-like forest, which teems with life. The sun-starved earth is a dense tangle of roots, tree trunks, and leaves, soaked in water and bathed in mud. Because it is such a rarified and isolated place, you should always arrange transportation in advance. Access is difficult, but most people feel that the mud and almost non-existent roads into the area are just part of the experience. To return to San José continue past Las Horquetas for another 30 minutes to the intersection with the Braulio Carrillo Highway, then make a right turn.

Map on pages 178–79

ABOVE: no through road.
BELOW: beware, Africanized bees can be very aggressive.

La Selva Biological Reserve

Continue for several kilometers past Puerto Viejo and then you will have to ask the help of a local resident for directions to the "OTS" (the Organization for Tropical Studies) in order to locate the gravel road to La Selva. The diversity and abundance of life in the lowland tropical forest of the Sarapiquí River region attracted tropical biologists more than 30 years ago. They subsequently founded the Organization for Tropical Studies and established the **Estación Biólogica La Selva** ❷ (La Selva Biological Reserve and Research Station).

In 1986 the Costa Rican government also made a major commitment to rainforest conservation by extending the boundaries of Braulio Carrillo National Park to meet the outer reaches of the 600-hectare (1,500-acre) La Selva Reserve. As a result of this decision, a total of 21,000 hectares (52,000 hectares) of virgin forest now preserves the migratory pathways and large territories required for the survival of several species of Costa Rica's rare and endangered birds and mammals.

Today, virtually all of the world's tropical biologists have spent time at La Selva as students, teachers or scientists – or at the very least they have been strongly influenced by the vast amount of scientific research that has been accomplished there over the past quarter of a century. Twice a year the Organization for Tropical Studies holds an eight-week course, open to students of ecology. It's not just biologists who are taught at La Selva, either; many Sarapiquí residents who work at ecotourist lodges were also trained as naturalist guides at La Selva.

The reserve is primarily a research and educational facility, but tours of the facilities and reserve trails can be arranged by calling La Selva (tel: 240 6696 or 766 6565). There is a well-developed trail system and some of the trails have

Sloths descend to the forest floor once a week to defecate – unusual behaviour that may be an attempt to move their scent away from their normal home.

BELOW: a stream in the lowland rainforest.

boardwalks in order to give access during the wet season. Although there are student-style rooms available at La Selva, the best choice for accommodations is at Selva Verde.

Map on pages 178–79

Selva Verde

In 1986, Giovanna and Juan Holbrook, conservationists from Florida, bought **Selva Verde** ㊸, which consists of 200 hectares (500 acres) of primary and secondary tropical lowland forest, along the banks of the Sarapiquí River, in order to save the land from deforestation. They designed their beautiful river lodge specially to have a minimal impact on the environment. It rests lightly on posts above the forest floor, resembling the jungle spiders that inspired its construction. Guests reside in tropical hardwood rooms at the end of covered corridors, which radiate from a central conference room into the forest. The jungle and its denizens are never more than a few feet away. This immersion in the lowland forest creates an extraordinary feeling of stillness, which encourages people to whisper as they speak.

Spectacular birds are commonplace at Selva Verde: keel-billed and chestnut-mandibled toucans can be seen feeding on the fruit of the nutmeg trees near the front porch of the lodge. A stroll along the path to the main lodge building is likely to be rewarded with the iridescent colors of several species of hummingbirds. Nearby, Montezuma oropendulas utter gurgling mating calls, which harmonize with the songs of other birds and countless frogs and insects in a continual symphony. In all, there are nearly 100 species of birds at Selva Verde. The Lodge's other main attraction is its incredibly slow-moving arboreal sloths, which have a metabolic rate of half of what is normal for an animal of its size. ❑

ABOVE keel-billed toucans are common at Selva Verde. **BELOW:** the canopy viewing system at Rara Avis.

MOUNTAINS OF FIRE

Vulcanologists are always busy in Costa Rica, which has nine active volcanoes and some 200 dormant and extinct ones

Costa Rica is a land of earthquakes and volcanoes, where time-strapped tourists, hikers and mountaineering enthusiasts can climb the Central Valley's four active cones in just two days. Visitors should remember, though, that an active volcano demands respect; proper equipment (good shoes, and in the case of Rincón de la Vieja, a compass) are essential. Taking a guided tour will ensure the greatest safety. Locals are proud of their explosive geology, and have made Poás and Irazú volcanoes the country's most visited parks.

The most dynamic and majestic of Costa Rica's active volcanoes is Arenal, a nearly perfect cone. The 1,633-meter (4,950-ft) high volcano rises above Alajuela's farmlands, adjacent to its own lake, and offers a spectacular show. Loud thunder-like explosions announce an eruption, and colorful clouds of gas and steam spew out of the top. While visitors to the conservation area find the explosions awe-inspiring and/or frightening, locals barely look up when Arenal thunders.

A VIOLENT PAST

Dormant until the late 1960s, Arenal was thought to be an extinct volcano until a series of earth-quakes began on July 28, 1968. Arenal blew the next morning, causing damage that stretched approximately 5 km (3 miles) west and shock waves that were felt as far away as Boulder, Colorado. More than 80 people died after being poisoned with volcanic gas and struck by rocks, and many homes were leveled. Since then, the volcano has continued to rumble and erupt on a more reduced scale, sometimes several times per day, spewing forth fiery cascades of lava and rocks the size of small houses.

▽ **GUANACASTE ERUPTS**
Rincón de la Vieja soars 1,900 meters (5,760 ft) above the forests of Guanacaste. One of its nine craters is active, and fumaroles bubble on the ground.

▽ **THE VIEW FROM IRAZU**
On a clear day, visitors to Irazú can see both the Atlantic and Caribbean. Its rich soils are excellent for growing potatoes, onions and other crops.

POAS VOLCANO IS IN ACTIVITY
YOU ENTER UNDER YOUR OWN RISK
SPN – MIRENEM

◁ **ACTIVE POAS**
Volcán Poás is just coming out of an active phase, and fumaroles are visible from the viewing point above the crater. However, sulfur gas emissions mean visibility is often poor.

▷ **SPRINGS OF DELIGHT**
One of the best places to view Volcán Arenal is from Tabacón Hot Springs.

◁ **DEADLY BEAUTY**
Arenal is most impressive at night, when incandescent rocks and lava cascade down the north slope, which is bare of vegetation most of the way down. There are explosions every few hours during the volcano's active periods, but it can rest for months without activity. The cone is often covered by clouds.

▽ **MOON WALK**
While the crater of Poás looks like the moon, the rest of the park is green: there is a dwarf cloud forest near the crater and a high-altitude wet forest also shelters the resplendent quetzal. The park has a good museum and hiking trails.

BELOW THE VOLCANOES

It's an ill wind that blows nobody good, and to observe Arenal in true luxury by day or night, pamper yourself at the Spanish colonial-style Tabacón Hot Springs Resort, built on the site of a 1975 hot avalanche deposit that provides the source of heat for the thermal waters.

Although vulcanologists feel there is a risk of future hot avalanches, this hasn't stopped the *Ticos* and tourists who flock here to exclaim excitedly over the activity of the volcano and soak their aching muscles. A dip in the waters is also supposedly beneficial for anyone suffering from skin problems and arthritis.

Twelve pools of varying depths and temperatures (the warmest is a sizzling 38°C/102°F), a jacuzzi, hot waterfall, slides and an individual tub tucked deep in the beautifully landscaped tropical gardens mean fun for everyone from kids to senior citizens.

A professional massage therapist also gives mud facials, and the resort has lockers, towel rental and showers. The hotel here is elegant and expensive. Book well in advance.

If you are on a tight budget, try the Baldi Termae just west of La Fortuna.

THE CARIBBEAN COAST

Map on page 230

Beautiful warm water glowing blue and turquoise, radiant sunshine and coconut palms rustling in the gentle breeze welcome you to Costa Rica's Caribbean coastline

The two-hour drive from San José to the Caribbean coast is on a good highway winding through the canyons, mountains, waterfalls and virgin forests of Braulio Carrillo National Park. Descending from the cool cloudiness of Braulio Carrillo into the tropical lowland forests of the Caribbean, the temperature rises and the air becomes heavy.

Puerto Limón

Puerto Limón ❶ (pop. 70,000) is pure Caribbean – with its rich, ripe jumble of sights and sounds and smells, it is a hot, steamy, laid-back place. Most middle-class *Ticos* who live in the Central Valley consider it something of a disgrace, while most young European and North American travelers are enamored with the idea of Puerto Limón, if not the place itself.

In the center of Limón you won't find the usual cathedral or soccer field facing a plaza such as you see in all the towns of the Central Valley. Instead **Vargas Park**, named after a local governor, is filled with huge banyan trees with buttress roots that the townspeople use for bus stop seats. If you occasionally notice cab drivers and children looking up, they are probably watching the family of *perezosos* (sloths) that live in the trees of the park.

Commerce began in Limón in the 17th century, when cacao plantations were worked by slaves. But pirates from Jamaica continually raided the area until production was finally abandoned in the early 1800s, and the region, which was impossibly hot, humid and swampy, was once again forgotten for several decades.

PRECEDING PAGES: the road to Cahuita. **LEFT:** tributary in Barra Colorado. **BELOW:** sloth at Aviaros del Caribe.

Coffee, bananas and the railroad

The growth of the coffee market meant that an Atlantic port was required for exporting to England and Europe, and in 1871, this was established on the site of "El Limón," a migrant black fishermen's village consisting of five huts. That same year, the government contracted the construction of the Atlantic railroad from San José to the Atlantic Coast. Laborers from Jamaica, Italy and China were brought in to work on the railroad and many made permanent homes in the area.

Meanwhile, Minor Keith, the North American responsible for building the railroad, had the bright idea of planting and cultivating bananas alongside the track in order to raise additional funds for the rising costs of construction of the Atlantic railroad.

Limón thus became a railroad and banana town, populated largely by Afro-Caribbean and Chinese immigrants who had come to Costa Rica looking for work. Since 1872, Limón and the banana industry have experienced great booms and busts: bumper

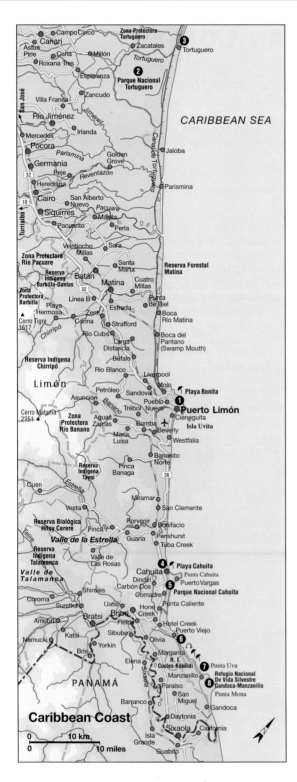

Caribbean Coast

0   10 km

0   10 miles

banana crops (even exceeding the value of Costa Rica's coffee exports); labor troubles and violent strikes; and hard times of high unemployment when the United Fruit Company abandoned the Atlantic Coast.

Yet Limón was effectively ignored by the Central Valley government of Costa Rica. The black workers and their families had no rights of citizenship; they were not permitted to work in the Pacific Zone nor in the Central Valley.

However, since the Civil War of 1948, living conditions have improved somewhat for the black residents of the city. Today, they are full-fledged citizens of Costa Rica, and can travel and work anywhere they wish.

Problems

There are few decent hotels in Limón. Most travelers stay at the Hotel Park or more upscale hotels north or south of the city center. Beware, however, that theft (particularly from cars) and muggings are a problem in the city and it is worth paying a little more for accommodations.

A severe earthquake in 1991 damaged much of Limón's infrastructure, but the roads and bridges have been repaired and the water distribution system is now functioning properly, making the water safe to drink.

Carnaval

For many people, Puerto Limón's annual *Carnaval* (Carnival) is the best reason to visit the place. This week-long jubilant event is held every October. Carnival first began in 1949, under the leadership of a barber called Alfred Henry King, who timed the festivities to coincide with the anniversary of Christopher Columbus's landing near Limón on October 18, 1502. *El Día de la Raza,* "the Day of the People," which falls during Carnival Week and traditionally includes the participation of the indigenous peoples who live in the region, has recently been re-named *Día de las Culturas* (Day of the Cultures) in recognition of the fact that not

Map on page 230

everyone remembers Columbus with equal affection and also as a tribute to the contributions made to Costa Rica by people of all cultures.

The highlight of Carnival Week is the parade, when local people and thousands of visitors take to the streets to join in a glorious music and dance spectacle. The drums, the heat, the beat, the shining bodies of dancers and drummers in bright costumes, urge spectators to abandon their inhibitions and to surrender to the Caribbean magic. And so they do, *Limonenses* and tourists alike, filling the streets, shimmying, shaking, singing and carousing, while the irresistible rhythms of steel drums fill the warm, humid air.

Tortuguero

Travel on the **Tortuguero canals**, up through the area north of Limón, has been likened to a trip on the *African Queen*, or to floating dreamily down the Amazon. It is certainly one of the most wonderfully lyrical trips to be taken anywhere. As you drift lazily amidst the fragrance of white ginger blossoms, lavender water hyacinths and the *Ilan Ilan* flower, there is a tranquility here that soothes all your cares away.

Look around and you may catch occasional glimpses of sloths, crocodiles and basking freshwater turtles. High up in the exuberant vegetation, green macaws and multi-colored parrots squawk noisily, while agile howler monkeys shake the branches. Around 19,000 hectares (47,000 acres) of the coast and hinterland have been designated as the **Parque Nacional Tortuguero ❷** (Tortuguero National Park). There are many ways to navigate its maze of waterways, including hitching a ride on a cargo boat, or by renting a dugout canoe or speedboat. The best way to tour the canals is on a boat guided by an expert nat-

ABOVE: some eating places in Costa Rica also cater for vegetarians.
BELOW: *Carnaval* revellers in Limón.

uralist. Or you can simpy take a package tour which will include a lodge room, meals, naturalist guides, and the trip through the canals. All the Tortuguero hotels offer guided river trips and transportation from San José.

Launches going up Tortuguero depart from Moín, just a few miles north of Limón. NatureAir and SANSA have short flights from San José to Tortuguero and **Barra del Colorado**, which is north of Tortuguero, near the Nicaraguan border. From there you can hire a boat to travel south through the canals.

The green sea turtle

Tortuguero, which means turtle, or *tortuga* in Spanish, is the main nesting area in the Caribbean for green sea turtles. The turtles have been listed as endangered since the 1950s and the **Caribbean Conservation Corporation** (CCC) has been established at Tortuguero for the purpose of studying and protecting these vulnerable creatures.

The CCC runs a **Natural History Center** between the village and the John H. Phipps Biological Field Station on the Tortuguero River. The center's large, colorful displays are packed with information about the region's plant and animal life, including, of course, the green sea turtle. The area has been known for its turtle-hunting grounds since at least the mid-16th century, and turtles were exploited for their meat, shells and eggs with impunity until as recently as 1970, when the area was established as a national park. Now at least the visiting green sea turtles and their leatherback cousins are afforded some degree of protection.

If possible, go to Tortuguero during the turtle-nesting season. And insist on having a knowledgeable naturalist guide to advise you of things to do (and things to avoid), in the spirit of understanding the habits and sensitivities of

Barra del Colorado is a wildlife refuge famous for its sport fishing. Tours are available, but beware high humidity, high temperatures, and a voracious mosquito population. Much of the refuge is unexplored with few marked trails.

BELOW: Tortuga Lodge, along the Tortuguero canals.

these magnificent creatures. Between July and October is the best time to view the prehistoric ritual of the nesting of the green turtles, and between March and May is best for the leatherback turtle. The enormous tractor-tread trails, which turtles leave in the sand as they laboriously make their way up the beaches to dig their nests, are easily visible even at night under a thick stormy sky. And following these freshly made trails to observe the nesting of one of these turtles is an experience that affects even the most worldly traveler.

At the southern entrance to Tortuguero National Park, at Jalova, the Parks Service has built a visitors' information center and a well-labeled 1-km nature trail providing information about the park's flora and fauna.

Another exciting option for turtle-watching is the beach at Parismina halfway between Tortuguero and Puerto Limón. Accessible only by boat from Siquirres or by small charter plane, this remote Caribbean village has opened a turtle hatchery to help the conservation of leatherback and green turtles. Tourists are warmly welcomed in this small community to help with the Save the Turtles of Parismina Project, and there are a few *cabinas* and rooms in the village to rent as well as two upscale fishing lodges *(see Where to Stay, page 281–282).*

Map on page 230

Tortuguero village

Further north, up the canals, the village of **Tortuguero** ❸ sits on a narrow spit of land bordered by the Caribbean Sea and the Tortuguero River. A brief history of Tortuguero is available at the information kiosk near the soccer field. The village is an interesting place to visit. Narrow paths wind through exuberant greenery. Palm trees rustle overhead. Wooden houses sit on stilts. Restaurants, shops, and *cabinas* catering to tourists have been constructed, but even so, village life seems to continue in a timeless way.

ABOVE: a guided tour of Tortuguero is recommended.
BELOW: paddling up a Talamanca tributary.

Antoinete Gutiérrez, one of the owners of the Jungle Shop, sells souvenirs and can answer your questions about Tortuguero. And if you're hoping to sample Caribbean rice and beans cooked in coconut milk, you can do so in one of the village's restaurants; Miss Junie's is one of the most popular (tel: 709 8102).

Talamanca

Most travelers who come to the Caribbean coast spend only a short time in Puerto Limón, and then quickly head south to the Talamanca coast. The drive south runs parallel to the Atlantic, with glimpses of rivers off to the right, and the sea to the left.

Somewhere near Tuba Creek begins the **Talamanca** region of Costa Rica, extending from the Caribbean coast and reaching into the mountains that run from the Central Valley southeast into Panamá. This area was the refuge of many indigenous people who fled the Spanish conquerors.

Until the 1970s, the Talamanca region was populated mainly by the Bribri and Cabécar who lived in the mountains, and by the descendants of English-speaking black immigrants from the Caribbean islands who settled along the coast. The black settlers were farmers and fishermen following the old ways brought from Jamaica, most affectionately described in their own words in Paula Palmer's fascinating folk history,

TIP

A good place to stay
between Puerto Limón
and Cahuita is
Aviaros del Caribe,
a comfortable bed
and breakfast, located
on a bird and wildlife
refuge in the middle
of tranquil canals and
islands. The star of
the place is Buttercup
the sloth.

What Happen. They developed a local cuisine based on the foods they grew, and planted the coconut trees that still line the beaches. For the little money they needed, they sold coconut oil, hawksbill turtle shells and cassava starch.

They spoke a creole English, played cricket, danced quadrilles, carved dugout canoes from local trees and recited Shakespeare for amusement. Isolated by the sea and the mountains, no roads connected these people with the rest of Spanish-speaking Costa Rica, and their life continued quite peacefully and independently. All that has changed now, with the opening of a slick new highway and other roads connecting the sleepy coastal towns of Talamanca with San José and the rest of the world.

Most black residents of the coast now speak both English and Spanish, but you'll have to listen carefully to pick up this local Caribbean patois form of English. A few of the more common expressions: "Wh'appen?" ("What's happening?") is the usual form of greeting, replacing the "Adios" of the Central Valley. "How de morning?" is "Good morning" and "Go good" is "Take care." The polite form of address is to use his or her first name preceded by Mr or Miss. For the most part, the indigenous peoples of the region now speak Spanish in addition to their own native language (of which there are several), and take part in regional political and economic life, although many maintain ancient beliefs and customs. There are three indigenous reserves in Talamanca: the large Talamanca-Bribri Reserve, the Talamanca-Cabécar Reserve and the smaller Kéköldi Reserve. Access to the reserves by non-indigenous people is limited, and you usually need to obtain permission in advance. Mauricio Salazar of Puerto Viejo's Chimuri Beach Cottages, however, is authorized to take visitors on walking trips through the Kéköldi Reserve.

BELOW: black beach at Puerto Viejo.

Cahuita

Local legend has it that in 1828 a turtle fisherman named William Smith (known as "Old Smith"), rowed and sailed north from his home in Panamá to fish for turtles. Finding a beautiful calm bay protected by a coral reef near Cahuita Point, he decided to settle there with his family. In those early days, green and hawksbill turtles were plentiful and, as they had not yet learned to fear man, made an easy catch. Old Smith is said to have been the first English-speaking Afro-Caribbean settler to the area, which at that time was populated with Amerindians, and frequently visited by pirates.

Cahuita ❹ is the largest and most developed of the Talamanca towns. Faded but dignified-looking wooden houses, once painted bright colors that are now soft pastels, with a touch of Caribbean whimsy in the gingerbread details, look out over dusty streets. Young travelers from Europe, Canada and the US, oblivious to more modest local sensibilities, amble along the beaches and roadways in scanty, bright beachwear.

Cahuita Tours, on Cahuita's main street, rents out snorkeling equipment and surfboards. It can also arrange fishing trips, jungle treks, and other excursions. A number of guides are usually available to show visitors around the sights.

Beware that Cahuita has drug problems, and petty crime against tourists is also rife, even though the authorities crack down every so often in an attempt to keep lid on the situation.

ABOVE: a bike is often a handy means of getting about on the coast.

Cahuita National Park

To the immediate south of Cahuita is **Parque Nacional Cahuita ❺**, famous for its fine, sandy beach and coral reef. The reef extends 500 meters (1,500 ft) out to sea from **Cahuita Point** and offers great snorkel-

BELOW: red-eyed tree frog, Cahuita.

ing, although the point of the reef was severely displaced during an earthquake. There are many species of tropical fish, crabs, lobsters, sea fans, anemones, sponges, seaweed and innumerable other marine creatures to observe amidst the coral formations. You can admire it all and keep your feet dry aboard a glass-bottomed boat, or you can swim from the Puerto Vargas end of the beach. Diving equipment may be rented in Cahuita town.

Camping is permitted in the park; to get to the **Puerto Vargas** camping area enter from the south side of the park, 5 km (3 miles) from Cahuita. Coatis and raccoons frequent the campgrounds looking for fruit and other edibles, and are not above overturning a tent to get them. Fresh water, outhouses, and picnic tables are available. From Puerto Vargas you can hike along a nature trail into the jungle or explore the wreck of a British slave galleon from which cannons, cannon balls, swords, copper and bronze manacles, and arm bands have been retrieved.

North of Cahuita is a black-sand beach where the waters are gentle and good for swimming. Accommodations, some with kitchens, are available throughout town and on the beach. Reservations are essential during Christmas, Easter and during Carnival, the second week in October. The best time to visit Cahuita is from February to April, and in October. Good food is served at Cha Cha Cha in the middle of town, and at Miss Edith's. Just ask anyone where Miss Edith's is: the place has an enviable reputation for good, down-home Caribbean cooking. The Hotel Jaguar is also known for its innovative French-Caribbean cuisine.

Coconuts and cacao

Heading south toward Puerto Viejo, along a pretty paved road that runs parallel to the beach, you pass houses of every style and class; but there is something magical about the Caribbean air and even the humblest shack has a picturesque quality when it is set amidst tall coconut trees. In many yards are low, wooden dryers with tin roofs, used for drying cacao and coconut. The roofs are opened to the bright sun on clear days, and closed in the rain.

Just before the turn-off to Puerto Viejo is **Hone Creek**. Hone is the name of a short palm with large roots. When the Jamaicans came to the Talamanca coast to work on the railroad in the 1890s, they began calling it "Home Creek," and today there are road signs in the area announcing both "Hone Creek" and "Home Creek."

There is usually a checkpoint with a guard at Hone Creek, seeking to stem the flow of contraband goods from Panamá. To get to Puerto Viejo take the gravel road to the left. Watch for cacao trees in the now-abandoned cacao plantations along the sides of the road. The fruit grows from the trunk of the tree and turns wonderful colors as it ripens: some become a soft turquoise color, others a brilliant coral. The seeds of the ripe fruit are slightly sweet and undeniably chocolatey, even in this raw state.

Puerto Viejo

While Cahuita has a certain shabby dignity, **Puerto Viejo** ❻ is a tumbledown community. It is a hodge-podge of dilapidated wooden houses amidst tall grass. At the entrance to the town you pass a rusted-out barge which is anchored just off the black-sand beach.

It wasn't long ago that there were no roads to Puerto Viejo: no cars, no tourists, no money. But things have changed. Puerto Viejo's beautiful undeveloped beaches and easy-going ways have been discovered. New *cabinas*, hotels, and developments throughout the area proclaim the arrival of tourism.

Puerto Viejo is famous in surfing circles for the **Salsa Brava**, a hot, fast, explosive wave that breaks over the reef from December to April and again in June and July. It attracts surfers from all over the world. At other times of the year the sea is quiet, particularly inside the reef, and good for snorkeling.

North of town is the road to Cabinas Chimuri – a collection of *cabinas* constructed of thatch over bamboo in the traditional Bribri style. Chimuri's owner, Mauricio, is wise in the way of the jungle and gives guided walking tours. El Pizote Surf Lodge, located on the right just before town, offers lovely cabins and rooms, well-groomed grounds with trails, and even California-Tico-style meals.

Restaurant Támara offers Caribbean-style fish or chicken served with tasty beans and rice, and a good

Along the roadside look out for stands advertising "Hay Pipas." They are selling green coconuts with refreshing juice inside. The vendor will slice one open for you with a wicked-looking machete.

BELOW: a beach near Punta Uva after a storm.

selection of fruit drinks. Stanford's on the beach is famous for its night-life and fish dinners. The Coral has what is easily the best breakfast in town, maybe in all of Costa Rica, and excellent pizza. And The Garden serves beautiful, exotically spiced dishes decorated with blossoms and fruit.

Map on page 230

To the south of town there are *cabinas* and sophisticated new hotels along the road across from beautiful stretches of white-sand beaches edged by palm and beach almond trees; award-winning Bungalows Cariblue at Playa Cocles is renowned for service, style and gourmet Italian food (tel: 750 0035). Rivers are bridged by precarious-looking wooden structures, which become slippery in the rain. Signs advertise bicycles for rent – a great way to get around Puerto Viejo and to the nearby beaches.

If you would like to learn a bit more about the Talamanca region, the non-profit **Talamanca Association for Ecotourism and Conservation** (ATEC; tel: 750 0398) provides environmentally and culturally oriented tours led by local guides who speak Spanish and English. Choices for outings include snorkeling, fishing, birdwatching, adventure treks, visits to the Talamanca indigenous reserves and visits to the houses of local people for home-cooked meals.

Punta Uva and Manzanillo-Gandoca

To the south of Puerto Viejo is heavenly **Punta Uva ❼**, probably the best easily accessible beach along Costa Rica's Caribbean coast. Crystalline, aquamarine water laps quietly on palm-lined beaches, and both the air and water temperature seem fixed at a constant, perfect 27°C (80°F). You can cycle here from Puerto Viejo and there are plenty of charming and affordable accommodations all the way down the road to Punta Uva. For people who like to

ABOVE: there is no shortage of rest and refreshment in Puerto Viejo.
BELOW: a Mexican hairy porcupine.

camp but don't want to rough it too much, there's Almonds & Corals Lodge, in the middle of a cool, shaded former cacao plantation. You'll sleep in comfortable tents nested within larger tents set on platforms and complete with electricity, hot-water showers and flush toilets (tel: 272 2024).

Further south, still on the beach, is **Manzanillo**, a tiny village which can be reached by walking along the sand for about two hours from Punta Uva, or 20 minutes from Puerto Viejo by car along the dirt and gravel road that terminates here. The two *tico* bars provide local dishes and idyllic views. Coral reefs offshore create a natural harbor. Surfers enjoy it for its fast beach break. Manzanilla is also a fisherman's haven. When news of a school of bait arrive, fishing boats appear from Puntarenas to take part in the days catch.

There is a cluster of houses, a restaurant, a bar, a grocery store, empty beaches, and very inexpensive *cabinas*. Local children play in the waves or bathe in the river, young men fish in dugout canoes, elders sit around and talk quietly in the shade, and not much more goes on around here. This is Costa Rica at its most relaxed. Local women will prepare meals for visitors in their homes if asked, and fishermen and farmers are usually happy to chat about their work and the land.

South of the village of Manzanillo is the **Gandoca-Manzanillo Wildlife Refuge ❽**, which protects swamplands, coral reefs, turtle nesting grounds and the only mangrove forest on Costa Rica's Caribbean coast. The Gandoca River Estuary is a nursery for tarpon. Most of the refuge is flat or has gently rolling hills, covered with forest and some farms. Hiking is limited to the coast. Bring your own supply of water since there are no facilities available in the refuge.

Family-owned Aquamor Talmanca Adventures is located in the refuge and offers a wonderful choice of scuba, kayaking and dolphin-watching trips.

ABOVE: snacking on the street is a way of life in Costa Rica. **BELOW:** United Fruit banana train, *circa* 1916.

Guests can stay at its Dolphin Lodge within the Wildlife Refuge and assist with conservation, marine research and the lodge's goal of promoting the respectful observation of dolphins in the area.

Map on page 230

Banana country

Sixaola is a banana town on the Panamá border. To get there continue along the paved road from Hone Creek to the south, instead of turning off to Puerto Viejo and Manzanillo. The road is paved until just outside of Bribri: the rest of the way it is gravel, in fair condition.

In the early 1900s, the United Fruit Company expanded its successful banana plantations from across the Panamá side of the Sixaola River into Costa Rica, and although the company has long gone, the area stretching from just outside the village of Bribri to the border at Sixaola is still very much Banana Land.

Banana-processing plants occur at intervals along the road: it's interesting to stop for a break at one of the open-air plants to watch the workers handling the large bunches, called *raicimos*, pulling the dried flowers off the ends of individual bananas, cutting bunches of bananas off the stalks, sorting, washing and putting them in boxes which no longer are labeled "United Fruit" but "Chiquita."

Mountains of green bananas, which look perfectly acceptable, but don't meet the specifications of Chiquita's North American and European consumers, are formed next to the sorting area. They are used for animal feed, banana paper, fibre in baby food or mulch. And some are left to rot. The smell of fermenting bananas is a familiar one here even though the fruit is used in a number of resourceful ways, from green banana *ceviche* to banana vinegar compresses, a folk remedy for sprained muscles.   ❏

ABOVE: six foot, seven foot? Even eight-foot!
BELOW: banana plantations near the Panamanian border.

CARIBBEAN BANANA REPUBLIC

Banana cultivation in Costa Rica began as a by-product of the Atlantic railroad. The crop was only planted by the side of the track in order to help finance its construction. However, the easy success of the banana venture quickly attracted foreign capital and export of the fruit in huge quantities was soon under way.

In 1889 Minor Keith, the Atlantic railroad pioneer, formed the United Fruit Company and turned Costa Rica into Central America's first banana republic.

United Fruit soon became a symbol of the evils of foreign domination and control over the local economy, making huge profits for the few at the top. The company's ruthless methods and exploitation of labor were widely reviled, but it was also highly successful. By 1913 the plantations were producing 11 million bunches a year and Costa Rica was the world's top exporter.

Unfortunately, banana disease on the Caribbean coast devastated the crop and in the 1930s United Fruit pulled out of Limón province for good, leaving behind a virtually destitute region that saw little economic activity until the 1970s. Nowadays, the area is once again producing bananas on a large scale, with more than US$500 million worth exported every year.

Sea Turtles

Sea turtles look more like their close but extinct relatives, the dinosaurs, than modern animals. Remarkable adaptations to life in the sea have enabled them to survive, largely unchanged, for more than 150 million years. They "fly" like birds through the water using front flippers as wings. Yet they retain terrestrial traits and must surface to breathe air and crawl ashore to nest and lay their eggs.

Costa Rica is home to five species of sea turtles: green, hawksbill, Olive Ridley, leatherback and loggerhead. They are more easily viewed here than anywhere else in the world. They nest at several well-known beaches on both Caribbean and Pacific shores. During the nesting season, if you happen to be in the right place at the right time, you may see one of the most amazing spectacles in the animal kingdom: *the arribada*, when 100,000 or more Olive Ridley turtles come ashore to nest simultaneously *(see*

page 202). Or, equally spectacular, the sight of a 680-kg (1,500-lb) leatherback hauling her massive body out of the water and up the beach to bury her clutch of eggs in the sand.

Tortuguero Beach, a 35-km (22-mile) stretch of sand on the Caribbean side of Costa Rica, is the most important nesting area for green turtles in the Western Caribbean. Here, you can see green turtles, hawksbill turtles and Ridleys.

Green turtles mate and nest several times from September through November. With the sharp hook on his front flippers, the male holds and mounts the female. If the sexually aggressive male can't locate a mate, he will eagerly clamber on top of anything that floats. Chunks of wood, other male turtles, even skin divers are not safe from a male's misguided passion.

An impregnated female waits offshore until dark before beginning her long struggle up the beach to the nesting site. During her crawl up the beach, disturbances such as noise and light will cause the female to abort the nesting procedure, and to return to the safety of the sea. But once she has begun digging the nest, nothing will distract her. Using her rear flippers, she scoops out a vase-shaped hole, approximately 1 meter (2–3 ft) deep. One hundred or more leathery, golf-ball-sized eggs covered with a mucus "fungicide" drop into the nest one or two at a time until the entire clutch is deposited. She covers the nest, tamps down the sand and begins her crawl back to the sea, leaving her progeny at the mercy of coatimundis, dogs, raccoons and human scavengers, known as *hueveros,* who steal the eggs and sell them to local bars.

In undisturbed nests, baby green turtles hatch in a couple of months. Using a temporary egg tooth, they tear open their shells. Soon the entire clutch is ready to rise to the surface. A critical mass of about 100 turtles all working together is needed to excavate the 1 meter (3 ft) of sand which is covering them. Usually before dawn, they erupt onto the beach, look for the brightest part of the horizon over the sea, and scramble for the water through a gauntlet of ghost crabs and birds, perhaps then only to be met by sharks and predatory fish once they do reach the water. Hundreds of thousands race for the sea and probably less than 3 percent survive. Those that do make it go offshore to floating rafts of Sargassum weed where they find shelter and food for their first and most difficult months at sea.

For several decades they live nomadic lives, migrating over vast distances of the open ocean to feed on turtle grass in the remote Miskito Keys off Nicaragua or at Cahuita on the Talamanca coast. Some navigate several thousand miles to the Windward Islands, using no apparent landmarks or visual cues. It is thought that crystals of magnetic iron located in the turtles' brains perhaps serve as internal compasses, guiding them across the seas, or more prosaically they may just follow a certain smell or substance.

Although no one knows for certain, marine biologists estimate that it takes 15–30 years for these turtles to reach sexual maturity, at which point they reconvene on the beaches where they were born to mate, nest and complete their incredible reproduction cycle.

To early explorers, fresh turtle meat was a welcome change from salt beef and sea biscuits. Tropical peoples still relish meat from the sea turtle. But sadly, the species is being endangered more from frivolous use than for subsistence purposes: six or seven species of sea turtle are on the brink of extinction. In bars from the Caribbean to Sri Lanka, sea turtle eggs are sucked from the shells as aphrodisiacs. Tortoiseshell has a high value when carved, polished and made into jewelry, combs and spectacle frames. Turtle skin is even being used as a substitute for alligator skin in shoes and purses.

Sea turtles remain on the endangered species list, although worldwide conservation programs are under way. Importation of turtle products into the US and other countries is illegal, and carries stiff penalties. But adult turtles are accidently caught in shrimp trawls and fishermen continue to hunt them, sometimes legally – the Costa Rican government grants permits to the people of Limón province to take 1,800 turtles a year.

Silt from illegally deforested land near Tortuguero washes onto the beaches, bringing weeds which grow and take valuable nesting space from the turtles. Floodlights from beachside hotels and developments frighten off females ready to nest, and disorient hatchlings trying to find the sea.

The future for many turtles is bleak, though in 1991 a new national park was created at Playa Grande on the Nicoya Peninsula and named Las Baulas, which means leatherback turtle. And the National Park authorities now take a very strict line on poaching. Perhaps this, plus the efforts of the many volunteer programs and the commercial demands of eco-tourism will yet save the turtles.

People tend to like turtles, even though they are not at first glance particularly lovable or even very attractive. In contrast to the modern way of life, the turtle's ponderous pace, non-violent nature and steady perseverance in getting from here to there seems a more reasonable way to conduct affairs.

Turtles even have a prominent place in the religious and folk histories of many cultures. Some Hindu sects venerate the turtle as a living god, the reincarnation of Shiva, creator and destroyer of all life. Myth states that a turtle brought the Buddhist world from the sea on its back. ❑

LEFT: struggling ashore to lay and bury eggs.
RIGHT: loggerheads are Caribbean dwellers.

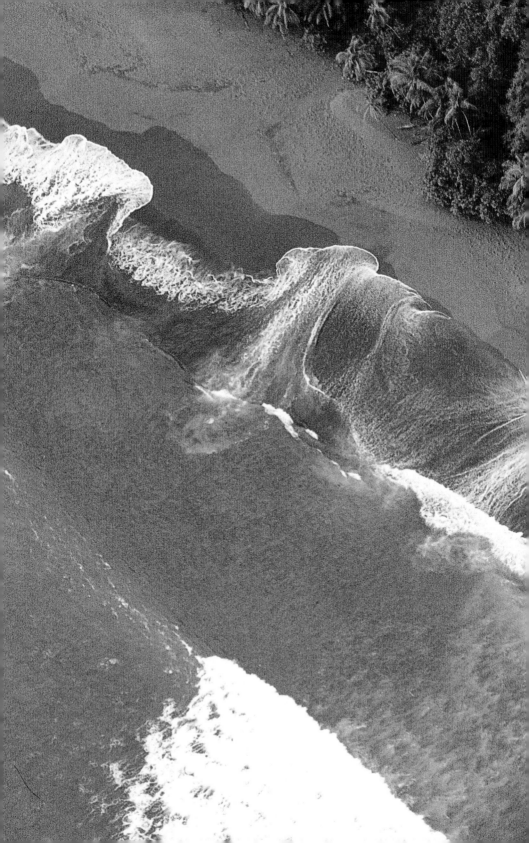

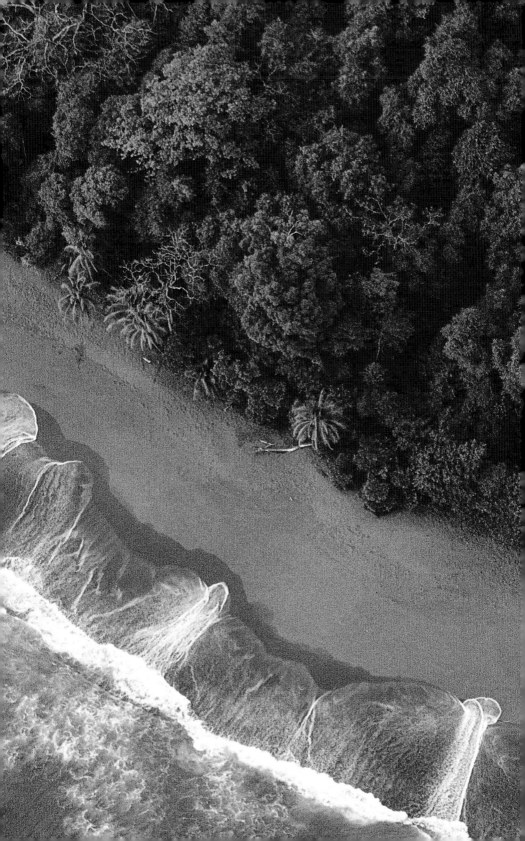

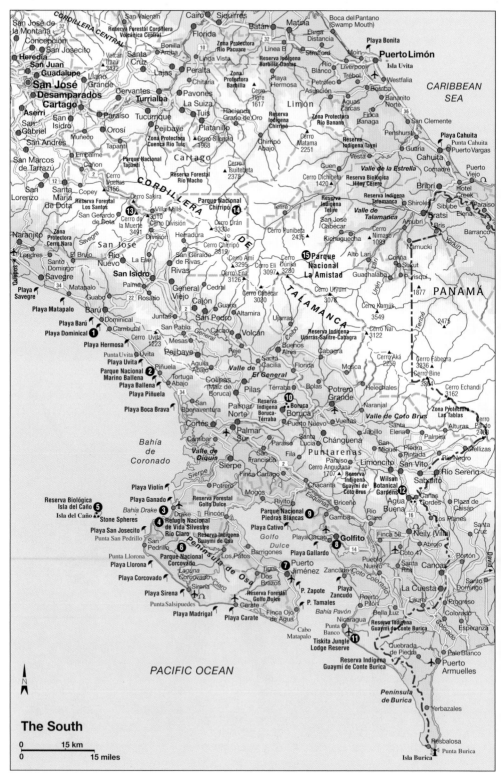

The South

THE SOUTH

Even by local standards, the south is a wild region. It includes the highest peak in Central America and the largest, most inaccessible national park with the most pristine tropical wet forest

T he *Zona Sur*, or Southern Zone, begins in the agricultural lands of the Valle de El General, rises to the highlands around the Cerro de la Muerte, then falls away to the valleys of the far south and ends at the Panamanian border. The Interamericana Highway runs like a spine through the whole region, joining up with the Costanera coastal highway at Palmar Sur. This is an area for hikers and nature lovers with a sense of adventure, who like exploring off the beaten path.

Playa Dominical and Marino Ballena National Park

A beautiful drive of 35 km (22 miles) on a paved road from San Isidro, through the southern section of the Valle de El General, brings you to **Playa Domini-cal ❶**. (The trip from San José to Dominical via San Isidro takes about four hours, including rest stops.) Dominical can also be reached by a two-hour drive along the coast from Quepos. The coast road from Quepos, the *Costanera Sur*, has been improved and the scenery is wonderful. Stop off for the night at the Cabinas Punta Dominical, set on a breezy headland that juts out into the ocean or at secluded Pacific Edge, set high on a forested ridge, with spectacular sea views. Or spend some time at Hacienda Barú, in the middle of a private forest reserve with miles of forest and beach trails.

The beach is a long stretch of brown, silty sand offering good waves for surfing, though beware dangerous currents when swimming. There are pleasant, shady places on the sand for camping. "Town" is a small, somewhat funky settlement, with a few trendy restaurants, surf shops, a health-food store and some comfortable hotels along with basic *cabinas* and hostels catering to young surfers. During the dry season Playa Dominical's weather can be impossibly hot and breezeless, and the landscape barren.

A horseback trip to **Nauyaca Falls**, also known as Santo Cristo and Barú Falls, takes about two hours. The falls consist of two cascades a total of 65 meters (210 ft) high, which tumble into a glorious warm-water swimming hole. The Finca Bella Vista and Don Lulo's Waterfall Tour both arrange horseback tours to the falls; Bella Vista also offers a sunset beach ride. Several area tour operators can book the tours for you, including Selva Mar in San Isidro de El General (tel: 771 4582).

Just south of Dominical is **Playa Dominicalito**, where there are good point-break waves for surfers. Swimming is best at low tide when beaches are exposed beyond coral rocks and there are beautiful views of the overlooking hills.

Some 17 km (11 miles) to the south of Dominical lies **Parque Nacional Marino Ballena ❷**, easily accessible along the recently widened and paved Costanera Sur. One of Costa Rica's smallest and most

Map on page 246

PRECEDING PAGES: Pacific breakers at Corcovado National Park; ox-cart on the Pacific coast. **BELOW:** ancient buttress roots.

recently dedicated national parks, Marino Ballena offers beautiful beaches, mangroves where you can spot raccoons, lizards and caimans, and coral reefs. Dolphins are commonly seen and the park's two sandy beaches provide nesting grounds for the Olive Ridley and hawksbill turtle.

The **Islas Ballenas**, also part of the park, provide refuge to humpback whales and their young from December through April. Two sandy beaches within the park sweep to a meeting point at Punta Uvita, and at low tide produce remarkably calm conditions for underwater exploration. Local boatmen will take visitors out to the reef for snorkeling, fishing or birdwatching, although at the north end of the park good snorkeling spots can be reached on foot at low tide.

In **Bahía Uvita**, the entry point to the park, there are a number of *cabinas* and *sodas*. Boats are available for diving, fishing and sightseeing trips. Just south of the park, on the east side of the Costanera, is a sign for Ojochal, a French-Canadian enclave with wonderful restaurants.

Further south along the **Costanera Sur Highway** are **Playa Piñuela** and **Playa Ventanas**. Delfin Tours, right at the park entrance in the village of Bahía, can get you out onto the water for snorkeling. Mystic Dive Center (tel: 788 8636) can get you under the water. And Skyline Ultra Flight can take you above the water for a bird's-eye view from aboard an ultralight plane (tel: 748 8036).

The Osa Peninsula

Jutting out more than 50 km (30 miles) into the Pacific, the Osa Peninsula shelters Golfo Dulce from ocean swells and creates a magnificent natural harbor. It is sculpted with picturesque beaches and rocky headlands, and is dissected by streams and rivers that cascade over volcanic cliffs on their way to the

Drake Bay is an unlikely spot for shopping, but the village of Agujitas is one of the few places in Central America which makes molas *– handmade reverse-appliqué stitched blouses and fabrics more often associated with Panamá.*

BELOW: messing about in the bay.

sea. The most majestic forests in all Costa Rica cover the hillsides and line the valleys of the Osa Peninsula and, in many cases, represent the last stronghold of nature and endangered animals and plants that are endemic to southern Pacific Costa Rica. It is an imposing, impressive and wild place.

Map on page 246

The Amerindians of the Diquis region were the first inhabitants of the peninsula, named Osa after one of their chiefs. They were accomplished goldsmiths and fashioned religious and ceremonial pieces from gold they found in the Tigre and Claro rivers. The Spanish made repeated explorations into Osa, killing the indigenous population, plundering their gold and searching for the legendary mines of Veragua. Gold continues to cause problems for the people of the Osa Peninsula. In the 1980s, the discovery of an 11-kg (25-lb) gold nugget created a gold rush and havoc in the Corcovado National Park. Farmers-turned-prospectors invaded the area, tore up creeks and rivers for flakes of placer gold, hunted wildlife and burned the forest to plant crops. Gold fever destroyed many thousands of acres of parkland, and Corcovado was plagued by the usual boom-town socioeconomic ills such as alcoholism and prostitution. In response, government officials closed the Corcovado National Park for years while they attempted to evict the trespassers. Then, after a minor civil war, officials reluctantly agreed to pay the miners a stipend to leave the park. Today, Corcovado is the jewel in the crown of Costa Rica's national park system. The park lodging facilities are very rustic and down-at-heel but the trails are worth the lack of comfort.

ABOVE: one of the region's mysterious giant stone spheres *(see page 251).*
BELOW: small insects often make the most noise.

Drake Bay

On the northern coast of the Osa Peninsula, **Drake Bay ❸** is said to be the place where Sir Francis Drake, the first English navigator to sail around the world, landed in 1579. Accessible only by water and air, it is a land of crystal-blue waters, pristine beaches and jungle. Your lodge will make your travel arrangements from San José, which usually involve a flight to Palmar, transfer to Sierpe, then an exciting, open motorboat ride to the lodge. New direct flights from San José to Drake airstrip pass over Manuel Antonio Park and provide aerial perspectives of the south Pacific coast en route to Corcovado. As you land on the grass airstrip, look for scarlet macaws. You can also travel to Palmar overland, by bus or car, a 5½-hour trip, or fly to Palmar Sur and take a taxi to nearby Sierpe.

Just south of Drake Bay, along the scenic coastal footpath, is the Delfin Amor Ecolodge, an enchanting colony of hillside screened *cabinas*. Sea kayaking, snorkeling and yoga sessions are offered, along with dolphin watching (tel: 394 2632).

A little farther south is Punta Marenco Ecolodge, in the 500-hectare (1,200-acre) **Río Claro National Wildlife Refuge ❹**. Guests reside in rustic but comfortable grass huts perched over the Pacific, with cool breezes, hammocks on private verandahs and views of Caño Island (tel: 234 1308). Drake Bay Wilderness Camp, just north of Marenco, is directly on the beach at Drake Bay and offers similar programs as well as offshore fishing, canoeing, ocean kayaking and whale-watching trips (during January and February). Romantic La Paloma Lodge is built into a hillside and offers

Ants in Your Plants

Should someone point out a "bull's horn acacia" to you, stop and have a close look at this thorny shrub. Measuring from between 1.5 to over 3 meters (4–10 ft) tall, along the branches are pairs of reddish spines that look like miniature replicas of a Texas steer's horns. Hence its name.

Of the many relationships that have evolved between tropical ants and plants, that of the bull's horn acacia and its stinging ants is one of the most curious. It is also one of the most dramatic examples of tropical co-evolution between species.

With some caution, shake the end of a branch. Ants burrow into the end of the spines (notice the tiny hole), excavate the inside of the branch, and set up a colony where they rear their young and go about the business of being ants. When the plant is disturbed, as in the case of your shaking the branch, the pugnacious ants charge aggressively from the spines, stingers armed and ready to defend their acacia host. It would only take one nasty sting to convince you that this unusual defense system works.

In addition to repelling would-be grazers, ranging in size from caterpillars to cattle, the ants manicure the ground around the acacia, keeping it clear of sprouts from other plants which might deprive their host of living space in a tropical forest containing 1,200 species of competing trees and countless other plants.

And the acacia is appreciative. Not only does it shelter its guardians, it also feeds them. Tiny, sausage-shaped pores hang from the ends of the leaflets. Loaded with sugar and protein, these are harvested gratefully by the ants.

On the forest floor you're almost sure to spot trails carved by leafcutter ants as they march through the jungle in search of tender leaves to attack. Their trails are veritable highways of activity. Imagine thousands of people walking home on the highway, each rushing along, carrying a 1.5 meter by 2.5 meter (4 ft by 8 ft) sheet of green plywood overhead, and you have the concept of these ants. Leafcutters are amazingly industrious insects. They can completely denude a full-grown mango tree overnight, carving circular slabs of leaf about 1 cm (½ inch) in diameter, hoisting them overhead and marching down the tree trunk back to the hive, which may be a kilometer away or more.

Several highways lead to their hive – often around the buttress roots of a large tree. Hives of over 100 sq meters, 2 meters (7 ft) deep in the forest floor, are not uncommon. In these hives, millions, perhaps billions, of ants chew the leaf fragments, mixing them with nutrient-rich saliva, into a gruel. From this gruel the ants grow and harvest mushrooms which provide their food source.

Large ant colonies can cut and process nearly 45 kg (100 lbs) of leaves a day. During the decades-long lifespan of an ant colony, tons of vegetation decomposes and is worked back into the forest floor. Constant rain and heat rapidly degrade tropical soils, and so the vast storehouse of nutrients and compost from the ant mounds create a rich oasis in the soil, without which the busy ants would be nearly sterile. ❑

LEFT: a leafcutter ant, found in the lowland forests of Costa Rica.

sweeping views of the ocean; its elegant and comfortable *cabinas*, with thatched roofs and private decks, blend unobtrusively into the jungle environs. From the lodge you can arrange expeditions to fish or dive, take dreamy trips up the river in sea kayaks and visit Corcovado and Isla del Caño.

Map on page 246

Isla del Caño and Parque Nacional Corcovado

The biological reserve of **Isla del Caño** ❺ sits low on the horizon, 15 km (9 miles) seaward of the Corcovado coastline, and is a pleasant 1-hour boat ride from either Marenco or Drake Bay. According to archeologists, the island was both a cemetery for indigenous peoples and a refuge for pirates. Spotted dolphins ride the boat's bow wave, and flying fish sometimes escort the traveler to the island. Between December and April, 40-ton humpback whales come from their feeding grounds in Alaska. Males sing haunting songs to attract females, and often leap high in impressive breaches during their procreative sojourn through Costa Rican waters. The island is ringed with turquoise water, tiny beaches and acres of coral-covered rock reefs. Brilliantly colored tropical fish are easily seen by skin divers within 15 meters (50 ft) of the shore at the park headquarters. Well-manicured trails lead through a rich forest drooping with epiphytes and enormous philodendrons.

Covering 40,000 hectares (100,000 acres), **Corcovado National Park** ❻ is an important sanctuary of biological diversity and endangered wildlife dominating the **Osa Peninsula**. It is the site of many of Costa Rica's most significant environmental conflicts. Wild animals live on the forest floor and in the tall trees that are draped with vines and lianas, supported by massive buttress roots, reaching out onto a forest floor teeming with life. Because Corcovado

The locals of Palmar take great pride in their stone spheres and when, in the 1980s, the San José authorities tried to remove a pair of them for display in the capital, they were prevented from doing so by student demonstrations.

BELOW: a gift from outer space or an ancient headstone?

MYSTERY OF THE SPHERES

At the highest point on Isla del Caño, where the forest thickens and becomes silent, dried leaves crackle underfoot as you approach the pre-Columbian cemetery of the Boruca people.

Two stone spheres sit among the trees. Green with moss and highlighted by shafts of sunlight from the forest canopy, the enigmatic spheres seem impossibly symmetrical in this forest of twisted plants. Thousands of spheres like this have been found in many locations in the south of Costa Rica and a few also in northern Panamá. They pose one of the country's great riddles. Though their exact origin and significance have defied explanation, it is speculated that they were made in villages on the Osa Peninsula near Palmar Norte, brought to Caño in canoes, then possibly rolled to the cemetery at the highest point of the island.

The smaller stone spheres, which are the size of oranges, were possibly toys but the huge spheres, over 2 meters (6 ft) in diameter, may have indicated the political or social standing of the deceased. Graves with spheres as headstones, oriented to the east, had secret chambers for precious ornaments and were covered with layers of sand, coral and pebbles. Many spheres found in groups have been placed to reflect the positions of the stars.

TIP

In Corcovado Park, you are largely on your own among such dangerous wildlife as coral snakes and fer de lance vipers. Although it is rare to come across these creatures, serious explorers may wish to carry an anti-venom kit on their travels.

BELOW:
a lonely beach on
Isla del Caño

Park is innundated with nearly 6 meters (20 ft) of rain a year, it is technically known as a "tropical wet forest." The simplicity of that classification belies the ecological complexity of the park. Thirteen distinct habitats here are each characterized by unique assemblages of plants, animals and topography. Five hundred species of trees – one quarter of all the species in Costa Rica, 10,000 insects, hundreds of species of birds, frogs, lizards and turtles, and many of the world's most endangered and spectacular mammals live in this place.

One of Corcovado's blessings is its inaccessibility. It is a park only for those who are prepared to make a considerable commitment in time and energy. There are several different ways to sample the beauties of Corcovado and the Osa Peninsula, from charter flights and accommodations at luxury eco-lodges to days of grueling hikes, fording rivers and battling insects, and sleeping in a tent.

At one end of the scale is **Lapa Ríos**, a renowned luxury eco-resort consisting of thatched-roof bungalows perched on the hillside of a 400-hectare (1,000-acre) reserve, with a calm and tranquil beach nearby. Like all the lodges this far south, Lapa Ríos is off the electrical grid, so there is no TV and few cellular or satellite phones. You really "get away from it all" here. **Bosque del Cabo** is smaller, but just as luxurious a place, and a favorite hangout for scarlet macaws. **Corcovado Lodge Tent Camp**, located within earshot of the crashing surf near La Leona, is an exciting place to stay in comfortable tents. Guests are driven from Puerto Jiménez or flown in a small charter plane to Carate, and make the rest of the journey on foot, while their luggage travels in horse-drawn carts.

The ideal time to go hiking and camping in Corcovado is in the dry season, December through April, and might include two nights at each of the three park stations, with days spent hiking from one station to the next. (Stations are joined

by trails, each of which requires from three to 10 hours of hiking time.) It is important to come well-equipped in the insect-battling department. A tent, mosquito net, insect repellent and long socks are essential. In addition to the usual camping gear, a machete is also a good idea. Make arrangements for visiting the park by contacting the park's administration office, next to the airport in Puerto Jiménez *(see page 254)*. The park stations will provide room and meals, but require at least one week's notice. The stations can be reached by charter plane, by hiking or by boat.

Map on page 246

The park stations

The **Sirena Station**, near the beach, has wonderful trails into the forest and along the beach. Swimming in the nearby Río Claro is refreshing, but sharks are said to frequent the ocean near the river mouth. The station itself, sadly, has been neglected and the accommodations and food here are very basic. **Los Patos Station** is an 11-km (7-mile) hike from Sirena on a wide trail that runs parallel to the El Tigre River. The trail allows relatively easy wildlife viewing. Even though it passes through thick forest, you stand a reasonably good chance of seeing at least tracks of jaguar, ocelot and tapir. Near Los Patos, there are simple accommodations available at the new Danta Corcovado Lodge, an airy, all-wood lodge with dormitory-style rooms as well as a few more private rooms (no phone). It's another 8 km (5 miles) to the park entrance at Los Patos. A road to the station, accessible by four-wheel drive vehicle, is open during the dry season.

ABOVE: strelitzia.
BELOW: Pacific brown pelican.

The trek to or from **San Pedrillo Station** and nearby **Llorona Waterfall** requires careful advance planning. Two rivers must be crossed at low tide during the 7–10 hour hike. Rangers at Sirena can provide estimates of transit times and tidal heights. Take a tide-table, food, water and camping gear, since you may need to use them en route. San Pedrillo is also accessible by a two-hour trail from Punta Marenco.

Of the estimated 250 jaguars remaining in the country, most are found in the forests of Corcovado, Tortuguero and the Talamanca Cordillera. An adult jaguar needs an enormous amount of land with abundant prey animals such as peccaries, deer and agouti to meet its food requirements. Since Corcovado Park was established, its jaguar population has more than tripled. Tracks are commonly seen on many of the trails, and are relatively easy to identify. The prints are wider than they are long, have three rear pads and four unequal toes showing no claw marks.

Herds of white-lipped peccaries roam the forest and root in the leaf litter for food. Evidence of their passing is easily seen: it will look like a bulldozer has gone through the forest.

Nearly 300 species of birds live in Corcovado of which scarlet macaws are the most spectacular. They loudly announce their arrival with gravelly shrieks. If you hear a cry like a puppy, look for a toucan, with its outlandish yellow bill, hopping through the trees. The spectacular red-breasted Baird's trogon and the melodious riverside wren are also denizens of these forests. Seeds or husks dropping through the forest will often reveal the presence of troops of squirrel

TIP

Peccaries (wild pigs) have an exaggerated reputation as the forest's most ferocious animal. Nonetheless, if a group of them approaches, or worse, surrounds you, then you would do well to climb the nearest tree.

monkeys or spider monkeys foraging in the canopy overhead. To improve your chances of seeing these animals, be on the trail before dawn.

Orchids, bromeliads, philodendrons and ferns grow attached to trees high in the forest where they find abundant light, airborne nutrients and water. Rich compost created by the epiphyte gardens is often exploited by the host tree, which sprouts roots from its branches and taps into the aerial soil. The dense growth of epiphytes creates a fantastic home for tiny red and blue poison-arrow frogs, who live in pools of water caught by bromeliad leaves. Females lay their eggs on land, and later carry the developing tadpoles on their backs over a distance of 30 meters (100 ft) or more up the trees to these pools, where they lay unfertilized eggs to feed their offspring.

Mushrooms and bracket fungi with strange shapes and astounding colors stud the rotting trunks of fallen trees. Fingernail-sized frogs and tiny salamanders live in the damp hollows of logs or under moist leaf litter.

Puerto Jiménez and inland to Sierpe

Just outside the Corcovado National Park to the east is **Puerto Jiménez 7**, the main town of the Osa Peninsula and a gateway to the park. It's a friendly, funky frontier town with a burgeoning tourist infrastructure and its own Ecotourism Chamber, which will recommend guides and assist you in planning your visit around the peninsula. Inexpensive meals and lodging are available in the town, and a number of lodges and ecotourism projects in all price ranges are to be found in the surrounding area. Puerto Jiménez is accessible by car or bus. It's about a 7-hour trip from San José and most lodges will arrange transportation.

An adventurous way to leave the Osa Peninsula is to charter a boat from one

BELOW: a naturalist gathers butterflies at the Golfito reserve.

of the lodges around Drake Bay and travel up the Sierpe River toward the little town of **Sierpe**. Luxurious Casa Corcovado Jungle Lodge brings all its guests to and from Sierpe by boat (tel: 256 8825). Beware, however, that the mouth (the *boca*) of the river is often very choppy. Make sure your boat is equipped with lifejackets and, as a precaution, put yours on when you near the *boca*.

The shores of the river are lined with mangrove trees. The maze of roots of these trees is inhabited by many species of small fish. Blue herons and flocks of snowy egrets may fly from the trees as the boat passes. Even these maritime mangrove forests are not immune to deforestation. They are cut and used to make charcoal, or the bark is stripped and tannin, used to cure leather, is extracted. Damage has been minimal so far, and the Sierpe mangroves continue to provide refuge for many animals.

A wide variety of boats ply their trade on the Sierpe. Weatherbeaten dugout canoes loaded with bananas and smoking cargo boats share the river with speedboats and naturalist tour vessels from nearby lodges. About two hours upriver at the Las Vegas Bar in Sierpe you can catch a bus to travel south to Golfito.

Golfito

On the eastern shore of the Golfo Dulce, **Golfito** ❽ is sheltered from the open sea by islands and peninsulas that form a perfect harbor within the gulf. In 1938, the United Fruit Company *(see page 239)* realized Golfito's potential, and built a major shipping port here. By 1955 over 90 percent of the bananas shipped from Costa Rica departed on the Great White Fleet of banana boats from Golfito. Boatloads of crewmen and 15,000 *Guanacasteco* immigrants came to work the plantations. They turned Golfito into a boomtown of brothels,

Map on page 246

ABOVE: raccoons are often eager for a human hand-out.
BELOW: "little mirror" butterflies in the act of mating.

Wild Cats of Costa Rica

Costa Rica is home to half a dozen kinds of wild cat. Secretive and nocturnal, they include some of the most endangered and elusive of the country's animals.

Costa Rica's wild cats – both big and small – are extremely wary of humans, and few visitors to the country are lucky enough to see them. Although they are now fully protected, their fear of people is understandable: over the years, hunting and deforestation have reduced their numbers to a fraction of their former level.

Like all cats, these animals are elegant and efficient predators. Most hunt on their own, and most hide away by day, camouflaged by beautiful spotted coats that, ironically, have made them such valuable quarry. They range in size from the jaguar – commonly known as *el tigre* – which can tip the scales at over 100 kg (220 lb) to the little spotted cat, which is smaller than many of

the domestic cats that people keep as pets.

For a cat, the jaguar shows an unusual liking for water. Its preferred habitats include mangrove swamps and the forested banks of rivers, and it seems to enjoy swimming. One of its favorite foods is peccary (a kind of wild pig), but it also catches fish and even turtles, breaking open their shells with its powerful teeth. Unfortunately, it also attacks cattle, particularly where new pasture has been created out of the former forest. As a result, many Costa Rican farmers view *el tigre* not as a national asset, but as a dangerous marauder. At one time, the jaguar was found throughout the entire country, but today its strongholds are in the national parks, particularly Santa Rosa, Tortuguero and Corcovado. You may not see a jaguar in the flesh, but you stand a chance of at least being shown its tracks.

Almost as large as the jaguar is the puma or mountain lion, one of the two Costa Rican cats that do not have spotted coats. It is a truly Pan-American animal, ranging from Canada as far south as Patagonia. The other unspotted cat, the jaguarundi, is much smaller, and has short legs and a curiously flattened forehead. Jaguarundis live in a range of habitats, but unlike pumas, they are most common in low-lying parts of the country.

The last three species have all paid a heavy price for the beauty of their coats but, with changing fashions and a ban on the trade in pelts, their future prospects look brighter than they once did. The ocelot – perhaps the most beautiful of them all – hunts mainly on the ground, although it climbs and swims well. The margay, which looks like a miniature long-tailed ocelot, is an extremely agile climber, and catches most of its food off the ground. It is the only cat that can climb head-first down a tree, instead of having to back down while holding on with its claws.

The little spotted cat is also a forest animal, sometimes living at altitudes of over 3,000 meters (9,850 ft). Although it was once widely hunted, relatively little is known about its habits in the wild. What is certain is that, despite its small size, it packs a punch: in encounters with domestic cats, the little spotted cat often comes out on top. ❏

LEFT: a young watchful puma (cougar), near La Pacífica reserve.

Map on page 246

smugglers and drunks. United Fruit or "Mamita Yunai," was seen to be funneling profits out of Costa Rica and into the pockets of rich North American stockholders and became the symbol for hated Yankee imperialism.

Following crippling strikes and conflicts with labor, United Fruit decided to close down and leave Golfito in 1985. Economic depression set in and former employees of the company found themselves leaving town or searching for work as fishermen or farmers. Recently, Golfito has begun to make a slow comeback and the old town, referred to as the **Pueblo Civil**, is regaining a touch of its boomtown atmosphere. Bars and prostitutes do business on the side streets; lively outdoor cafes overlooking the pier have taken over the main street. And in the recently classified "duty-free zone" on the waterfront, known as *El Depósito*, consumer durables sell at about 40 percent off the San José price. If you're searching for bargains, try the huge outdoor mall with air-conditioned shops. (But you must stay in Golfito at least 24 hours in order to shop here.) The **American Zone** of Golfito has a sleepy, suburban atmosphere. This former United Fruit Company neighborhood comprises large wooden plantation-style homes on stilts, with screened porches and hipped roofs.

Before leaving Golfito, drive to the top of **Golfito Forest Reserve**. A sign marks the road in Barrio Invu across from the Plaza Deportes soccer stadium. Watch for toucans and sloths in the trees beside the steep, winding gravel road. At the top, the panoramic views of **Golfo Dulce** are spectacular. Piedras Blancas National Park and the Golfito National Wildlife Refuge lie just north of town; they are important wildlife corridors where birders and nature lovers can roam along miles of trails. There are regular flights to Golfito; check with the airline offices for their current schedules. For the more patient traveler, the very scenic 7-hour bus ride from San José to Golfito is a memorable experience.

TIP

If you would like to learn more about the harsh conditions of the banana plantations, read the exuberant *Mamita Yunai*, written by pioneer labor organizer Carlos Luis Fallas and set in the 1930s and 1940s in Limón province.

BELOW: giant philodendrums.

North of Golfito

Beside the Golfo Dulce, accessible only by boat, are beautiful pebbled beaches, and dense jungle that starts almost at the water's edge. Rainbow Adventure Lodge, on Playa Cativo, is aptly named. A 45-minute speedboat ride from Golfito, this open-air, pagoda-style lodge is filled with art-nouveau antiques and stained-glass panels. Nearby is luxurious, Playa Nicuesa Rainforest Lodge, handcrafted with more than eight kinds of tropical wood. Secluded cabins are scattered around a lush tropical garden. There is kayaking, snorkeling, fishing and dolphin-watching out the front door of the lodge, and hiking, bird-watching and waterfalls in the mountain forest just steps behind the back door. In the next cove over is **Casa Orquidea**, a beautiful landscaped garden of ginger, cacao, papaya, orchids and tropical plants. Tours last one hour (open daily; entrance fee).

In 1991, 1,200 hectares (3,000 acres) of rainforest on the west side of Golfo Dulce was declared the **Parque Nacional Piedras Blancas** ❾. However, as the government didn't have the funds to compensate the landowners, the possibility remained that title could revert to the former owners and that the logging operations which had been under way could resume.

Michael Schnitzler, an Austrian violinist and Golfito homeowner, solicited contributions from his countrymen and women, and with additional funds contributed by national and international groups, the money was raised to pay the landowners and ensure the continuation of Piedras Blancas as a national park. It is incorporated into Corcovado National Park, and appears under this name on some maps. Even more confusingly, it is also known as Esquinas National Park, for the river that flows through it, and it has also been given the nickname of the "Rainforest of the Austrians." A biological station owned and operated by the University of Vienna offers basic accommodations for a minimal fee, and students and scientists from around the world are invited to stay and contribute to research into the park's biodiversity. More luxurious accommodation is available at Esquinas Lodge. Guides for park exploration are available and are strongly recommended since the trails are sometimes hard to follow.

If you continue on the Interamericana Highway past Palmar Norte, and just past Puerto Nuevo, a rough track leads to **Boruca** ⑩. This is a small village located in a valley near Buenos Aires, where life moves at a leisurely pace. Over the New Year's holiday, Borucas celebrate the *Fiesta de los Diablitos* (Celebration of the Little Devils), a re-enactment of the war between the Spanish and indigenous population – only this time the Amerindians win.

South of Golfito

Between the mouth of the Río Coto Colorado (which lies just south of Golfito), to Punta Banco, the last major point of land before the Panamanian border, lie some of Costa Rica's most inaccessible and remote beaches. Take the old cable ferry across the river. Then, in Pueblo Nuevo, turn right for **Playa Zancudo**, an 8-km (5-mile) long, sandy crescent with excellent swimming and surfing, and several nice places to stay. Cabinas Sol y Mar is friendly and serves good food. Continue on the road parallel to the coast to **Pavones**, just before Río Claro. The beach is not suitable for casual swimming, but this is a renowned surfing spot. Basic lodging is available, along with more comfortable rooms at Cabinas La Ponderosa (tel: 824 4145).

After the seemingly endless potholes, bogs and washboard bumps in the road, continue on for another 30 minutes to **Punta Banco**. Wide intertidal flats of volcanic and sedimentary rock, riddled with tidepools full of marine life and battered by continual surf characterize Punta Banco.

At the end of the point, a pasture and gate on the left mark the entrance to **Tiskita Jungle Lodge** ⑪, Peter Aspinall's private rainforest reserve, experimental tropical fruit farm and eco-lodge.

The tortuous drive (a four-wheel drive vehicle is essential) can be avoided by using a package tour, which includes a private airplane charter that sets down on a grass airstrip near the lodge. Isolated cabins with ocean views are a short walk from the main lodge. Well-designed trails lead to waterfalls, idyllic swimming holes and various points of natural history interest in Tiskita's 162-hectare (400-acre) forest. More than 100 species of fruit trees from around the tropical world are under cultivation here.

BELOW:
capuchin monkey.

Wilson Botanical Gardens

Map on page 246

For a more academic experience in tropical botany, visit **Wilson Botanical Gardens** ⓬ in Las Cruces, some 6 km (4 miles) south of San Vito on Highway 16. The gardens, adored by botanists and non-botanists alike, are operated by the Organization for Tropical Studies (OTS) as a center for research, scientific training and public education (open daily 8am–4pm; entrance fee). Designed by an Italian landscape architect, trails wind through extensive collections of "lobster claw" heliconias, bromeliads, tree ferns, orchids and palms, and ultimately lead into the wild forest reserve behind the gardens. This offers splendid mountain vistas and hiking to rocky pools around the Río Jaba. The gardens offer simple, dormitory-style accommodations, as well as comfortable private rooms with verandahs for bird-watching. You can talk with visiting scientists in residence or attend seminars by horticultural societies from around the world.

The **Villa Neilly-San Vito Road** was built in 1945 by the USA as a strategic protection point, due west of the Panamá Canal. The paved road rises sharply into the cool mountains that lead to **San Vito** at 960 meters (3,150 ft) above sea level. San Vito was founded by immigrants from post-war Italy, who were encouraged by the Costa Rican government to settle there. It's a clean, modern town of 45,000 inhabitants (including the surrounding area), high in a mountain valley, where you can get a good Italian meal and hear Italian spoken on the streets. Pizzería Liliana, in the center of town, is the most popular restaurant.

Valle de El General

Since colonial times, people had attempted to find a pass through the Talamanca Mountains to join the Central Valley with the unknown lands on the

ABOVE: giant bromeliad at Wilson Botanical Gardens.
BELOW: a moment of jungle quietude.

The country estate of former president Don Pepe (José) Figueres lies just off the highway as you start to climb Cerro de la Muerte. The house is called La Lucha Sin Fin *(the Endless Struggle) since it was here that he formulated many of the political views that led to the Civil War.*

BELOW: Mount Chirripó, the tallest peak in southern-Central America.

other side of the Dota Mountains. But it was not until the end of the 1860s that Don Pedro Calderón, responding to a prize offered by the government, found a way through. The opening of the road led to the colonization of the **Valle de El General**, and later, to the building of the Interamericana Highway, which connects San José and the Central Valley with the southern Pacific zone of Costa Rica. If you are traveling south to the Valle de El General, start early to avoid the fog and rain that often appear later in the day. From San José take the Interamericana Highway toward Cartago, veering right to take the road to San Isidro.

The route to the Valle de El General passes over the spectacular **Cerro de la Muerte ⑬** (Death Mountain), which rises to 3,350 meters (11,000 ft). Named for early foot travelers who died here from exposure, today the mountain is not as inhospitable as its name suggests. Still, it is not difficult to imagine the hardships the early pioneers endured on the week-long journey. Rain, cold and fog can make the first half of the drive miserable, but the road quickly rises above the clouds to cool, crisp sunshine, fields of flowers and hillside farms. Foxglove, azalea, hydrangea and white cala lily grow wild. Clouds swirl through the valleys and over peaks. There are a number of small hotels just off the highway. One of the first, just as you start climbing the mountain, is Genesis II, a private cloud-forest reserve, which is recommended for birdwatchers. More than 150 species have been spotted at Genesis II, including the quetzal (tel: 381 0739).

For almost-guaranteed quetzal sightings, visit the affordable Albergue Mirador de Quetzales, just off the main highway at Km 70. Lodging here is in quaint, A-frame cottages with hot-water showers and hot-water bottles to warm beds for the chilly nights. Miles of trails are great for both hikers and birdwatchers. Camping sites are also available (tel: 381 8456).

Map on page 246

Villages of the Valley

Down the road to the right from Empalme is **Santa María de Dota**, a small town with a beautiful little park. The paved road, which continues toward San Marcos de Tarrazú, San Pablo de Léon Cortes and San Cristóbal Sur, is called **La Ruta de Los Santos** (The Route of the Saints), and is best tackled in a four-wheel drive vehicle. In **Copey**, a village in the mountains above Santa María, you can rest at a waterfall and lake, fish for trout at one of the many local trout farms or lodge comfortably at El Toucanet Lodge (tel: 541 1435).

Continuing on the Interamericana Highway, about half an hour from Empalme, is a sign that says "San Gerardo." This is the turn-off for **San Gerardo de Dota**, 9 km (6 miles) down a good, partially paved road that runs parallel to the Río Savegre. In the midst of the valley, Don Efráin Chacón and his family offer comfortable *cabinas* and delicious homemade meals at the **Albergue Montaña de Savegre**. Look for a bridge and some clean white buildings painted with bright red apples on the left just above the river. The area is known for its cloud forests and offer one of the best opportunities in the world to see the resplendent quetzal. The quetzals feed in trees almost in Don Efráin's backyard, and the guest book is full of enthusiastic comments such as: "8 quetzals today!"

There are miles of challenging trails here, including a hike to a magnificent waterfall. Bring plenty of warm clothing as it becomes surprisingly chilly at night. The drive to **San Isidro de El General** is beautiful once the fog clears from Cerro de la Muerte. San Isidro is the commercial center for this agricultural area, a busy town with a large central park and lots of noisy traffic. Explore the numerous plant nurseries, coffee and cattle farms that are sprinkled on its slopes.

BELOW: downtown San Isidro.

Map on page 246

Parque Nacional Chirripó

Situated 150 km (94 miles) south of San José, **Chirripó National Park**  covers 43,700 hectares (108,000 acres). Its main attraction is its diversity of landscapes, including *páramos* – flatlands with stunted growth; oak forests; fern groves; cloud forests; swamps; crystal-clear glacial lakes; and the highest peak (3,800 meters/12,500 ft) in southern Central America.

Only those willing to brave a long day of hiking in the cold, and quite possibly rain, make the ascent to the very top of **Mount Chirripó**. A rustic lodge and several trails, which are regularly maintained, make the ascent, if not easy, at least possible. Daytime temperatures reach over 27°C (80°F) but at night-time they can drop to almost freezing. The best months to attempt Chirripó are February and March, the driest time of year, but during the rainy months the flora is splendid. Visits to Chirripó require advance reservations, which you can make by booking through the office in **San Isidro de El General** (tel: 771 3155) or by going to the ranger station near the village of **San Gerardo** in the low season. The hike to the top of Chirripó, including a day on the summit, takes at least four days. It costs $10 to enter the park and $10 for each day you are there.

You can spend the first night in the national park in San Gerardo at any number of inexpensive *cabinas*. The owner of **Posada del Descanso** is very knowledgeable about the area. Before entering the park, check in at park headquarters in San Gerardo. Park maps are available there, but they are basic and abbreviated, and rangers often do not have the information hikers request. Good, large-scale topographical maps are available in San José. Rangers can put you in touch with locals with horses who will haul your pack to the hut ahead of you. Río Chirripó Retreat has cozy cabins within sound of the rushing Río Chirripó (tel: 771 7065). Rio Chirripo's natural setting is inspirational for yoga and meditation workshops.

The area around San Gerardo is well worth visiting, even if you do not attempt to climb Chirripó. Bird-watching is good, with frequent sightings of quetzals, and hiking is very satisfying, with beautiful lush scenery, natural hot springs to relax your sore muscles and waterfalls.

ABOVE: close to nature, but with creature comforts.
BELOW: mist-clad foliage in Cerro de la Muerte.

Parque Nacional La Amistad

La Amistad National Park  is an enormous protected area that covers approximately 12 percent of Costa Rica's total territory. Adjacent to Chirripó, in the interior of La Amistad Biosphere Reserve, the park is for the most part inaccessible. La Amistad (which means "Friendship") has been declared a Biosphere Reserve and a World Patrimony site because of the diversity of its flora and fauna, and because of its great scientific value. There are over 20 species of hummingbird and you'll find 3 inch (7cm) grasshoppers. More than half of La Amistad has yet to be explored. Hiking near **Las Tablas Forest Reserve** is safe and rewarding, but only experienced tropical trekkers should venture into the interior. There is a ranger station with camping facilities at the Altamira park entrance (tel: 200 5355). Day trips are possible from San Isidro or San Vito, or you can stay at the eco-friendly La Amistad Lodge. ❑

Isla del Coco

Isla del Coco is the most remote of Costa Rica's territories, adrift in the Pacific Ocean nearly 600 km (over 360 miles) southwest of the mainland, on the same latitude as Colombia. Because of this isolation it only counts its visitors in the hundreds, yet millions have seen it on film, in the opening moments of *Jurassic Park*. In all senses, this is a place of high drama.

At its crown is a thick coniferous forest full of springs and rivers. The cliffs that tower over 100 meters (300 ft) around the entire island are covered with incredibly thick tropical vegetation with magnificent waterfalls plummeting straight down to the sea. In all, there are 200 waterfalls on the island. Lionel Wafer, a pirate physician who visited over 300 years ago wrote "what most contributes to the loveliness of the place is the number of clear, freshwater springs that fill the entire lower part of the island." And there are rocky crags and wondrously formed islets that have been shaped by the wind and water. No wonder then that it inspired Steven Spielberg, to whom it was "Isla Nebular."

Measuring roughly 12 km by 5 km (8 miles by 3 miles), Isla del Coco is the largest uninhabited island in the world. It is now a National Park and the richest in endemic species belonging to Costa Rica.

As if these facts were not sufficiently alluring, the island's history is also full of pirate stories. Many insist that there is treasure hidden here still, yet in more than 500 expeditions none has ever been found.

Two bays, Wafer Bay and Chatham Bay, offer a way to tie up and gain entry to explore the island. Chatham Bay is small, with a rocky beach. Here, the ghosts of past explorers, and of pirates, are almost tangible. Today's visitors are mostly treasure hunters, divers and environmentalists.

Most visitors consider Wafer Bay to be the best access route to the island. From here, ancient natural paths follow steep cliffs all the way to the highest part of the humid forest. There are bountiful bromeliads, giant ferns, orchids, unnamed flowering plants, mosses and ferns covering almost everything. And from a high peak there are views of an unbelievably blue sea above an impossibly green landscape, with white, angel-like doves moving gently, hovering and fluttering in the air. Every natural path, every river, every waterfall, every beach has some rare treasure. The peace is astounding and deafening. And the views of the coral reef, the crisp clarity of the water, the lushness of the landscape, all somehow contribute to an atmosphere where the mysterious legends of the past come alive.

Camping is not permitted on the island: you must sleep on your boat. There is drinkable water, however; and hiking, although the trails are not marked. Contact the National Parks Service for information and permission to enter. Specialist tour companies operate out of Puntarenas but be warned: the price of a trip is very high. For the majority of people, Isla del Coco remains just a dream – and perhaps that is no bad thing. ❑

RIGHT: the dense, deep, little-known jungle interior of Isla del Coco.

INSIGHT GUIDES
TRAVEL TIPS

CONTENTS

Getting Acquainted

Area: 51,000 sq. km (19,700 sq. miles).
Capital: San José.
Highest mountain: Mount Chirripó, 3,820 meters (12,500 ft).
Coastline: More than 1,200 km (750 miles) of Caribbean and Pacific coastline.
Population: 3.8 million.
Language: Spanish. English (Creole) is spoken by Costa Ricans of Caribbean descent, most of whom live near the Caribbean coast.
Religion: Catholic (76.3 percent); most others are Protestant and there is a small Jewish community.
National flower: *Guaria Morada* (orchid).
Time zone: GMT -6 hours. No Daylight Savings change.
Currency: colón.
Weights and measures: metric.
Electricity: 120 volts, 60-cycle current. Two-prong flat and round plugs.
International dialing code: 506.

Climate

Costa Rica has two seasons; the rainy or green season, which Costa Ricans call winter *(invierno)*, and the dry season or summer *(verano)*. In the Central Valley, the rainy season lasts from May to November and the dry season from December through April. Even during the rainy season, most mornings are bright and sunny.

Many people visit during the rainy season and take advantage of green-season discounts in hotels and fewer tourists.

Rain can fall at any time on the Caribbean coast; October being the driest month to vist. It is generally more humid on the Caribbean.

The average temperature in San José is 24°C (75°F). In the highlands, temperatures drop approximately 0.6°C for each 100 meters (500 ft) of elevation. The temperature on the coasts varies from the mid 20s°C (70s°F) to the 30s°C (low 90s°F).

The Economy

Tourism, pineapples, coffee, bananas, electronics, and textiles are the staples of Costa Rica's economy. Costa Ricans enjoy one of the highest standards of living in the Americas. They have socialized health care and public education, and one of the highest literacy rates (95 percent) in Central, South, or North America.

Government

Costa Rica is a democracy governed by a president who is elected every four years. A president may be re-elected eight years after completing his original term. There are two vice presidents and a cabinet of 12 ministers. Members of the Legislative Assembly are elected every four years. The Constitution, adopted in 1949 after a civil war, abolished the military. There is no capital punishment.

Courtesies & Customs

Greeting
People shake hands with each other when first introduced. Women usually greet each other with a kiss on the cheek and say goodbye in the same fashion; this also applies when a friendly relationship exists, and men and women often greet in the same way. Children are very affectionate and greet their elders with a kiss. However, among adults, excessive demonstrations of affection in public are not well received. Note that in Costa Rica, the "*Usted,*" or formal pronoun for "you" is used even between parents and their children.

Nude bathing
There are no nudist beaches in Costa Rica and topless bathing is not acceptable to Costa Ricans; nor is wearing bathing suits on the streets.

Prostitution
Prostitution is legal in Costa Rica; pimping is not. Some years ago the government tried to implement a system to certify the health of prostitutes and keep medical records on them, but this has long since been abandoned and health risks are high. Some beautiful "women" are in fact transvestites. Aids is a formidable reality in Costa Rica and safe sex is encouraged. Sex with a minor is illegal and punishable by imprisonment. The children's rights group Casa Alianza, led by Bruce Harris, has kept consistent pressure on the government to crack down on pedophiles, with some success.

Planning the Trip

Visas & Passports

US, Canadian and UK citizens
To enter Costa Rica, you need a valid passport, as the Costa Rican government has discontinued tourist cards. Travelers may remain for 90 days. Visa extensions are no longer possible, although if you leave the country for 72 hours, when you return you will be given another 90-day visa. Immigration is cracking down on "perpetual tourists," however, so repeated exits and entries are not advisable.

Identification: always carry your passport (or at least a photocopy of it and the page that contains your entry stamp) in case of immigration authorities' spot checks. Report lost identification immediately.

Travelers from other nations
Contact the nearest Costa Rican consulate or embassy, or try the website: www.rree.go.cr.

Customs Regulations

Personal effects may be taken into the country and up to six rolls of film, 500 g (18 oz) of tobacco, 2 kg

Embassies Abroad

US: 2114/S Street, NW, Washington DC 20008. Tel: 202-234 2945.
Canada: 325 Dalhousie Street Suite 407, Ottawa, Ontario, K1N 7G2. Tel: 1-613-562 2855. www.costaricaembassy.com.
UK: 14 Lancaster Gate, London, W2 3LH. Tel: 020-7706 8844. www.costarica.com

(4 lbs) of candy, and 3 liters (106 fl oz) of wine or liquor (if over 21). Carry prescription drugs in original containers. Anyone caught with illegal drugs can face 8–20 years in jail and no bail.

Exit Regulations

Costa Rica, like many other Latin American countries, does not permit minors (up to and including 17 years of age) born in Costa Rica or living in Costa Rica for extendend periods of time to leave the country unaccompanied without the permission of Immigration. These restrictions do not apply to foreign tourists

Health

Costa Rica ranks near the United States, Canada, and other Western nations in health-care standards.
Inoculations: no inoculations are required for visiting Costa Rica.
Water: in San José and the Central Valley, water is treated. It is, with some exceptions, potable throughout the country. If you have persistent intestinal problems, take a stool sample to the Clínica Americana (tel: 222 1010, same-day results) or the Clínica Bíblica (tel: 221 3922, results in minutes) to be analyzed (about US$8–10).
Illness: malaria is not generally a problem in Costa Rica, except in the remote regions of Talamanca. Cholera is not usually a problem, either, due to Costa Rica's strong public health efforts. There have been incidences of dengue fever, however. Dengue symptoms include the sudden onset of fever, headache, severe joint and muscle pains followed in most cases by a rash which starts on the trunk of the body and spreads to the limbs and face. The fever subsides in a few days and recovery begins, usually with no serious side effects. Dengue is spread by the *Aedes aegypti* mosquito, which bites principally at dusk. There is presently no prophylactic treatment available for dengue.

Pets

To bring in pets, an import permit is required, and obtaining this permit can take from three days to three or four months. You must fax your request to the following number, and bring with you the returned permit and updated health and vaccination certificates when you enter the country with your pet. Contact: **Vigilancia de la Salud,** Ministerio de Salud, Costa Rica. Tel: 255 1427. Fax: 221 1167.

Money Matters

The currency unit is the colón. The current rate of exchange can be found in the English-language *Tico Times* business pages or the same section of the daily *La Nación*. Or call a private bank for the current rate.
State Banks: the main ones are Banco Nacional (tel: 222 2000) and Banco de Costa Rica (tel: 287 9000), with offices throughout the country.
Private banks: the main ones are Banco Banex (tel: 257 0522) and BAC San José (tel: 295 9797/256 9911). Other private banks include. Bancrecen, Interfin, Scotiabank, and Citibank.
Cash and travelers' checks: cash machines are available in the bigger shopping centers and petrol stations of the Central Valley. Only machines marked ATH, such as at Scotia Bank or Coopealianza, will accept foreign cards; these banks are largely in the Central Valley. If you travel to the beach or the mountains, you will probably need cash or travelers' checks for expenses, other than at large hotels. It is advisable to have some travelers' checks, notes, and change in small denominations. You may not be able to break 5,000 colón notes when paying for taxis and such. US dollars in small denominations are often accepted in taxis and shops, particularly in towns and cities.
Credit cards: American Express, Visa, and MasterCard are widely

Public Holidays & Festivals

January 1 Culmination of week-long festivities in San José and other locations *(Fiestas del Fin del Año)*. Celebrations continue on the following day.

Mid-January Fiestas in Santa Cruz (Nicoya Peninsula), and rodeos, bullfights, music, and dancing in Palmares (Alajuela).

February/March Annual Orchid Show; also the best time to see orchids in bloom at Lankester Gardens, Cartago. San José National Theater Symphony season begins in March. Rodeos in San José. The Caribbean and Monteverde have impressive music festivals in March.

Mid-March National Handicraft Fair, downtown San José. Feast of San José (St Joseph), patron saint of San José. *Día del Boyero* (Day of the Ox-cart Driver) parade and blessing of the ox-carts *(carretas)*, San Antonio de Escazú.

March/April *Semana Santa*, Holy Week: banks, post offices, and government offices, as well as most shops and restaurants, are closed Thursday and Friday. *Jueves Santo*, Holy Thursday; start of Holy Week ceremonies. *Viernes Santo*, Good Friday: religious processions at 1am and 4pm. "Roman soldiers," biblical personages, and black-clad mourners, in San José, Cartago, Heredia, Escazú, and especially San Joaquín de Flores.

April 11 Juan Santamaría Day; hero of Costa Rica, died in the Battle of Rivas in action against William Walker in 1856; celebrated especially in Alajuela.

May 1 Labor Day: Worker's March in San José. Election of the President of the Parliament.

May/June Feast of Corpus Christi on the Thursday after Trinity Sunday.

June 29 Feast of Saints Peter and Paul.

July 25 "*Anexión de Guanacaste*." The President and his cabinet commemorate the "*Partido de Nicoya*." Horseback parades and concerts.

August 2 *Nuestra Señora de los Angeles*, Feast of Patroness of Costa Rica, at the Basilica in Cartago. The pilgrimage of thousands the days before is impressive.

August 15 Feast of the Assumption and Mother's Day.

September 15 Independence Day. Independence from Spain since 1821 is celebrated nationwide. All traffic in San José stops at 6pm on the 14th, and everyone sings the national anthem.

October 12 Columbus Day, *El Día de la Raza* (also called *El Día de las Culturas*). Week-long Carnival in Puerto Limón with floats, dance contests, and an elaborate parade.

October 31 National Masquarade Day with parades, clowns.

Mid-December: Festival of Lights: gigantic Christmas parade, fireworks throughout the month.

December 25/last week of year Christmas Day. Opening of the *Festejos Populares,* with fireworks and activities in Zapote. Parade of horses *(tope)* on the 26th; San José Carnival on the 27th.

accepted in the Central Valley area. Hotels and other establishments usually add a surcharge of 7–8 percent to credit card purchases, so check before you book.
Changing money: money can be changed on arrival at the airport until 5pm. State banking hours are weekdays 9am–4.30pm. Private banks, as well as offering more extensive opening hours, are a much better option for changing dollars and dollar travelers' checks than state banks, where having to wait in line for an hour is not uncommon. Your hotel may change money for you.
It may be advisable to exchange colónes back into dollars before departing Costa Rica. The airport bank may cash only US$50 worth back into dollars for departing travelers.

What to Bring

Clothing and footwear: plan to dress in layers. Sweaters and jackets are needed for activities in the mountains and cool evenings. Shorts are worn for athletic activities or at the beaches, not normally in the cities. Bring weatherproof gear and boots if you plan to do much hiking. Have a comfortable pair of walking shoes that are already broken in. Sidewalks are non-existent in many areas, and uneven at best.
    Costa Rican women are always well groomed, even the poor majority who can be seen emerging perfectly made-up from one-room shacks. Bring dressy clothes for upmarket San José restaurants and nightlife.
    Personal items: a folding umbrella will often be welcome. Bring what medications and specialty film you need. It is a good idea to bring insect repellent, sunscreen, tampons, and contraceptives with you: they are often expensive and difficult to find outside San José.
    Repellent, natural brands included, is easily available in San José. Avon bath oil, Skin-So-Soft, rubbed on the skin, is reputedly effective at keeping the "no-see-'ems" at the beach from biting; also check out the Avon Skin-So-Soft sunscreen.

Getting There

BY AIR

International flights arrive in Costa Rica at Juan Santamaría Airport, located in the Central Valley about 16 km (10 miles) from San José, the capital city. Delta, Continental, and American arrive at Daniel Oduber Airport in Liberia, Guanacaste Province (also called Tomás Guardia). Several charter companies fly directly there. Make reservations as far ahead as possible, especially December–February, as these flights are usually booked well in advance. Confirm flights 72 hours before departure. For the budget traveler, or those making last-minute reservations, a number of discount "bucket shops" should be considered. Check the Sunday editions of the *New York Times* and *Los Angeles Times.* To lessen the chance of getting "bumped" by overbooking, arrive two hours before your flight.

Weight limits per checked bag are usually 23–30 kg (50–66 lbs), two maximum. If necessary, determine how the airline is equipped to handle surfboards, bicycles, etc. Have your luggage well tagged and identified. Be prepared in case your luggage is lost. There is a US$26 airport exit tax for tourists when departing Costa Rica.

It is a 20-minute ride (about US$12 by taxi) to San José from the airport. Prices are standardized; passengers pay at a kiosk at the airport, not the taxi driver. A bus into town is available for under US$1.

Airlines

Air Canada,
tel: 0 800-052 1988,
www.aircanada.ca.
American, tel: 257 1266
fax: 442 0545
www.aa.com.
America West,
tel: 290 5222,
www.americawest.com.
Continental Airlines, tel: 296 4911, fax: 296 4920
www.continental.com.

Delta, tel: 257 4141/0880-056 2002.
www.delta.com.
Iberia, tel: 257 8266,
fax: 223 1055.
www.iberia.com
Lufthansa, tel: 243 1818,
fax: 233 9485
cms.lufthansa.com.
Martinair, tel: 232 3246,
fax: 296 7360
www.martinair.com.
Mexicana, tel: 295 6969,
fax: 295 6919
www.mexicana.com.
Natureair (domestic and Nicaragua flights),
tel: 220 3054,
fax: 220 0413
www.natureair.com.
SANSA (domestic flights only),
tel: 221 9414
fax: 255 2176
www.flysansa.com.
TACA Costa Rica, US and Canada:
Tel: 443 3555/296 9353
tel: 1-800-535 8780;
UK: 0870-241 0340
www.taca.com.
United Airlines, tel: 220 4844,
fax: 220 4855
www.united.com.
US Airways,
tel: 430 6690,
www.usairways.com.

BY BUS

There are bus services to Costa Rica from Panamá or Nicaragua. **Tica Bus,** Ca 9, Av 2/4, tel: 221 8581/221 9229, www.ticabus.com provides a comfortable, reliable service throughout Central America. Daily buses from Nicaragua and Panamá. **Trans Nica,** Ca 14, Av 3, tel: 223 4242.
Nicaragua, tel: 505-278 2090. El Salvador, tel: 503-240 1212.

BY CAR

The Interamericana Highway allows fairly rapid transit into Costa Rica via Panamá or Nicaragua. Avoid traveling at night. Bringing a vehicle into the

country must be noted in your passport. Departing without a vehicle that has been registered in your passport will be difficult. Make certain your car is in good working order. Be sure you have good tires and carry a spare.

BY SEA

Cruise ships come into Puerto Limón on the Caribbean coast and Puerto Caldera and Golfito on the Pacific. Check with a travel agent about which companies currently sail to Costa Rica. Private yachts are popular as a means to visit. Check into a port of entry with four copies of the crew and passenger lists, ship's papers and a notarized statement from the owner (if not on board). Fly a yellow quarantine flag as well as a Costa Rican flag (can be small) upon arrival and wait until boarded and cleared by both immigration and customs before going ashore.

BY RIVER

NOTE: This is extremely difficult and rarely attempted.
The truly adventurous can travel through Nicaragua down Río San Juan, which is the border between Nicaragua and Costa Rica. To do this, take a bus from Managua to Granada on Lake Nicaragua. The boat to the village of San Carlos, where the Río San Juan begins, leaves from the pier twice a week. Use a hammock for the overnight trip, which arrives at dawn.
Buying a canoe: negotiate in San Carlos for a dugout canoe that will be large enough to be comfortable, but not so heavy as to be unmanageable; or purchase passage on the river boat to El Castillo and buy a dugout there. Ensure that the paddles are well seasoned, otherwise they will be heavy and tiring to handle. If the river is raging because of recent rains, wait until it is manageable.
Food and drink: small amounts of cash can be exchanged for food

and a covered place for your hammock at many of the small farms along the river. Be prepared to camp. Do not drink any untreated water or eat uncooked food or unpeeled fruit.

Crossing the border: about halfway through this trip you will enter Costa Rica. Have your passport stamped (or signed if the official cannot find his inkpad) at the *aduana* shack. It is less than a two-week trip from

Lake Nicaragua to the Caribbean coast where you can take the protected and fairly well-traveled coastal canal. Alternatively, descend on a coconut barge or other river traffic to Limón.

Specialist Tours

Aventuras Naturales
Tel: 225 3939
Fax: 253 6934
E-mail: avenat@racsa.co.cr
www.toenjoynature.com.
Specialist in adventure tours within a natural setting. Offers rafting, kayaking, cycling, and hiking.
Diving Safaris
Tel: 672 0012
Fax: 672 0231
Toll-free: 877-853 0538
www.costaricadiving.net.
Long-established dive and adventure operator. Comprehensive website.
Costa Rica Expeditions
Tel: 257 0766
Fax: 257 1665
www.costaricaexpeditions.com.
The original whitewater rafting company. Offers nature tours to Tortuguero, Corcovado, and Monteverde, with knowledgeable, bilingual guides.
Coast to Coast Adventures
Tel: 280 8054
Fax: 225 6055
www.coasttocoastadventures.com.
Adventure tourism and races; cycling tours.
Costa Rica Sun Tours
Tel: 255 3418
Fax: 225 8842
www.crsuntours.com.
Off-the-beaten-track tours with a naturalist focus. Volcanoes, national parks, cloud forests, rainforests, beaches. Turtle-watching tours. Whitewater rafting, hiking, biking, and horseback riding tours.
Costa Rican Trails
Tel: 225-6000
Fax: 225-4049
From US: 888 803 3344
www.costaricantrails.com.
Friendly company that offers a

variety of nature, family, and adventure tours including motor-cycling.
Discovery Costa Rica
Tel: 394-3257/228-9261
Fax: 289 7124
E-mail: discovcr@racsa.co.cr
www.discoverycostarica.com.
Design your own package from a large range of tours.
Horizontes
Tel: 222 2022
Fax: 255 4513
www.horizontes.com.
Customized nature tours of all types throughout Costa Rica, including tours for families. Day trips in the Central Valley.
Intertur
Tel: 253 7503
Fax: 234 6308.
Natural history tours including fishing, birding, diving, ballooning. Tours to volcanoes and rafting trips.
The Original Canopy Tour
Tel: 291 4465
www.canopytour.com.
Sail through the treetops via a system of pulleys and cables. Several sites.
Ríos Tropicales
Tel: 233 6455
Fax: 255 4354
www.riostropicales.com.
Leading tour company for rafting and kayaking.
Serendipity Adventures
Tel: 558 1000
Fax: 558 1010.
From US: 877 507 1358
www.serendipityadventures.com.
Specialists in hot-air ballooning.
Swiss Travel
Tel: 282 4898
Fax: 282 4890
www.swisstravelcr.com.
Upscale ecotourism and adventure.

Insurance

It is essential to have comprehensive insurance when traveling to Costa Rica. Some bank and credit cards may include insurance, but this may not provide adequate medical cover. In Costa Rica, you need a minimum of US$2 million of cover for medical expenses and repatriation.

Insure yourself against theft of personal items and loss of passport and money.

Certain sporting activities may necessitate paying an additional insurance premium – always read the small print to make sure that you are adequately covered for any accidents.

Practical Tips

Business Hours

Business hours are generally 9am to 5pm, with a lunch break between noon and 1pm. State banks are usually open from 8.30am until 4.30pm.

Taxes & Tipping

Restaurants and hotels add 13 percent tax to the bill. Hotels also charge a 3 percent tourism tax on room charges and restaurants add a 10 percent service charge.

Hotel bellboys should be tipped. In restaurants tipping is not expected.

Media

Radio

Radio stations in English include 107.5 FM , which plays classic rock and has news and other information in English, and Radio Dos (99.5 FM), a Spanish-language station that plays British pop and rock classics, has a morning show in English and news in English, every other hour.

Television

There are more than 50 cable TV channels listed in the local TV guide; more are available. Programming includes approximately 30 channels in English, one in German, one in French, and one in Chinese. There are also programs in Hindi, Japanese, and Tagalog, as well as selections from many Latin American countries.

Newspapers & magazines

Available in English, Spanish, and other languages, at bookstores, supermarkets, newsstands, and hotel outlets.

Weekly English-language publications include:
The Tico Times (tel: 258 1558 www.ticotimes.net), published on Friday. Widely available. For the week's news in Costa Rica, up-to-date listings of what's happening, and where.

An annual *Exploring Costa Rica* guidebook gives an overview of the country.
Costa Rica Outdoors (tel: 282 6743 www.costaricaoutdoors.com). Bimonthly magazine featuring fishing, birding and Tico Culture. Daily Spanish-language newspapers include: *La Nación*, *La Prensa Libre*, *La República*, and *Al Día*.

Telecommunications

Costa Rica has one of the best telecommunications systems in Central America. Fax machines are popular, with public access from most post offices around the country. E-mail is easily sent and received at a number of Internet cafés around the country, ranging from US$1–$5 per hour. Remote areas that use satellite connections charge much higher rates.

For written telecommunications contact:
Radiográfica Costarricense, S.A. (RACSA), Ave 5, Calle 1, tel: 287 0087, www.racsa.co.cr. Services include telegraph, telex, fax and e-mail.

Making telephone calls

Most telephones work with telephone cards, which can be bought at many small shops or supermarkets.

Ten or 20 colón coins, and the public phones that use them, are being phased out but can still be found. Place the coin(s) in the slot on top of the phone, then dial the number; the coin will drop down when the connection has been made. Extra coins placed in the slot will fall automatically, only as needed.

International calls

See the telephone white pages under *Lista de países por zonas de códigos* MIDA for the codes for various countries. International phone cards are available at various locations. If you do not have access to a telephone, international calls can be made from Radiográfica (Calle 1, Ave 5) or Telecomunicaciones Internacionales (Ave 2, Calles 1 & 3).

Tourist Offices

Costa Rican Tourism Institute (ICT), open 8am–4pm, staffed by bilingual operators, tel: 1-800 343 6332 (from the US) or 506-223 1733 (from the UK), fax: 223 5452. www.visitcostarica.com
Don't miss the ICT office in the Gold Musem on the pedestrian walkway (tel: 222 1090) open Mon–Fri 8am–5pm; good information and maps. Also convenient is the desk at the Costa Rica post office (tel: 258 8762), open 8am–4pm.
National Parks Information, tel: 257 2239, fax: 222 4732, e-mail fpn_cr@racsa.co.cr. Fundación de Parques Nacionales; extensive information on all national parks.
Corcovado Park Administration, office in Puerto Jiménez, tel: 735 5036.
Santa Rosa National Park Headquarters, tel: 666 5051.
Ostional Wildlife Refuge: locals have formed an association. Call 682 0470 for information on accommodation and turtle activity.
Curú Wildlife Reserve, call ahead for information about staying in a rustic beach cabin on the privately owned reserve. Contact the Schutt family, tel: 710 8236/641 0014, e-mail: refugiocuru@yahoo.com.

Medical Services

Costa Rica has an excellent health care system, much less expensive than in the US. Many doctors are trained in the US or Europe and speak English, especially those at private clinics.

Useful Numbers

Local collect calls: 110
Information: 113
International information: 124
Operator assistance
(international calls): 116
Airport information: 437 2626
Tourist information: 222 1090
Rate of exchange: 243 4143
Time: 112
Fire, police, ambulance: 911
National Parks: 192

Public medical centers
Hospital Dr Calderón Guardia
Tel: 257 7922.
Hospital de los Niños
Tel: 222 0122 (for children).
Hospital México
Tel: 232 6122.
Hospital San Juan de Díos
Tel: 257 6282.

Private medical centers
Clínica Americana
Tel: 222 1010.
Clínica Bíblica
Tel: 257 5252.
Clínica Católica
Tel: 283 6616.
Clínic Santa Rita
Tel: 221 6433
Fax: 225 1248.
Specializes in maternity and
gynecology.
Hospital San José Cima
Tel: 208 1000
Fax: 208 1001.
Hospital Cristiano Jerusalem
Tel: 216 9191.

Plastic surgery
Plastic surgery is a big business in
Costa Rica, with people coming
from North America and Europe for
reconstructive and cosmetic
procedures, which often cost less
than half of US prices. Consult *The
Tico Times* for ads placed by
English-speaking plastic surgeons.
   There are lots of useful websites
to research cosmetic surgery
including:
www.healthcostarica.com
www.plasticsurgeryincostarica.com
www.villaplenitud.com
You can also contact the Costa

Rican Plastic Surgery Association,
Silvia Quiros, tel: 831 1024, e-mail
sqdr@hotmail.com.

Dentists
Costa Rican dentists provide
competent and inexpensive
cosmetic as well as general
dentistry.
A new emergency hotline (tel: 800-
336 8478) puts you in touch with
English-speaking dentists.
The *Tico Times* contains ads placed
by English-speaking dentists.

Credit card calls
Visa, MasterCard, Diners Club, and
American Express are handled by
local credit card firm **Credomatic**,
tel: 295 9000.
   Access numbers for international
credit card calls are:
AT&T: 0-8000-114114
MCI: 0-8000-122222
Sprint: 0-8000-130123
Canadian cards: 0-8000-151161
British Telecom: 0-800-0441044

Postal Services

Airmail between the US or
Europe and Costa Rica should
take about five days, but a wait of
two or more weeks is not
uncommon. The Central post
office is located at Calle 2, Av 1–3,
tel: 223 9766. Mail can be
received there in the general
delivery section *(Lista de Correos)*.
Outgoing mail should be posted at
either a hotel desk or a post office.
It is usually difficult, time-
consuming, and expensive to
receive packages in the mail.
Outrageous duties are sometimes
applied and you can spend
days trying to deal with numerous
officials. A receipt showing a
low value may help if included
with the package. There are
agents *(agencias de aduana)*
listed in the phone book who

Emergencies

For emergencies requiring police,
fire, and ambulance (bilingual
operator), tel: **911**

will handle the hassles of customs
clearances for a fee.
Couriers: there are many
international courier services. Some
of the most popular include: FedEx,
DHL, UPS and TNT Expresso Mundial.
Consult the *Yellow Pages* for
numbers.
Aero Casillas
Tel: 208 4848
Fax: 208 4872
www.aerocasillas.com
Central offices are at Trilogia
Building 3, across from PriceSmart
in Escazú, is a mailing service that
uses a Miami address to send and
receive mail for a monthly fee. You
are billed for US postage according
to weight of packages received, and
have the benefit of reliable and
timely service. Has seven counters
around the country.

Security and Crime

Theft is a growing problem in Costa
Rica. Pickpocketing, chain and
watch snatching, backpack
grabbing, and other kinds of theft
are becoming more common,
especially in downtown San José. It
is, for the most part, non-violent,
snatch-and-run thievery. Do not
become paranoid and frightened,
but do be vigilant.
● Do not take valuables with you
when you walk on the streets of
San José. Carry only as much cash
as you will need. Leave your
backpack, passport, jewelry,
cameras, watches, and even
sunglasses at your hotel. Keep an
eye on wallets and shoulder bags. If
you buy valuable items, make your
return trip by taxi.
● While walking on the street, be
aware of who is around you, and act
confidently.
● When driving through the city by
car, keep your windows rolled up
high enough that no-one can reach
inside.
● Avoid the streets at night.
● Avoid walking in isolated areas.
● Be especially watchful in the
following areas: from Plaza de la
Democracia to the San Juan de
Díos Hospital; near the Coca Cola
bus terminal; the Plaza de la

Consulates

Canada
Oficentro La Sabana, Building 5
San José
Tel: 242 4400
Fax: 242 4410
www.sanjose.gc.ca
UK
11th Floor
Edificio Centro Colón
San José
Tel: 258 2025
Fax: 233 9938
www.embajadabritanica.com
US
Ca 120, Av 0
Pavas
San José
Tel: 220 3939/220 3127
Fax: 220 2305
www.usembassy.or.cr

Cultura; Parque Central; Av 4 and
Av Central; and Ca 12 from Av 10
to Av 5.
● Thefts from rental cars, which
bear license plates identifying them
as such, are common in all parts of
the country. Do not leave anything
unattended in your car. Do not
assume items in a locked trunk are
safe: they are not. Whenever
possible, park in a guarded area.
● Do not leave things unattended
on the beach. This includes towels,
clothing, tents, and camping gear.

Getting Around

Finding Your Way

San José uses a grid system for its
streets. North–south-running
streets are *calles*, east–west-
running streets are *avenidas*.
Avenida Central (Av Ctl) divides the
city north and south; it becomes
Paseo Colón west of Hospital San
Juan de Díos. Calle Central (Ca Ctl)
divides San José east and west.
The southern avenues and western
streets are numbered evenly. The
northern avenues and eastern
streets have odd numbers.
　Abbreviations used for
addresses: Av = avenida,
Ca = Calle, Ctl = central, Apto or
Apdo = apartado (post office box,
for mailing addresses). When an
address is given using the street
and avenues, the first part is the
street or avenue on which the
building is located, and the second
part of the address indicates the
streets or avenues the building is
between. For example: the location
of the Metropolitan Cathedral is Ca
Ctl, Av 2–4. That is, the Cathedral is
on Calle Central between Avenidas
2 and 4. *(See San José city map,
page 130.)*
　For the most part, there are no
addresses nor are there street
names in Costa Rica. Although
downtown San José has numbered
avenues and streets, Costa Ricans
do not refer to them. Homes and
buildings are not numbered. Usually
an address is given as the distance
in meters *(metros)* north, east,
south, or west from a known
landmark. When it comes to
walking, remember that cars have
the right of way, not pedestrians, so
look twice before crossing the
street.

By Air

Domestic flights *(vuelos locales)*
are fairly inexpensive and can
provide a comfortable alternative to
many hours on bad roads.
SANSA
Tel: 221 9414
Fax: 255 2176.
www.flysansa.com
Offers service to Coto 47, Golfito,
Puerto Jimenéz, Palmar Sur,
Tortuguero, Barra del Colorado,
Nosara, Sámara, Tamarindo, Punta
Islita, Quepos, Tambor, Liberia, and
Drake Bay. Credit card payment for
phone reservations must be
confirmed by fax. If you have not
paid for your flight, your seat will be
sold as the flight fills up. Extra
charge for surf boards.
Natureair
Tel: 220 3054
Fax: 220 0413.
www.natureair.com.
Flies to Liberia, Tamarindo, Nosara,
Carrillo, Tambor, Quepos, Palmar
Sur, Golfito, Puerto Jiménez, Barra
del Colorado, Limón, Drake Bay,
Carate, Punta Islita, Tortuguero, and
Granada, Nicaragua. Surf boards
accepted if there is space available,
with an extra charge. Slightly more
expensive than SANSA but worth it.
Aerotaxi Alfa Romeo
Tel/fax: 735 5178
Air taxi from Puerto Jiménez into
Serena Ranger Station in Corcovado
National Park.
Paradise Air
Tel: 296 3600
Fax: 296 1429.
e-mail: paradiseair@racsa.co.cr
Pavas Airport. Charter flights and
flights to other North, Central, and
South American destinations.

Airports

Juan Santamaría (international
flights), tel: 443 2622.
Daniel Oduber, Liberia
(international flights), tel: 668
1010.
Tobias Bolaños, **Pavas** (domestic
flights), tel: 232 2820.
Limón (private flights only),
tel: 758 1379.

Flying Crocodile
Tel: 656 8048
Fax: 656 8049
E-mail: flycroco@racsa.co.cr
www.flying-corcodiles.com
Operates from Crocodile Lodge in Sámara. Scenic flights in an ultralight plane over sea, beaches, and tropical forests. Lessons on how to fly ultralights.
Skyline Ultra-Flight
Tel: 743 8036
Fax: 743 8037
www.flyultralight.com
Individual flights around southern Pacific and Sierpe; flying lessons.

By Bus

You can go virtually anywhere by bus in Costa Rica; it is the way most Ticos travel. Drivers take great pride in their vehicles. The main bus stop in the center of San José is the "Coca Cola" terminal, located near a former bottling plant at Ca 16, Av 1–3. Departure places and times may change. The Costa Rican Tourist Institute (ICT) office located below the Plaza de la Cultura has a list of bus companies' names and telephone numbers, tel: 222 1090. Or call INFOtour, tel: 223 4481.

By Taxi

Taxis are widely used and inexpensive. All should have operational meters (marías); be sure the drivers use them. If not, negotiate before getting in. If you are greatly overcharged, write down the driver's name and license number, and call the taxi company number marked on the outside of the cab, or tell the driver to find a policeman. Overcharges can be taken to the Transportation Department.

Arrangements can be made to take trips by taxi to places outside San José. Beware – taxi drivers who are parked in front of major hotels will always charge more. Taxis are red and have a "Taxi" sign on the roof of the car. If they are not red and have no numbered yellow triangle on the door, then they are pirate taxis, or *piratas,* and are unlicensed.

Taxi Companies
CGT, tel: 254 6667.
Coopetaxi, tel: 235 9966.
Coopetico, tel: 224 7979.
Coopeirazu, tel: 254 3211.
Coopeguaria, tel: 226 1366.
San José Taxis, tel: 221 3434
Taxis Aeropuerto, tel: 443 9333.
Taxis Unidos, tel: 221 6865.

By Ferry

Peninsula de Nicoya
de Coonatramar R.L.
Tel: 661 1069,
fax: 661 2197
www.coonatramar.com.
Puntarenas to Playa Naranjo
Departs 6am, 10am, 2.20pm, and 7pm.
Playa Naranjo to Puntarenas
Departs 7.30am, 12.30pm, 5pm, and 9pm.
Puntarenas to Paquera
Departs 4.30am, 8.30am, 12.30pm, and 5.30pm.

Driving: A Survival Guide

Four-wheel drive (doble tracción) is recommended for many areas as the roads outside the Central Valley, especially during the rainy season, are muddy and rutted. Chains work well in the mud; try letting some air out of your tires, to increase traction, if the car is stuck.
Licenses: operating a motor vehicle without a license is a serious violation of Costa Rican law and invalidates any insurance carried on the vehicle. A valid driver's license from another country can be used for three months. Always carry your passport (photocopies, including that of your entry stamp, usually suffice).
Import: foreign vehicles brought into Costa Rica for a period over 6 months must pay a large import tax. If you enter with a vehicle, you will have to leave with it or show papers proving you have sold it.

Driving habits: drivers weave all over the road to avoid the many ruts and holes, called *huecos.* Two headlight blinks usually indicate the other driver is giving you the right of way (especially when you are making a left turn); on the highway two headlight blinks may mean that the police are ahead. Radar is often used. If waved over by the police, don't try to get away. They will radio ahead to have you stopped.
Accidents: Costa Rica has a high accident and death rate. Always drive defensively. Don't drive an uninsured vehicle. The law requires motorists to carry a set of reflecting triangles. If you are in an accident, do not move your car until the police and INS, the government insurance agency, arrive. Give no statements, but take witnesses' names.
Parking: be careful not to park illegally. A yellow curb means no stopping. Even if you are in the car, police may prevent you from leaving and call a tow truck (grúa). You can ride in the car to the yard, where you will be required to pay the towing charges. It is better to park in one of the inexpensive parking lots (parqueos). This will reduce the chance of theft.
Corruption: unfortunately, there are corrupt police who target foreign drivers for the purpose of extracting some colones. You may be stopped for no apparent reason. Have all necessary automobile documents in the car and be polite. It is illegal for the police to demand payment on the spot. If you are badly treated, or if the policeman solicits a bribe or asks that you pay the fine immediately, ask for the ticket ("Deme el parte"), then ask for the officer's identification. Write it down, and report to the Dirección de Tránsito as soon as possible.

Paquera to Puntarenas
Departs 6.30am, 10.30am, 3pm, and 8.30pm.

By Bicycle

Mountain bikes are a good way to see Costa Rica's back country, especially on the lightly traveled dirt roads which crisscross the rural areas. Bicycle riding can be dangerous on the roads as they have no shoulders. Check with the consulate about import taxes. Consider installing KEVLAR inner tube protectors (such as Mr Tuffy). Bring a good lock. Check with your airline about shipping.

By Car

Car rental
Renting a car makes sense for trips outside San José. Reserve a car well in advance and get written confirmation. Prepayment is advised, especially during high season. Rates generally start around US$60 per day, including insurance. Four-wheel drive vehicles start around US$80 per day. Renting without a credit card usually involves a large deposit. When reserving four-wheel drive vehicles, find out what kind of vehicle you are getting. **Elegante** is one of the few companies that provides non-deductible insurance, as an option. All other insurance is deductible for the first US$750–$1,000. The following agencies all accept American Express, MasterCard, and Visa. **Europcar** (formerly Prego) is recommended. Most agencies insist that the driver is over 21 years of age, they hold a valid tourist card or passport and driver's license, and have a valid credit card for a deposit (not cash).
Alamo Rent a Car, Ca 11–13, Av 18, tel: 233 7733; US toll-free: 1 800-570 0671; Costa Rica toll-free: 800-232 7368; fax: 290 0431 www.alamocostarica.com.
Budget, Paseo Colón, tel: 223 3284; fax: 255 4966, www.budget.co.cr.

Discovery, tel: 293 2865/293 2866; fax: 293 2932.
Dollar, Paseo Colón, Ca 34/36, tel: 257 0671; www.dollarcostarica.com.
Economy: Sabana Norte, Tel: 231 5410, fax: 232 7041, www.economyrentacar.com.
Elegante, 5 km (3 miles) south of Liberia airport, tel: 668 1054; toll-free from US: 1-800-582 7432; toll-free from Canada 1 800-283 1324; www.eleganterentacar.com. Also office in Tamarindo (tel: 653 0015.
National, La Uruca, shares building with Alamo head office. tel: 290 8787; fax: 290 0431; reservations: 800-CAR RENT; e-mail: reservations@natcar.com; www.alamocostarica.com. Bilingual chauffeurs available.
Europcar, Paseo Colón, Ca 36–38, tel: 257 1158; fax: 255 4492; www.europcar.co.cr.
Toyota, Ca 30–32, Paseo Colón, tel: 258 5797, fax: 221 2688; www.toyotarent.com.

Private tour drivers
An alternative is to hire a knowledgeable bilingual driver, experienced with Costa Rican roads. Ask at your hotel or consult *The Tico Times*.

Where to Stay

The airport ICT desk can help if you arrive without advance hotel reservations, but only if you arrive between 9am and 5pm. Downtown San José is very noisy and polluted, so you may well prefer to stay out of the center. Escazú, Santa Ana, Alajuela, Heredia, and other Central Valley towns are less expensive, more enjoyable, and still give a good taste of Costa Rican life.

Reservations made, but not paid for, especially during high season, may not be held, especially near the beaches and Monteverde. Discounts may be given for stays of more than one night. Ask at your hotel about green (wet) season discounts.

The Tourist Institute has a system of classifications for lodging based on size and facility; however, there is a wide range of popular names used unofficially:
Apartotel Apartments with cooking facilities and living area in a hotel-style complex. Weekly and monthly rates.
Cabina Usually a one-room cabin with a shower and bath, often close to the beach in coastal resorts. *Cabinas* vary widely in quality and price.
Bed & Breakfast Price and quality vary widely, from a modest room in someone's own house to elegant guest houses all to yourself with pools and tennis courts.
Lodge Popular in more remote areas, usually near parks or natural attractions. Price usually includes meals.
Villa or Chalet Often indistinguishable from a hotel.
Inn Often a B&B, but with more extensive amenities.
Resort Usually a luxurious, self-contained hotel complex.

Hotel Anything with more than 10 rooms.
Hostel In Costa Rica there is a small youth hostel system. Prices vary.
Albergue/Pensión Modest, small hotels.

CENTRAL VALLEY

Expensive
Casa Turire
Turrialba
Tel: 531 1111/531 2244
Fax: 531 1075
E-mail: turire@racsa.co.cr
www.hotelcasaturire.com
Luxurious plantation-style hotel on the grounds of a sugar cane, coffee and macadamia nut plantation. Spring-fed swimming pool.
Finca Rosa Blanca Country Inn
Near Heredía
Tel: 269 9392
Fax: 269 9555
E-mail: info@fincarosablanca.com
www.finca-rblanca.co.cr
A lovely, small hotel in the foothills of Heredia.
Hotel Alta
Santa Ana
Tel: 282 4160
Fax: 282 4162
www.thealtahotel.com
Distinctive luxury hotel with pool.
Hotel & Villas La Condesa
San Rafael de Heredia
Tel: 267 6001
Fax: 267 6200
E-mail:
reservation@hotellacondesa.com
www.hotellacondesa.com
Mountain hotel with luxury rooms, conference center, pool, good restaurants; hiking and horseback riding trails.
Hotel Chalet Tirol
Heredia
Tel: 267 6228
Fax: 267 6373
E-mail: tirolcr@racsa.co.cr
Tyrolean-style A-frame cottages in the cloud forest above Heredia, bordering a National Park.
Hotel Grano de Oro
Ca 30, Av 2–4

San José
Tel: 255 3322
Fax: 221 2782
www.hotelgranodeoro.com
Elegant, restored mansion in a quiet area. Excellent restaurant.
Hotel and Spa Xandari
Alajuela
Tel: 443 2020
Fax: 442 4847
www.xandari.com
Exclusive oasis, fantastic views, full spa, beautiful grounds.
Poás Volcano Lodge
Varablanca, Heredia
Tel: 482 2194
Fax: 482 2513
www.poasvolcanolodge.com
Fireplaces, hot bathtubs, cozy rooms, and mountain views; birdwatching, hiking, horseback riding.
Vista del Valle Plantation Inn
Grecia
Tel: 450 0800
Fax: 451 1165
www.vistadelvalle.com
Coffee/orange plantation, with botanical garden, wonderful views.

Moderate
Hotel II Millenium
Alajuela
Tel: 430 5050
Fax: 441 2365
E-mail: bbmillenium@racsa.co.cr
www.bbmilleniumcr.com
Bed and breakfast, 1 km (⅔ mile) from Juan Santamaría International Airport and close to the bus stop. English-speaking owner, well-run and friendly atmosphere. Monthly rates on request.
Hotel Bougainvillea
Santo Domingo de Heredia
Tel: 244 1414
Fax: 244 1313
E-mail: info@bougainvillea.co.cr
This is a perfect setting for nature lovers who like tranquility. 5 hectares (12 acres) of tropical gardens with reading area, heated pool, sauna, and lit tennis courts. Eighty tastefully decorated rooms.
La Providencia Ecological Reserve
Poás
Tel/fax: 232 2498
Pleasant, rustic *cabinas* on a former dairy farm located near the

top of Poás Volcano. Rates include breakfast.
Volcán Turrialba Lodge
20 km (12½ miles) above Turrialba
Tel: 273 4335
Fax: 273 0703
www.volcanturrialbalodge.com
Cabins with wood stoves; lofty setting; horseback rides and hiking to extinct crater.

Budget
Albergue El Marañon
Ciudad Colón
San José
Tel: 249 1271
Fax: 249 1761
E-mail: cultourica@racsa.co.cr
www.cultourica.com
A typical country house in the small town of La Trinidad. There is a tropical garden with fruit trees and butterflies. The restaurant serves local and vegetarian dishes.
B & B Cinco Hormigas Rojas
Ca 15 Av 9–11bis
San José
Tel: 255 3412
Tel/fax: 257 8581
E-mail:
cincohormigasrojas@hotmail.com
Funky, verdant hideaway owned by artist.
Casa Ridgeway
Av 6 bis, Ca 15,
San José
Tel: 233 6168
fax: 233 6168
e-mail: friends@racsa.co.cr
Small *pensión* managed by the Society of Friends (Quakers). A pleasant place to stay. Use of kitchen and laundry.
Hostal Toruma
Av Central, Ca 29/31,
San José
Tel: 234 8186
Fax: 224 4085
E-mail: recajhi@racsa.co.cr
www.hicr.org
Costa Rica Youth Hostel Network headquarters in a mansion near downtown. Shared baths, hot water, Internet service. Includes breakfast. Use of kitchen.
Hotel Aranjuez
Ca 19, Av 11–13
San José

Tel: 256 1825
Fax: 223 3528
www.hotelaranjuez.com
A labyrinth-like historic building in older part of town.

Turrialtico
Turrialba
Tel: 538 1111
www.turrialtico.com
Charming. Rooms above the restaurant have private baths and heated water. Hilltop location. Beautiful views.

CENTRAL PACIFIC

Expensive

Best Western Jaco Beach
Tel: 643 1000
Fax: 643 3246
www.bestwesterncostarica.com
Beachfront property with 125 rooms and a wide range of sports facilities.

Heliconia Hotel
Monteverde
Tel: 645 5109
Fax: 645 5007
www.hotelheliconia.com
Southern European atmosphere.

Hotel Amapola
Jacó
Tel: 643 2255/3668
www.barcelo.com
Close to the beach; 53 rooms, pool.

Hotel Karahe
Manuel Antonio
Tel: 777 0170
Fax: 777 1075
E-mail: karahe@racsa.co.cr
www.harahe.com
Nine air-conditioned bungalows surrounded by 600 hectares (1,500 acres) of grounds. Swimming pool, restaurant. Outdoor pursuits.

Hotel Punta Leona
Punta Leona
Tel: 231 3131
Toll free: 800-231 3131
Fax: 232 0791
www.hotelpuntaleona.com
Resort with access to good beaches. Restaurant, three pools. Kitchens available.

Hotel Villa Lapas
Near Carara National Park
Tel: 637 0232
Fax; 222 3450

Price Categories

Price categories are for double occupancy per night without breakfast:
Expensive: US$70 and up
Moderate: US$40–70
Budget: US$40 and under

www.villalapas.com
All-inclusive, comfortable hotel; pool, mini-golf, suspension-bridge hike, canopy tour.

La Mariposa
Manuel Antonio
Tel: 777 0355
Fax: 777 0050
www.lamariposa.com
The area's first hotel, beautiful view, excellent staff; recommended.

Sapo Dorado
Monteverde
Tel/fax: 645 5010
E-mail: elsapo@racsa.co.cr
www.sapodorado.com
Nice *cabinas* with fireplaces.

Sí Como No
Manuel Antonio
Tel: 777 0777
Fax: 777 1093
www.sicomono.com
Romantic rainforest setting, movie theater, two restaurants; stylish.

Tango Mar Beach and Golf Resort
Tel: 683 0001
Fax: 683 0003
www.tangomar.com
Resort on Playa Quizales with thatched-roof cabins. Two restaurants. Kitchens available. Tennis, diving, seaside golf course.

Villa Caletas
Near Jacó
Tel: 637 0606
Fax: 637 0404
www.hotelvillacaletas.com
A luxurious French colonial fantasy retreat on a mountaintop overlooking the Pacific. Lovely pool. Amphitheatre with regular cultural performances.

Villas Nicolás
Manuel Antonio
Tel: 777 0481
Fax: 777 0451
www.villasnicolas.com
Terraces with beautiful views.

Moderate

Arco Iris Lodge
Monteverde
Tel: 645 5067
Fax: 645 5022
www.arcoirislodge.com
Small lodge near Monteverde cloud forest. Rooms with hot water and private bathrooms. Great breakfast buffet. Laundry. Tours offered.

Belmar
Monteverde
Tel: 645 5201
Fax: 645 5135
E-mail: belmar@racsa.co.cr
www.hotelbelmar.com
Chalet style and homey. Views.

El Bosque
Monteverde
Tel: 645 5221
Fax: 645 5129
Cabinas and campsites with toilets and hot water.

El Establo
Monteverde
Tel: 645 5110
Fax: 645 5041
www.hotelelestablo.com
Comfortable. Horseback riding.

El Mono Azul
Near Manuel Antonio
Tel: 777 1548
www.monoazul.com
This popular 9-room hotel is friendly and clean and has a Kids Saving The Rainforest souvenir shop.

Hotel Amor de Mar
Montezuma
Tel/fax: 642 0262
www.amordemar.com
Close to Montezuma; located on a rocky point overlooking the Pacific.

Hotel Tioga
Puntarenas
Tel/fax: 661 0271
www.hoteltiogo.com
Garden, casino, and restaurant.

Budget

Cabinas Doña Alicia
Quepos
Tel: 777 0419
Clean and friendly. Private bathrooms, cold water, and ceiling fans.

Cabinas Las Olas
Playa Hermosa (near Jacó)
Tel/fax: 643 3687

Price Categories

Price categories are for double occupancy per night without breakfast:
Expensive: US$70 and up
Moderate: US$40–70
Budget: US$40 and under

www.cabinaslasolas.com
Rooms have private baths, heated water, ceiling fans, and kitchens. Pool. Friendly surfers' hang-out.
Hotel Ancia de Oro
Cabuya de Cobano
Tel/fax: 642 0369
Close to the National Reserve. Seven rooms with bathroom and hot water. No credit cards.
Hotel Ceciliano
Quepos
Tel/Fax: 777 0192
Well kept and pleasant. Rooms with shared/private bathrooms and ceiling fans.
La Felicidad Country Inn
Esterillos Beach
Tel/fax: 778 8123
www.lafelicidad.com
Nice *cabinas* and rooms. Pool. Tours offered.
Hotel Moctezuma
Montezuma
Tel/fax: 642 0058
Overlooks the beach. Shared bathrooms, ceiling fans. Restaurant downstairs.
Nature's Beachfront Aparthotel
Manuel Antonio
Tel: 777 1473
Fax: 777 1475
www.maqbeach.com/natures.html
Studio apartments with kitchens; on the beach.

GUANACASTE

Expensive
Capitán Suizo
Tamarindo
Tel: 653 0075
Fax: 653 0292
E-mail: capsuizo@racsa.co.cr
www.hotelcapitansuizo.com
Elegant, well-designed rooms and bungalows in lush garden. Pool, beach.

Colores del Pacifico
Playa Potrero
Tel: 654 4769
Fax: 654 4976
www.coloresdelpacifico.com
Small, exquisitely decorated hotel overlooking Flamingo Bay; pool, yoga, aqua exercise sessions.
El Jardín del Edén
Tamarindo
Tel: 653 0137
Fax: 653 0111
Red-tile roofs and Mediterranean touches in the hills above the beach. French cuisine.
El Ocotal Resort
Playa Ocotal
Tel: 670 0321
Fax: 670 0083
www.ocotalresort.com
Elegant and secluded hotel overlooking the beach; two restaurants, tennis, pools, sportfishing.
Harbor Reef Lodge
Playa Guiones, Nosara
Tel: 682 0059
Fax: 682 0060
www.harborreef.com
Comfortable rooms in garden property, perfect for surfers with good breaks nearby; pool, restaurant with healthy food options.
Hotel Flor Blanca Resort
Santa Teresa
Tel: 640 0232
Fax: 640 0226
www.florblanca.com
Gorgeous, ultra-luxurious, and romantic. Private outdoor tub, shower, yoga, gourmet restaurant, and art studio.
Hotel Las Tortugas
Playa Grande
Tel/fax: 653 0458
E-mail: surfegg@cool.co.cr
Turtle-friendly hotel on a long, wide beautiful beach. Conservationist management. Good restaurant. Pool. Excellent surfing directly in front of hotel.
Hotel Sugar Beach
Sugar Beach
Tel: 654 4242
Fax: 654 4239
E-mail: sugarb@racsa.co.cr
www.sugar-beach.com
Great views, secluded beach,

oceanfront restaurant. Arranges fishing and snorkeling trips.
Villa Casa Blanca
Playa Ocotal
Tel/fax: 670 0448
E-mail: vcblanca@racsa.co.cr
www.hotelvillacasablanca.com
Romantic B&B. Sumptuous breakfasts.
Land Ho! at Hotel Villa Serena
Playa Junquillal
Tel: 658 8430
Fax: 658 8091
www.landho.com
Pleasant small hotel facing the beach. Meals included.
Punta Islita Hotel
Punta Islita
Tel: 661 3332
Fax: 661 4043
www.hotelpuntaislita.com
Wonderful ocean views, swimming pool, private porches with hammocks, luxury spa.
Sueño del Mar
Playa Langosta
Tel/fax: 653 0284
www.sueno-del-mar.com
Romantic, original rooms, great breakfast, cool gardens.
Sano Banano Beachfront Hotel
Montezuma
Tel: 642 0638
Fax: 642 0631
www.elbanano.com
Ten-minute beach walk north, romantic bungalows and suites, beautiful gardens. Also runs moderate B&B in town.
Villas Playa Sámara
Playa Sámara
Tel: 256 8288
Fax: 221 7222
E-mail: info@villasplayasamara.com
www.villasplayasamara.com
Rambling complex of villas on the beach. Many activities.

Moderate
Cabinas Zully Mar
Tamarindo
Tel: 653 0140
Fax: 653 0028
E-mail: zullymar@racsa.co.cr
www.tr506.com/zullymar
Clean rooms, friendly management. Rooms with hot water, refrigerator or air-conditioning are more expensive.

Hotel El Velero
Playa Hermosa
Tel/fax: 672 0036
www.costaricahotel.net
Graceful, breezy, white beachfront hotel. Sailboat.
Hotel Giada
Playa Sámara
Tel: 656 0132
Fax: 656 0131
www.hotelgiada.net
Colorful garden, artistic Italian touches.
Hotel Hibiscus
Playa Junquillal
Tel/fax: 658 8437
Very comfortable bungalows. Rate includes breakfast.
Hotel Las Brisas del Pacífico
Playa Sámara
Tel: 656 0076
E-mail: info@brisas.net
www.brisas.net
Pleasant and well designed. Pool fronts the beach. Good restaurant.
Lagarta Lodge Biological Reserve
Nosara
Tel: 682 0035
Fax: 682 0135
www.lagarta.com
Botanical trails, views of reserve and ocean, restaurant, Internet.
La Ensenada Lodge
Palo Verde
Tel: 289 6655
Fax: 289 5289
www.laensenada.net
Breezy *cabinas* overlooking the Gulf of Nicoya. Meals, horseback rides and boat tours included.
La Guacamaya Lodge
Playa Junquillal
Tel: 658 8431
Fax: 658 8164
www.guacamayalodge.com
Bungalows, pool, restaurant/bar, Swiss specialties.
Rincón de la Vieja Lodge
Rincón de la Vieja
Tel/fax 661 8198
www.rincondelaviejalodge.com
Rustic and comfortable. Restaurant. Tours to the park.

Budget
Cabinas Marielos
Tamarindo
Tel: 653 0141
Quiet garden; some air conditioning.

Hostel La Botella de Leche
Tamarindo
Tel: 653 0944
www.labotelladeleche.com
New dorm-style lodging, large communal kitchen, big-screen TV, surf racks, lockers.
Hotel Brasilito
Playa Brasilito
Tel: 654 4237
Fax: 654 4247
www.brasilito.com
Vintage, wooden hotel on beach; new restaurant.
Hotel Playa Hermosa
Playa Hermosa (Guanacaste)
Tel: 672 0046
Fax: 672 0019
On the beach, with a good seafood restaurant. *Cabinas* have private bathrooms, heated water, and ceiling fans or air conditioning.
Rinconcito Lodge
Rincón de la Vieja
Tel: 666 2764
rinconcito@racsa.co.ca
Thermal baths, waterfalls, restaurant, cold water.

THE NORTH

Expensive
Arenal Volcano Observatory Lodge
La Fortuna area
Tel: 290 7011
Fax: 290 8427
E-mail: info@arenal-observatory.co.cr
www.arenal-observatory.co.cr
Best site for volcano viewing. The more expensive rooms have views of the volcano. Lots of observation decks. Pool, jacuzzi, trails. Includes breakfast.
Hotel Occidental El Tucano
San Carlos area
Tel: 248 2323
Fax: 255 0919
Resort built around natural hot springs. Olympic-size swimming pool, jacuzzis.
Hotel Bosques de Chachagua
San Rafael de Peñas Blancos
Tel: 239 6464
Fax: 239 6868
www.chachaguarainforesthotel.com
Cabañas on a 150-hectare (380-acre) cattle and horse ranch. Trails, pool.

Hotel Tilajari Resort
Near Muelle
Tel: 291 1081
Fax: 291 4082
www.tilajari.com
Spacious rooms and acres of rolling lawns on the San Carlos River. Tennis, swimming, horses, pool.
La Garza
Platanar (overlooking the Platanar River)
Tel: 475 5222
Fax: 475 5015

Homestays

If you would like a better understanding of the people and culture of Costa Rica, try the **Home Stay Service**. It is designed to offer a cross-cultural experience to both visitors and Costa Ricans. Visitors are lodged in the guest room of a host family and participate in as much (or as little) of the family activities as they wish. Families have been chosen on the basis of the quality of their homes and their hospitality, and most speak English. Most are in the San José area, close to public transportation, and are quite inexpensive.

Visitors receive an information pack with their reservation, including data on Costa Rica, a map with directions to the host residence and an introduction to the host family. Airport and hotel pick-up service is available.

The best homestay agency is **Bells' Home Hospitality**, PO Box 1771–2050, San José, Costa Rica, tel: 225 4752, fax: 224 5884, www.homestay.thebells. org. Or, in the US, Department 1432, PO Box 25216, Miami, Florida 33102-5216.

Local families sometimes rent rooms at a price including meals and laundry. Check around the university and the bulletin board at the Costa Rican/North American Cultural Center, see the *Tico Times* or the local papers, or call the language schools.

National Parks

Name	Distance from San José	Highlights	Accommodation	Topography	Facilities
Volcán Arenal	128 km NW	Active volcano	None	Rainforest	Toilets, visitor center
Ballena	189 km SW	Diving and snorkeling	None	White sand, mangroves, reef	None
Barra Honda	137 km NW	Deep caves	Lodge, meals	Mixed forest	Toilets
Guanacaste	264 km NW	Howler monkeys	Lodge	Mixed forest	Biological station
Palo Verde	218 km NW	Waterbirds, monkeys	Lodge, meals	Dry forest, wetlands	Toilets, Biological station
Santa Rosa	288 km NW	Turtles, sandy beaches	Lodge, meals	Dry forest	Historical museum
Rincón de la Vieja	242 km NW	Active volcano, hot springs	Camping area	Mixed forest, savanna	Toilets
Las Baulas	286 km NW	Turtles, beach	None	Sandy beach, mangrove	None
Corcovado	329 km SW	Macaws, monkeys	Lodge, meals	Rainforest	Toilets
Manuel Antonio	182 km SW	Sandy beaches	None	Transitional forest	Visitor center, showers
Braulio Carrillo	20 km NE	Good hiking	Camping	Mixed forest	Museum, toilets
Cahuita	211 km SE	Coral reef, sloths	Camping area	Rainforest, coral reef	Toilets, showers
Volcán Irazú	54 km E	Active volcano	None	Páramo	Toilets
Volcán Poás	56 km NW	Volcano crater	None	Páramo	Museum, cafe
Tapantí	49 km SE	Good hiking, birding	Camping	Rainforest	Toilets, Exhibits
Tortuguero	189 km NE	Turtles, canals	None	Rainforest	Exhibits, toilets
Guayabo	85 km E	Archeological site	Camping area	Rainforest	Museum
Chirripó	151 km SE	Highest peak, good hiking	Lodge	Cloud forest, páramo	Toilets,
Isla del Coco	550 km SW of Cabo Blanco	Diving, hiking	Anchorage	Rainforest	None
La Amistad	259 km SE	Experienced hikers	Camping	Rainforest	Toilets, exhibits
Juan Castro Blanco	80 km NW	Active volcano	None	Mountain forest	None
Volcán Turrialba	40 km E	Hike to crater	Camping	Humid forest	Trails
Piedras Blancas	300 km SW	Biological diversity, borders Corcovado	None	Tropical rainforest	Trails, several lodges border park
Barbilla	200 km NE	Wildlife	Camping	Mixed forest	None
Tenorio	240 km N	Waterfalls	None	Tropical humid forest	Toilets
Carara	91 km SW	Turtles	None	Transitional forest	Visitor center

www.hotellagarza.com
Riverside *cabinas* on a large
working cattle and horse ranch.
Beautiful gardens. Horseback
riding, fishing.
Las Cabiñitas
La Fortuna
Tel: 479 9400
Fax: 479 9408
E-mail: cabinita@racsa.co.cr
www.cabanita.com
One of La Fortuna's nicest places
to stay. Comfortable, traditional tile-
roofed *cabinas*. Includes breakfast.
Rara Avis
Near Las Horquetas
Tel: 764 3131
Fax: 764 4187
www.raraavis.com
Three-hour tractor ride to arrive.
House, lodge, and cabin.
Tabacón Resort
Lake Arenal
Tel: 256 1500
Fax: 221 3075
www.tabacon.com
Luxury resort famous for hot
springs in landscaped gardens with
views of Arenal Volcano.
Villa Blanca
Near San Ramón
Tel: 461 0301
Fax: 461 0302
www.villablanca-costarica.com
Well-appointed *casitas* modeled
after colonial-era workers' homes.
Fireplaces, generous bathtubs.
Located adjacent to Los Angeles
Cloud Forest Reserve.
Villa Decary
Tel: 383 3012
Tel/fax: 694 4330
www.villadecary.com
Country inn, lake view, great
birding, no credit cards.

Moderate
La Catarata Lodge
La Fortuna area
Tel: 479 9522
Fax: 479 9168
catarata@racsa.co.cr
Pleasant modern cabins with
volcano views. Restaurant.
Lake Coter Eco-Lodge
Nuevo Arenal
Tel: 440 6768
Fax: 440 6725
www.ecolodgecostarica.com

Comfortable cabins with Lake
Arenal views, grand fireplace in
lodge; great hiking, horseback
riding, kayaking, and canopy tour.
La Ceiba Tree Lodge
Nuevo Arenal area
Tel/fax: 692 8050
ceibaldg@racsa.co.cr
Lovely bed and breakfast on a
hilltop with goats and an organic
garden. Trails; sailboat.
La Laguna del Lagarto
San Carlos area
Tel: 289 8163
Fax: 289 5295
www.adventure-
costarica.com/laguna-del-lagarto/
Remote lodge on a hill with views,
with comfortable rooms. Hiking,
horseback riding, boat trips on the
Río San Carlos.
La Quinta de Sarapiquí Country Inn
North of La Vírgen
Tel: 761 1300
Fax: 761 1395
www.laquintasarapiqui.com
Birding, reference library,
restaurant, insect/butterfly gallery.
Selva Verde Lodge
Near Puerto Viejo de Sarapiquí
Tel: 766 6800
Fax: 766 6011
www.selvaverde.com
Beautiful river lodge. Great
birdwatching, nature walks,
horseback riding. Meals are
included.

Budget
Eco Center La Finca Lodge
South of Puerto Viejo de Sarapiquí
Tel/fax: 476 0279
Two wooden country homes, each
with five rooms. The owners are
trying to breed macaws. Daily tours
with bilingual guides available.
Hotel Don Goyo
Ciudad Quesada
Tel: 460 1780
Fax: 460 6383
Pleasant modern hotel, in town.
Hotel Mi Lindo Sarapiquí
Tel/fax: 766 6074/6281
Small hotel close to the rainforest.
Clean rooms, TV and hot water.
Student discount.
Hotel Sierra Arenal
La Fortuna
Tel: 479 9751

Eight rooms, volcano view, camping
area, cable TV.
Rancho Leona
Puerto Viejo de Sarapiquí area
Tel: 841 5341
www.rancholeona.com
Basic lodging with shared bath, cold
water, pool, and sauna. Kayaking
and hiking. Friendly ambiance and
good food. Recommended.
Xiloe Lodge
Nuevo Arenal/Tilarán
Tel: 692 1101
Fax: 259 9882
piensos@racsa.co.cr
Cabinas with private bathrooms.
Hot water, refrigerators, some with
kitchens. Disco, restaurant.

THE CARIBBEAN

Expensive
Bungalows Cariblue
Tel: 750 0035
Tel/fax: 750 0057
www.cariblue.com
Award-winning hotel, bungalows on
stilts, gourmet restaurant.
Hotel Maribú Caribe
Limón area
Tel: 795 2543
Fax: 795 3541
Circular, thatched-roof *cabinas* on a
cliff, with beautiful views.
Restaurant, tours.
Mawamba Lodge
Tortuguero
Tel: 223 2421
Fax: 222 5463
www.mawamba.com
Pleasant *cabinas* and good meals.
Offers package deal including
meals and transportation from
San José.
Tortuga Lodge
Tortuguero
Tel: 257 0766
Fax: 257 1665

Price Categories

Price categories are for double occupancy per night without breakfast:
Expensive: US$70 and up
Moderate: US$40–70
Budget: US$40 and under

www.costaricaexpeditions.com
Pleasant lodge 2 km (1 mile) from the village. Package deal including meals and transportation from San José available. Fishing trips.
Villas del Caribe
Puerto Viejo
Tel: 233 2200
Fax: 221 2801
www.villasdelcaribe.com
Delightful two-story condominium-style units on a lovely white-sand beach. Kitchens.

Moderate

Almonds and Corals
Manzanillo
Tel: 272 2024
Fax: 272 2220
www.almondsandcorals.com
Furnished tents. Rates include three meals. Restaurant; nestled in rainforest.
Avarios del Caribe
Off coastal highway to Cahuita
Tel: 750 0775
Fax: 798 0374
Comfortable bed and breakfast and wildlife sanctuary on the Río Estrella. Canoe trips through miles of freshwater canals and lagoons. Good for watching birds and butterflies; sloth rescue center.
B & B El Encanto
Cahuita
Tel/fax: 755 0113
www.elencantobedandbreakfast.com
Bungalows, affordable house for six, Zen garden, yoga, homemade bread.
El Pizote Lodge
Puerto Viejo
Tel: 750 0088
Fax: 750 0226
www.pizotelodge.com
Wooden bungalows and rooms with pleasant grounds across the road from a black-sand beach. Trails.

Hotel Park
Av. 3, Ca. 2–3
Limón
Tel: 798 0555
Fax: 758 4364
irlixie@racsa.co.cr
Best option in town; ocean views, air conditioning and safe parking.

Budget

Cabinas Arrecife
Cahuita
Tel/fax: 755 0081
Diagonal to Restaurant Edith, with clean rooms and shared verandah with hammocks.
Cabinas Chimurri
Playa Negra
Tel/fax: 750 0119
www.greencoast.com/chimurribeach.html
Afro-Caribbean beach houses.
Cabinas Iguana
Cahuita
Tel: 755 0005
Fax: 755 0054
www.cabinas-iguana.com
Nice *cabinas* with kitchens. Ceiling fans, porches, hammocks.
Colibrí Paradise
Cahuita
Tel: 755 0263
Pleasantly designed and furnished, with private baths, heated water, and ceiling fans. Kitchens and hammocks.
Escape Caribeño
Puerto Viejo area
Tel/fax: 750 0103
www.escapecaribeno.com
Cabinas near Salsa Brava. Porches, communal cooking area, private bath, table fans.
Hotel Cocorí
Limón area
Tel/Fax: 795 2930
Rooms, spa, pool.

THE SOUTH

Expensive

Bosque del Cabo
Puerto Jiménez/Corcovado
Tel/fax: 735 5206
www.bosquedelcabo.com
Small, friendly inn where you can watch macaws. Meals included.

Cabinas La Ponderosa
Pavones
Tel: 824 4145
www.cabinaslaponderosa.com
All-inclusive comfortable cabins; surfing, hiking, bicycling.
Casa Corcovado Jungle Lodge
Corcovado
Tel: 256 8825
Fax: 256 7409
www.casacorcovado.com
Remote luxury, 69 hectare (170-acre) reserve, nature tours. On edge of Corcovado Park.
Drake Bay Wilderness Resort
Drake Bay
Tel/fax: 770 8012
Fax: 221 4948
www.drakebay.com
Cabins and tent/cabins on the beach. Guided explorations of the area. Meals included.
La Paloma Lodge
Drake Bay
Tel: 293 7502
Fax: 239 0954
E-mail: lapaloma@lapalomalodge.com
www.lapalomalodge.com
On a hillside, with sweeping views. Comfortable thatched-roof *cabinas* with private decks. Pool. Tours to Isla del Caño. Fishing trips. Meals included.
Lapa Ríos
Puerto Jiménez/ Corcovado
Tel: 735 5130
Fax: 735 5179
E-mail: laparios@racsa.co.cr
www.laparios.com
Luxurious thatched-roof bungalows built on the hillside of a large reserve. Meals included. Resident nature guides.
Las Esquinas Rainforest Lodge
Golfito area
Tel/fax: 775 0901
www.esquinaslodge.com
Rainforest jungle lodge with *cabinas*, pool, and large, comfortable common areas. Excursions and activities. Profits are used to finance projects in the nearby village of La Gamba.
Playa Nicuesa Rainforest Lodge
Golfo Dulce
Tel: 735 5237
www.nicuesalodge.com
New, palatial tree-house lodge;

secluded cabins. Accessible only by boat. Trails, tours, watersports.

Punta Marenco Lodge
Drake Bay
Tel: 234 1308
Fax: 234 1227
www.corcovadozone.com
Simple but comfortable grass-roofed cabins with Pacific views from hammocks on verandahs; meals included; miles of hiking trails in Rio Claro National Wildlife Refuge with naturalist guide.

Tiskita Jungle Lodge
Near Pavones
Tel: 296 8125
Fax: 296 8133
E-mail: info@tiskita-lodge.co.cr
www.tiskita-lodge.com
Rustic and comfortable *cabinas* with great ocean views and sea breezes. Over 100 varieties of tropical fruit trees attract many birds and monkeys. Trails and waterfalls. Meals included.

Moderate

Albergue Jinetes de Osa
Bahía Drake Bay
Tel: 826 9757/241 2906
Tel/fax: 236 5637
E-mail: crventur@costaricadiving.com
www.costaricadiving.com
On the beach. Original canopy tour of the rainforest. Includes meals.

Albergue de Montaña Tapantí
Cerro de la Muerte area
Tel: 231 3332
Tel/fax: 232 0436
Cozy, old-fashioned *cabinas* and good restaurant.

Cabinas Punta Dominical
Dominical
Tel: 787 0016
Fax: 787 0241
Pretty *cabinas* overlooking the ocean. Ocean breezes and tranquility.

Complejo Turístico Samoa del Sur
Golfito
Tel: 775 0233
Fax: 775 0573
www.samoadelsur.com
Air-conditioned rooms on the water, restaurant, craft and shell museum, yacht club.

Corcovado Lodge Tent Camp
Corcovado
Tel: 257 0766
Fax: 257 1665
www.costaricaexpeditions.com
Large tents on wooden platforms. Beautiful location on the beach. Meals included.

Delfín Amor EcoLodge
Drake Bay
Tel: 847 3131
www.divinedolphin.com
Pretty hillside cabins with dolphin-themed décor; all meals included; yoga, dolphin-watching, sea kayaking from beach at bottom of hill.

Hacienda Barú
North of Dominical
Tel: 787 0003
Fax: 787 0057
www.haciendabaru.com
Private refuge, 133 hectare (330 acres), restaurant, renowned eco-lodge.

Pacific Edge Cabins
Near Dominical
Tel: 381 4369
www.pacificedge.info
Stunning views, pool, comfortable cabins.

Savegre Hotel de Montaña
San Gerardo de Dota
Tel: 740 1029
Fax: 740 1027
www.savegre.co.cr
Remodled rooms in the cool mountains near Cerro de la Muerte. Spot quetzals and enjoy fresh trout. Set in 600 hectares (1482 acres); restaurant. Meals included.

Wilson Botanical Gardens
San Vito
Reservations: OTS
Tel: 773 4004/240 6696
Fax: 240 6783
www.ots.ac.cr
Bunk rooms and cabins in botanical gardens and reserve. Trails. Meals included. Discounts for Costa Rican residents, children, students, and researchers.

Budget

Albergue Mirador de Quetzales
Tel/fax: 381 8456
www.exploringcostarica.com/mirador/quetzales
High-altitude, rustic A-frame cabins with hot water; great hiking trails

and birdwatching for Resplendent Quetzal; breakfast and dinner included.

Cabinas Sol y Mar
Playa Zancudo
Tel: 776 0014
www.zancudo.com
Tranquil *cabinas*, private bathrooms, and fans. Friendly atmosphere.

Hotel Canto de Ballenas
Near Ojochal
Tel/fax: 743 8085
www.turismoruralcr.com
Wooden rooms, rural cooperative; flat paths – one room is wheelchair accessible.

Hotel El Ceibo
San Vito
Tel/fax: 773 3025
Pleasant accommodations with private bathrooms and heated water. Good restaurant. Attractive views.

Poor Man's Paradise
San Josecito
Tel/fax: 771 4582
www.mypoormansparadise.com
Book through Selva Mar. Equipped tents, including meals. The best deal near Drake; also more expensive cabins. Camping, restaurant, helpful owner.

Posada del Sol
Dominical
Tel: 787 0067
Fax: 787 0085
Comfortable, basic lodging.

Where to Eat

Eating Out

While Costa Rican cuisine may not rank among the world's greats, there are lots of very good things to eat all around the country. Refer to chapters on *Tico Cooking (see page 108)* and *Fruits of Costa Rica (see page 112)*.

Restaurants

SAN JOSÉ AND ENVIRONS

Expensive

Bakea (Mediterranean)
300 meters/yards north of Parque Morazán, Barrio Amón
Tel: 221 1051
New, upscale local favorite in restored mansion. Creative, well-executed gourmet fare.
Ile de France (French)
Hotel Le Bergerac, Ca 35, Los Yoses
Tel: 283 5812
Indoor and outdoor seating, good service, good intimate option.
Le Chandelier (French)
100 meters/yards east and 100 meters/yards south of ICE, Los Yoses
Tel: 225 3980
Elegant atmosphere in a restored mansion.
Le Monastère (French)
Escazú mountains
Tel: 289 4404
www.monastere-restaurant.com
View of the Central Valley and, with a bit of luck, the Golfo de Nicoya. Elegant atmosphere with cheerful bar in the basement with live shows Thurs–Sat.
Ram Luna (International and Costa Rican)
On the way to Tarbaca
Tel: 230 3060

Exceptional mountain views in clear weather. Dinner only Mon–Fri, weekends lunch too. Folkloric performances and buffet on Wed.
Tin Jo (Asian)
Ca 11, Av 6/8
Tel: 221 7605
Wide selection, vegetarian menu, creative Pan-Asian cuisine, classy ambiance. Long-time local favorite.

Moderate

Ave Fenix (Chinese)
San Pedro, 175 meters/yards west of the church
Tel: 225 3362
Delicious soups and sauces, delicate Chinese vegetables.
Café Mundo (Fusion)
Barrio Amon
Tel: 222 6190
New fusion cuisine in an attractive old house in this historic district.
Capriccio (Italian)
300 meters/yards south of Periféricos, Los Anonos, 150 meters/yards east of San Rafael de Escazú
Tel: 228 9332
Real Italian food. Exceptional pastas. Vegetarians will enjoy the extensive antipasto buffet.
Chango (International)
Escazú
Tel: 228 1173
Known for US-style ribs and steaks. Features sporting events on large-screen TV.
El Exótico Oriente (Indonesian and Thai)
25 meters/yards west of El Cruce, San Rafael de Escazú
Tel: 228 5980
Indonesian and Thai classics.
Grano de Oro (International)
Calle 30, Ave 2–4, Paseo Colón
Tel: 255 3322
Excellent, friendly service and good food served in the covered garden of an elegant, restored mansion.
Las Orquídeas (International and Costa Rican)
On the road to Guápiles
Tel: 268 8686
Fax: 268 8989
Large restaurant with views over the exotic garden, surrounded by the mists of the rainforest.

Los Adobes (Costa Rican)
San Antonio de Belén
Tel: 239 0957
Classic Costa Rican home-cooked food served in a 100-year-old adobe, and its pleasant, covered garden. Music on weekends. Casual.
Lubnán (Lebanese)
Paseo Colón (in front of Mercedes-Benz)
Tel: 257 6071
Sparse decor with a Middle Eastern flavor. Good food.
Machu Picchu (Peruvian)
Calle 32 Ave 1–3, 150 meters/yards north of Kentucky Fried Chicken, Paseo Colón
Tel: 222 7384
Casual, sometimes boisterous ambiance. Good food. Try a pisco sour and book a driver to get you home.
La Casa de Doña Lela (Costa Rican)
Road to Guápiles
Tel: 240 2228
Large portions, traditional food and good ambiance.
News Café (North American)
San José
Hotel Presidente
Tel: 222 3022
US-style sandwiches, meals, and desserts. Some tables overlook pedestrian walkway: good for people watching.
Olio (Mediterranean)
200 meters/yards north of Bagelmen's, Barrio Escalante
Tel: 281 0541
Upscale bohemian atmosphere, tapas, warm brick walls and stained-glass fixtures; popular with university crowd.
Ponte Vecchio (Italian)
Just east of Mall San Pedro
Tel: 283 1810
Award-winning food ("one of Central America's top 100") from a New York-Italian chef.

Price Guide

Prices are for dinner for two, including wine:
Expensive: US$50 plus
Moderate: US$25–50
Budget: US$25 or less

Taj Mahal (Indian)
1 km (⅔ mile) west of Centro
Comercial Paco, old road to Santa
Ana
Tel: 228 0980
The only Indian restaurant in the
country. Remodeled mansion with
indoor and outdoor seating. Will
spice up dishes on request.

Budget
Cafe Ruiseñor (International)
150 meters/yards west of Mall San
Pedro, Los Yoses
Tel: 225 2562
A casual place for lunch, dessert,
or a snack. Espresso and
cappuccino. Walls hung with
contemporary art.
Il Pomodoro (Italian)
Two blocks north of San Pedro
church, also in Escazú
Tel: 224 0966; delivery: 283 1010
Good pizzas (try the *panzanella*
which has cubes of mozzarella
cheese and fresh tomato).
La Criollito (Costa Rican)
Near INS, downtown San José.
Tel: 222 3232
Hearty local fare; breakfast
specialties.
Pane e Vino (Pizza/Italian)
Centro Comercial El Cruce, San
Rafael de Escazú
Tel: 289 7325
Vast menu of pizza and calzones.
Newer, larger sister restaurant in
San Pedro.
Princesa Marina (seafood)
On the north side of the Catholic
church in Barrio San José de
Alajuela (and in Curridabat,
Moravia y La Sabana).
Tel: 296 7667
Fresh fish and mixed rice served in
a casual atmosphere. Eat in or take
away.
Rosti Pollo (Nicaraguan-style
chicken roasted over coffee wood)
Several locations around town.
Casual, good and fast. Take out or
eat in.
Rincón Mexicano (Mexican)
Next to Gimnasio Fitzsimmon,
Sabana Sur.
Tel: 291 1744
Welcoming bakery with light
Mexican fare. Good option before or
after a walk in La Sabana Park.

Sale e Pepe (Italian)
San Rafael de Escazú, El Cruce
Tel: 289 5750
Great pizza.

For good, inexpensive food, also try
the neighborhoods around the
University of Costa Rica in San
Pedro or the National University in
Heredia, and the *sodas* (diners) in
the Central Market downtown San
José and Heredia. Best to go after
mealtime rush hours.

THE PACIFIC

Expensive
The Rico Tico (Costa Rican and
Mexican)
Si Como No Hotel,
Manuel Antonio
Tel: 777 0777
Casual outdoor dining surrounded
by jungle gardens and with ocean
view. Buffet breakfast. Fresh fish
and lobster.

Moderate
Los Faroles (Mexican)
In the town of Jacó Beach
Tel: 643 3167
Restaurant with bar area. Various
tacos feature among other dishes.
El Gran Escape (seafood)
Entrance to Quepos
Tel: 777 0395
Good value, good sushi, generous
portions, popular hangout.
Poseidon (international/fusion)
Hotel Poseidon
Downtown Jacó
Tel: 643 1642
Excellent, varied seafood menu;
open kitchen.
Vela (vegetarian)
Vela Bar/Hotel
Manuel Antonio
Tel: 777 0413
Wooden bungalow with palm roof.
Seafood, vegetarian, and Costa
Rican dishes. Fresh fruit juices.

Budget
Flor de Vida (international/
vegetarian)
Monteverde
Tel: 645 6081
Delicious homefries, desserts,

Boca Bars

Bocas (literally "mouths") are
Costa Rica's equivalent of
Spanish *tapas*. Just about every
bar has its version of savory
snacks to be served with drinks.
  Two of the best are:
Bar Mexico
Opposite corner from the Barrio
Mexico Church, tel: 221 8461.
Bar Los Parales
Curridabat, tel: 272 2241.
Famous for its variety of *bocas*.

excellent meal selection. Good
place to lounge when it rains.
La Yunta (seafood)
Puntarenas
Tel: 661 3216
Good option on ocean drive, breezy
verandah; classic surf and turf.
Mar Luna (seafood)
Manuel Antonio
Tel: 777 5107
On a hill. Simple but reasonable
seafood.

GUANACASTE

Expensive
Playa de Artistas (Mediterranean)
Montezuma
Tel: 642 0920
Arguably the country's most
romantic eatery. Dramatically rustic,
excellent food and service.
Puesta del Sol (Italian)
Junquillal
Tel: 658 8442
Four tables, intimate upscale Italian
home flavor. Fresh pasta and
authentic ingredients.

Moderate
Café de Paris (international)
Guiones Beach, Nosara
E-mail: info@cafedeparis.net
Fresh bread baked daily. French and
North American-style breakfasts.
Lunch and dinner choices include
pizza, paella, beef filet and fish.
Lazy Wave Food Company (seafood/
fusion)
Tamarindo
Tel: 653 0737
Creative, affordable, and fun.

Sol y Luna (Italian)
Hotel La Puerta del Sol
Playas del Coco
Tel: 670 0195
Alfresco dining, authentic flavor.

Budget
Coopetortillas (Costa Rican)
Santa Cruz
Women's cooperative, handmade
tortillas, traditional favorites.
El Dulce Momento (Italian)
Nicoya
Tel: 686 4585
Forty pizzas to choose from, housed
in a 1930s movie theater.
Homemade pasta, good value.
La Frontera
Peñas Blancas on the North Border
Tel: 679 9156
Fax: 679 9271
Country-house atmosphere. Unusual
and tasty Tico-style rice dishes. Next
to the immigration office.

Price Guide

Prices are for dinner for two:
Expensive: US$50 plus
Moderate: US$25–50
Budget: US$25 or less

THE NORTH

Moderate
Restaurant Colbert (French)
Varablanca
Tel: 482 2776
Fantastic food, decadent pastries.
Perfect stop when visiting Volcán
Poás or La Paz Waterfall Gardens.
El Mirador (Costa Rican)
On the road to Zarcero, Alajuela
Tel: 451 1959
E-mail: taf@arweb.com
Great wood-roasted cuisine.
Delicious cheese tortilla with sour
cream. Try the spicy potato dish
picadillo de papa.
Tramonte Pizza (Italian)
Nuevo Arenal
Tel: 694 2828
Wood-oven baked pizzas, pastas.

Budget
Toad Hall (natural foods)
Arenal Lake
Tel: 692 8020

Gorgeous lake views, natural juices,
fresh food. Quality Costa Rican art.
Restaurant Caballo Negro
(German/vegetarian)
3 km (2 miles) outside Nuevo Arenal
Tel: 694 4515
Schnitzels, sausages, and good
vegetarian food. Gallery includes
art by owner's daughters; proceeds
go to animal welfare projects.

THE CARIBBEAN

Expensive
La Pecora Nera (Italian)
Playa Cocles
Tel: 750 0490
Top Italian restaurant on the
Caribbean coast; good service,
fresh pasta, creative chef.

Moderate
Amimodo (Italian)
Puerto Viejo
Tel: 750 0257
Creative Italian-by-the-sea cuisine,
including specialties such as
lobster ravioli.
Cha Cha Cha (international)
Cahuita
Tel: 394 4153
Interesting Mediterranean and Thai
mix. Laid-back vibe, excellent service.
Kelly's Creek Restaurant (Spanish)
Cahuita
Tel: 755 0007
Convenient, airy restaurant
serving up delicious paella
and other traditional Spanish
favorites.

Budget
Elenas (Caribbean)
Chiquita Beach, Limón
Tel: 750 0265
Dancing, live music, and satellite
TV. One of the most popular places
on the way to Puerto Viejo.
Miss Edith's (Caribbean/
Costa Rican)
Cahuita
Tel: 755 0248
Local institution and local cuisine
worth the wait.
Soda Tamara (Caribbean)
Downtown Puerto Viejo
Tel: 750 0148
Delicious Caribbean dishes and

seafood. Small, friendly restaurant
that plays reggae.

Drinking Notes

There are several beers made
in Costa Rica: Imperial, Pilsen,
Rock Ice, Bavaria, and Heineken.
All are good, but none is
exceptional.
   Try Cafe Britt's extraordinary
coffee liqueur. You'll never again
even consider the likes of Kahlua.
   Guaro, the local sugar cane-
based firewater, is cheap and can
strip paint.

Bars
In San José try the following:
Café Loft, Av 11, Ca 3, tel: 221
2302. New York-style chic.
Cielo, Av 1, Ca 21, tel: 222 7419.
Funky upstairs lounge, good mix of
rock and alternative.
Henry's Beach Café and Grill, San
Rafael de Escazú, tel: 289 6250.
Good mix of locals and expatriates;
sophisticated crowd.
Jazz Café, next to the old Banco de
Costa Rica, tel: 253 8933. Best live
music venue, varied menu.
Raices, across from Mall San
Pedro, tel: 280 4964. Best roots
reggae around.
Calle de la Amargura (Street of
Bitterness), near the University of
Costa Rica, is lined with a variety of
spots, from cheap college drinking
holes to outdoor bar/restaurants.
Extremely popular.

Opening Times
From Monday to Saturday, most
bars open any time from 8.30am to
11am, and stay open until around
midnight or 2am. On Sunday, some
may close earlier, and others do not
bother to open at all. Friday and
Saturday nights are very busy, but
earlier in the week you may find
happy hours and other attractive
offers.

Legalities
You must be 18 years of age
to drink alcohol in Costa Rica.
Some bars may require you to
show some identification before
admitting you.

Culture

Art Galleries & Music

This is a continually changing scene. Check *The Tico Times* for a listing of shows and exhibitions in the Central Valley.

Dance

Costa Rica's modern dance scene is one of the best in Central America. The **National Dance Company** performs both classical and modern works, some by Central American choreographers. The **Teatro Melico Salazar** on Av 2, Ca Ctrl in San José stages productions several times a month; another regular venue for this company is the **Teatro Nacional** on the Plaza de la Cultura. Tickets can be bought at very reasonable prices.

Theater

San José has a lively theater scene, with productions in both English and Spanish. See *The Tico Times* for information.

Movies

Most cinemas show major US movies with Spanish subtitles.
San Pedro Mall, San Pedro.
Plaza Colonial, San Rafael de Escazú.
Magaly, Ca 23, Av Ctrl.
Multiplaza Mall, Guachipelín, Escazú.
Mall Internacional, Alajuela.
Multiplaza del Este, Curridabat.
Omni, Ca 3, Av Ctrl–1
Outlet Mall, San Pedro.
Plaza Liberia, Liberia.
Plaza Mayor Mall, Rohrmoser.
Real Mall Cariari, General Cañas Highway.

Terramall, Curridabat.
Variedades, Ca 5, Av Ctrl/1.
Two specialist theaters, next door to one another, screen art films from different countries. Check *The Tico Times* as to what language the dialogue and subtitles are in.
Sala Garbo
Av 2, Ca 28, tel: 222 1034
Teatro Laurence Olivier
Av 2, Ca 28, tel: 223 1960.

Libraries & Bookstores

Mark Twain Library, Centro Cultural Costarricense/ Norteamericano, Los Yoses,
tel: 207 7500; fax: 224 1480;
www.cccncr.com. 200 meters/yards north of La Gasolinera Los Yoses, near Auto Mercado. Also has branches in La Sabana and Cartago. English-language reference books, magazines, fiction and non-fiction.
7th Street Books, Ca 7, Av Central 1, tel: 256 8251.
Best-known English-language bookstore in San José. Helpful owners.
Librería Internacional, Multiplaza, Escazú; Barrio Dent; Mall Internacional, Alajuela; Zapote and Rohrmoser. Tel: 253 9553. English and Spanish books.
Libromax, several stores around San José, tel: 800 542 7662. Low-priced books, large English stock.
Mora Books, Omni Bldg, San José, tel: 255 4136.
Popular with travelers. Used English books, magazines, and comics.
Universal, Av Ctrl, Ca 1–Ctrl, tel: 222 2222.
Large selection of English books.

Latin Dance Classes

Centro Merecumbé, tel/fax: 224 3531. Has studios in San Pedro, Guadalupe, Rohrmoser, Heredia, and Alajuela.
Costa Rican Latin Dance Academy and Language School, tel: 233 8914; fax: 233 8670.
www.crilang.com

Nightlife

Nightclubs & Dancing

Castro's, Av 13, Ca 22, tel: 256 8789. Crowded. Good place to practice Latin dance moves. While the bar is safe, the area is not so hot – take a taxi.
Centro Commercial El Pueblo
Near Villa Turnon on the highway to Heredia.
A complex full of boutiques, galleries, restaurants, nightclubs, bars, and discos. Musical offerings range from jazz and Latin Fusion to Argentine Tango and Andean music. Popular place to finish off a night, as some bars are open until 4 am.
El Cuartel de la Boca del Monte
Av 1, Ca 21–23
Tel: 221 0327.
Situated downtown, close to Cine Magaly, this is a popular singles bar. Good live music, packed on Mondays.
La Caribeña
Zapote, tel: 253 9276.
Caribbean music and food.
Planet Mall
Mall San Pedro, tel: 280 4693.
One of the biggest clubs in town playing a variety of Latin and pop music.
Trejos Montealegre shopping center
Escazú, several bars, Frankie Go most popular with young, upscale crowd.

Gay Spots

La Avispa
Ca 1, Av 8–10, tel: 223 5343.
Salsa/Merengue. Three dance floors and pool tables. Women only last Wednesday of the month.

Dejá Vu
Ca 2, Av 14–16, tel: 223 3758.
Mostly for men, but women are
welcome too. Cabaret. Pop music.

El Bochinche
Ca 11, Av 10–12, tel: 221 0500.
Pop music.

Casinos

Herradura
Cariari
Next to the Hotel Cariari on the
highway to the airport
Tel: 239 0033
Fax: 239 2992.

Gran Hotel Costa Rica
Downtown San José
Tel: 221 4000
Fax: 221 3501.
www.granhotelcr.com
24-hour casino.

Hotel Fiesta
Puntarenas
Tel: 663 0808
Fax: 663 1516.

Hotel Irazú
San José
General Cañas Highway
Tel: 232 4811
24 hours.

Hotel San José Palacio
San José
Tel: 220 2034
Fax: 220 2036.

Hotel Corobicí
Sabana Norte
Tel: 232 8122
Fax: 231 5834.

Club Colonial
Downtown San José
Tel: 258 2807
Fax: 233 3827.
24 hours.

Shopping

What to Buy

Coffee
Costa Rican coffee is excellent and
relatively inexpensive. Café Britt is
recognized as one of the best in the
world. It is available in
supermarkets and gift shops. Café
Britt also makes a delicious coffee
liqueur.

Woodwork
Wooden items, including bowls,
plates, cutting boards, and boxes,
are widely available. Most gift
shops carry them. The mountain
town of Sarchí is known for
its woodwork. The finest
quality wooden boxes and bowls
are made by Barry Biesanz
of Biesanz Woodworks.
He welcomes visitors to his
beautiful, light-filled studio in
Bello Horizonte, near Escazú:
www.biesanz.com.

Leatherwork
Leather bags, wallets, and
briefcases are a good choice. They
are available in many stores
throughout the Central Valley.

What to Avoid

Visitors **should not** purchase any
of the following:
● Coral
● Tortoiseshell items
● Furs (such as ocelot or jaguar)
● Items made from tropical
hardwoods (such as mahogany,
laurel, and purple heart – if in
doubt, ask the seller what kind of
wood has been used)
● Anything made from crocodile,
cayman, or lizard skins

Woven bags
Look out for interesting woven bags
coloured with natural dyes by the
indigenous Bribri; these are
available at many locations.

Jewelry
Inexpensive handmade earrings and
jewelry are sold at street artisans'
stalls in San José.

Paper
Beautiful handmade papers, made
from recycled plant materials and
and using natural dyes, are sold in
many gift stores.

Other items
Of course there is the usual array of
tourist souvenir goods: T-shirts,
painted feathers, watercolors of
country life, ceramics, and so on.

San José

There are craft stalls in the Plaza de
la Democracia, next to the national
museum, at La Casona, Ca Central,
Av Central–1, and at the central
market. At Plaza Esmeralda in
Pavas, tel: 296 0312, browse
through a number of stalls and
watch artisans at work.
Galería Namú, Av 7, Ca 5/7, tel:
256 3412, has an excellent
selection of local art and
indigenous crafts.
Annemarie Boutique, in Hotel Don
Carlos, Av 9, Ca 9, tel: 221 6707,
sells ceramics, wood souvenirs,
and jewelry.

San Rafael de Escazú

Sabor Tico, behind Plaza Colonial.
Well-selected crafts of Central
America.

Moravia

100 meters/yards south of the Red
Cross (Cruz Roja). Souvenir shops
and arts and crafts gallery, line two
city blocks in the center of town.

Sport

Bungee Jumping

Costa Rica Bungee and Rappel Adventures, tel/fax: 494 5102 www.bungeecostarica.com.
Tropical Bungee, tel: 248 2212 www.bungee.co.cr

Cycling

You can rent a bicycle from bike rental shops around the country; mountain biking is only feasible in certain areas.
Aventuras Naturales, tel: 225 3939. Single and multi-day tours.
Bi.Costa Rica, tel/fax: 446 7585.

Diving

Underwater visibility is best during the dry season (November–April). October is usually the best month on the Caribbean. Costa Rican waters are still largely uncharted.
Buceo Aquatour. Located on the main road through Punta Uva, 20 minutes south of Puerto Viejo. Reservations through the Pizote Lodge, Hotel Punta Cocles, and Villas del Caribe.
Diving Safaris, Playa Hermosa, tel: 672 0012, fax: 672 0231, www.costaricadiving.net. Costa Rica's largest and oldest operation. Diving expeditions, equipment rental, and diver certification classes.
Ecotreks Adventure Co., Osa Peninsula, tel/fax: 735 5723, e-mail: tervoz@racsa.co.cr. Diving trips, diver certification classes, equipment rental.
Mundo Acuatico, tel: 224 9729, fax: 234 2982, e-mail: mundoac@racsa.co.cr. San Pedro and Pavas. Sales and rental of scuba equipment. Spare parts and repairs. Tank refills. Classes.

Fishing

Fishing permits are required and are usually taken care of by fishing guides. On the Pacific, permits are paid for just before boarding the boat. On the Caribbean, they're bought at lodges; some lodges provide all-inclusive deals. Freshwater permits are more expensive than saltwater permits. If you encounter rangers while fishing, they will ask you to present your permit and your passport (a copy of which may suffice).

To arrange permits before arriving at your fishing destination, check with tackle shops in San José. Good sources of information on fishing in Costa Rica are:
Carlos Barrantes, La Casa del Pescador, a tackle shop at Ca 2, Av 16–18, tel: 222 1470.
Deportes Keko, Calle 20, Ave 4–6, tel: 223 4142.
Jerry Ruhlow, a fountain of fishing information (tel: 282 6743/800-308 3394, email: jruhlow@costarica outdoors.com, publishes fishing columns bimonthly in *Costa Rica Outdoors* and weekly in *The Tico Times* and arranges fishing expeditions around the country.

Golf

Costa Rica Golf Adventures, tel: 239 5176 or 877-258 2688, www.golfcr.com, is a great one-stop information source for golfing in Costa Rica.
Barceló Playa Tambor, tel: 683 0303, Tambor. 9-hole course.
Cariari Country Club, tel: 293 3211, Cariari, northwest of San José. 18-hole course. Use can occasionaly be arranged by the Hotel Cariari.
Four Seasons Resort, tel: 696 0000, Papagayo, on the Northern Pacific coast. 18-hole Arnold Palmer-designed course.
Hacienda Pinilla, tel: 680 7000, outside of Tamarindo. 18-hole course, wide fairways.

Los Reyes Country Club, tel: 630 9000, Guácima, Alajuela. 9-hole course, open to the public Mon–Fri.
Marriott Los Sueños Golf Resort, tel: 630 9000, Playa Herradura on the Central Pacific. 18-hole Ted Robinson-designed golf course.
Paradisus Playa Conchal, tel: 654 4123, Playa Conchal. 18-hole course.
Parque Valle del Sol, tel: 282 9222, Santa Ana. 18-hole course.
Tango Mar Resort, tel: 683 0001, Nicoya Peninsula near Tambor. 9-hole course.

Horseback Riding

Horseback riding is widely available in Costa Rica, from hour-long rides on the beach to a riding break on a working cattle ranch. The following offer interesting options:
Caballeriza El Rodeo, book through Desafío Adventures, tel: 479 9464, www.desafiocostarica. com. Horse-friendly option for Monteverde-La Fortuna ride.
Finca Los Caballos, Montezuma, tel/fax: 642 0124. Four-hour trail rides through beautiful scenery.
Hacienda Los Inocentes, La Cruz, Guanacaste, tel: 679 9190; fax: 679 9224, www.losinocentesranch.com. Lodge with guides. Well-trained horses.
La Garza, Planatar, tel: 475 5222, fax: 475 5015, www. hotellagarza.com. Large working ranch with *cabinas*.

Hot-Air Ballooning

Available through **Serendipity Adventures,** tel: 558 1000, fax: 558 1010. Balloon trips originate from Turrialba and near Ciudad Quesada.

Mountaineering

Mundo Aventura, tel: 221 6934, www.maventura.com. Tours, gathering spot for fledgling climbing culture, climbing wall.
Vesa Tours, www.vesatours.com. Arranges climbing expeditions.
Ríos Tropicales, tel: 233 6455.

Rafting & Kayaking

Costa Rica Expeditions, tel: 257 0766, www.costaricaexpeditions. com.
Costa Sol Rafting, tel: 293 2150, fax: 293 2155, www.costasolrafting.com.
Desafío Adventures, tel: 479 9464, www.desafiocostarica.com. Focus on Northern Zone waters.
Ríos Tropicales, tel: 233 6455, www.riostropicales.com. Rafting and sea kayaking.

Sailing

Allegro Tours, tel: 395 6090, www.costarica-realestate.com. Trimaran, catamaran, monohulls. Pacific cruises.
Costa Rica Yacht Club, Puntarenas, tel: 661 0784, fax: 661 0035, cryacht@racsa.co.cr.
Hotel El Velero, Playa Hermosa, tel/fax: 672 0016, www.costarica hotel.net. Beachfront house/hotel with sailboat.

Island cruises

Calypso Tours, tel: 256 2727; fax: 256 6767, www.calypsocruises. com Catamaran cruises from Puntarenas to Isla Tortuga, or the private reserve of Punta Coral.
Bay Island Cruises, tel/fax: 258 3536; e-mail: bayisland@ racsa.co.cr, www.bayislandcruise. com.
One day tour to Isla Tortuga. Departs from San José by bus.

Swimming & Surfing

There is good swimming and surfing on both the Caribbean and Pacific coasts, although some beaches may not be suitable all year round. Dangers include rip tides *(see page 291)* and large waves, caused by heavy swells, that may hit you when leaving the water. Always ask the locals before entering the sea.

The following are good surfing beaches:
Pacific coast: Boca Barranca near Puntarenas, Tamarindo, Jacó, Hermosa, Dominical, and Pavones.

Caribbean coast: Puerto Viejo, Punta Uva, Salsa Brava, Black Beach.

For up-to-date information on surfing conditions, call **Alacrán Surf**: tel: 232 9597 or see www.surf.co.cr and www.surf-costarica.com.

Tennis

Costa Rica Tennis Club, Sabana Sur, tel: 232 1266.
Parque Valle del Sol, Near Santa Ana. The 10 exceptionally good courts are open to the general public.
Parque La Sabana, 4 courts open to the public.

Hiking & Camping

Campsites

There are few established campsites with facilities in Costa Rica, and those that do exist are not generally very well advertised. Property owners in rural areas are often willing to permit visitors to use their land for camping.

Sometimes rural hotels, for a small fee, will permit campers to stay on their grounds. While campers face little risk of prosecution if they bunk down on the beach, recent conflicts between campers and resorts have thrust beach camping into the public spotlight. Government officials and lawyers are still debating its legality. Some parks and reserves permit camping. Call the National Parks Information Service (tel: 257 0922).
Camping Rincón de los Monos
Montezuma
Tel: 642 0634
Well-kept grounds on the beach.
Hotel Jungla y Senderos Los Lagos.
Tel: 479 8000, fax: 479 8009, www.hotellagos.com
Moderate hotel also offers campground and park on the lower slopes of Volcán Arenal just a few kilometers northwest of La Fortuna. Feel the volcano rumble as you drop off to sleep. Camping price includes access to pool and hot springs. Crowded on weekends.
Poor Man's Paradise
San Josecito
Tel/fax: 771 4582
www.mypoormansparadise.com
Book through Selva Mar. Equipped tents, including meals; the best deal near Drake. Also more expensive cabins. Camping spots also available. Restaurant, helpful owner.

Camping Equipment

Alumicamping, Moravia, tel: 225 1532. Purchase, rental, and repair of tents and other equipment.
Centro de Aventura, North side of the former Guadalupe rotunda, tel: 257 0253, www.centrodeaventura.net. One of the best-equipped stores. Sells camping gear. Helpful staff speak English.
Taller La Casita, Pavas, tel: 231 7426. Manufacturers of camping equipment.

Outdoor Safety

Rip tides

Several beaches throughout Costa Rica are known for their strong rip tides. Rip tides or rip currents are forceful ocean currents that travel 5–10 km (3–6 miles) an hour, faster than even very strong swimmers.

If you are unfortunate enough to get caught in a strong ocean current, relax and don't fight it. Let it carry you. Its strength will eventually diminish. Once it does, swim parallel to the beach, toward the incoming waves, and let them carry you ashore.

The following beaches are famous for their rip tides:

On the **Pacific** coast: Jacó, Esterillos, Junquillal, Dominical,

Manuel Antonio's North Espadilla. On the **Caribbean** coast: Cahuita, Playa Bonita.

Plants

On the beach, you should avoid the **manzanillo** tree, a small evergreen with many branches. The leaves, bark and small, yellowish fruit produce a white latex which stings and causes blisters. Sometimes fatal if ingested, one antidote is large quantities of bitter lemon juice. About one person in 10 is allergic to the skin of the **mangos**. Reactions are similar to those described above. Like **mango**, **cashews** are related to poison ivy. Plentiful along the beaches, cashews are tempting to campers who gather them without proper precautions to roast over a fire – a mistake, as even the smoke from these roasting nuts can give someone a bad rash.

Snakes

There are around 136 varieties of snake in Costa Rica. Of those, 18 are poisonous. Snake bites are uncommon, but the following may be helpful. The only poisonous snake in the San José area is the coral snake (coralito), with distinctive red, yellow, and black stripes. All other snakes found in this area are harmless.

Snake Bites

Although snake bites are rare, to avoid being bitten follow these suggestions:
● When walking in the countryside, wear closed, preferably high-top shoes or boots.
● Walk with a stick in hand. Use it where visibility of the ground is blocked to probe before you step.
● Try to choose paths clear of high grass and debris.
● Never reach into areas you can't see into.
● If you encounter a snake, remain calm and retreat immediately. Never tease a snake or chase a retreating one. Snakes attack

people only when they perceive a threat.
If, despite all these precautions, you are bitten:
● Remain calm and try to immobilize the area of the bite.
● Do not apply ice to the affected area; it can worsen the wound.
● Do not cut the wound or attempt to suck the venom out with your mouth.
● Go immediately to the nearest clinic, hospital, or Red Cross agency for an injection of antivenin. It is not necessary to know what kind of snake bit you. Doctors can tell by the wound which kind of antivenin to give.

Bee Attacks

If attacked by bees, call 911 for assistance. Remember:
● You can outrun them (run in a zigzag pattern)
● They hate water (jump into a river)
● They can't see light colors well (get under a sheet)
● They can't see at night
● They are excited by noise
● They can and will follow you into a house

Outside San José and its environs, the fer-de-lance or terciopelo is responsible for more human bites than any species in the country. Few of these bites result in fatalities, however, and some of the strikes can be "dry bites," meaning that the skin is punctured but no venom is injected. Antivenin exists for all of Costa Rica's land snakes. Currently there is no antidote for the venom of the sea snake, distinguished by its prominent oar-shaped tail. The only two reported cases of sea snake bites on record entailed severe pain and swelling, but resulted in complete recoveries.

Africanized bees

Africanized bees are quite indistinguishable from classic European honeybees and their venom is no more poisonous, but they are easily excited, extremely aggressive, and will attack en masse. All of Costa Rica's bees should now be considered to be Africanized. There have been human fatalities in Costa Rica due to Africanized bee attacks. Attacks on tourists are as yet unknown, but it might be helpful to know the following things about them:
● They nest in hollow trees, gutters, or holes in walls or in the ground.
● They are not dangerous when swarming in search of a new home, but become very defensive when they are protecting a hive.
● Attacks are more frequent during the dry season.

Conservation

Costa Rica tries very hard to do a great deal with few resources. The following are some of the more popular environmental organizations that are actively involved in saving and protecting Costa Rica's natural resources.

APREFLOFAS (Association for the Preservation of Wild Flora and Fauna) is a private, non-profit, non-governmental organization for nature conservation and has chaired the Costa Rican Members Committee of the World Conservation Union. It helped establish Braulio Carrillo National Park. Welcomes volunteers. Tel: 240 6087, fax: 236 3210, www.preserveplanet.org.

Asociación ANAI: Active organization working in Talamanca region, linking social development with conservation among indigenous peoples. Projects include a marine turtle conservation program, bird conservation and biological corridor, training and advocacy. It works through grass roots organizing and volunteers, both general and highly qualified. Donations are tax-deductible in the US, or through supporting European organizations. Sells beautiful nature-oriented souvenirs to support the organization. Tel: 224 3570 (828-524 8369 in Franklin, North Carolina), fax: 253 7524, www.anaicr.org.

Caribbean Conservation Corporation: this group runs the green turtle tagging project at Tortuguero Beach on the Caribbean coast, which is the largest nesting colony of this endangered species in the western Caribbean. For an annual membership fee members receive a quarterly newsletter.

Further information from the Caribbean Conservation Corp., PO Box 2866, Gainesville, FL 32602, tel: 352 373 6441, www.cccturtle.org. Or tel: 297 5510.

CEDARENA (Environmental and Natural Resource Legal Center): this center educates the public and government officials on the use of the law to protect the environment. Contributions are tax-deductible. Contact: CEDARENA, Apartado 134–2050, San Pedro, San José de Costa Rica, tel: 283 7080, www.cedarena.org.

Conservation International: the goal of this US-based organization is to integrate people as part of the worldwide ecosystem. It works closely with government agencies throughout the world. In Costa Rica, it gives technical and financial support to the 81,000-hectare (200,000-acre) La Amistad International Biosphere Reserve, which makes up 14 percent of Costa Rica's territory. Membership entitles you to a quarterly newsletter. More information from Conservation International, 1919 M Street, NW Suite 600, Washington DC 20036, USA, tel: 202-912 1000, www.conservation.org.

Fundación de Parques Nacionales (National Parks Foundation): the leading organization devoted to protecting and expanding Costa Rica's reserves. They accept contributions to help maintain Costa Rica's world-famous national park system. Tel: 257 2239, e-mail: fpn_cr@racsa.co.cr.

Fundación Neotrópica (Neotropic Foundation): this group works to foster "sustainable development" in communities near Costa Rica's wildlife preserves, parks, forest reserves, and other protected areas. The annual membership fee brings a quarterly newsletter and gives members a 10 percent discount on its Heliconia Press publications. Tel: 253 2130, fax: 253 4210. www.neotropica.org.

INBio (National Biodiversity Institute): this private non-profit organization promotes

awareness of the value of biodiversity. In recognition of its research it has received two important awards: the Prince of Asturias Award for Scientific and Technical Research and the Saint Francis of Assisi Award for environmental studies. It runs the 5.5 hectare (14–acre) INBioparque in Santo Domingo de Heredia. Experienced guides take visitors on an interactive tour, providing them with information on biodiversity in Costa Rica. Since 1989 the institute has cataloged many insects, plants, mushrooms, and mollusks. Tel: 507 8107, fax: 507 8139, www.inbio.ac.cr/inbioparque

Kids Saving The Rainforest: Based in Manuel Antonio, conservation projects and public education with a kid focus. Co-founder Janine Licare has been featured as "person of the month" in *Teen People*. Projects include reforestation, including an adopt-a-tree program ($20 to sponsor a planting), and Titi monkey bridges. Profits from the gift shop, featuring artwork by kids, go to rainforest projects. Tel: 777 2592, fax 777 1954, www.kidssavingtherainforest.com.

Monteverde Conservation League: this group, a community conservation organization in Monteverde, works on reforestation, environmental education and sustainable development projects. It co-ordinates the International Children's Rainforest Project (Bosque Eterno de los Niños), which is 22,000 hectares (54,000 acres) in size. A US$100 contribution helps pay for a guard in the reserve. Tel: 645 5003, www.acmonteverde.com or www.childrensenternalrainforest.org.

In the UK, the Children's Tropical Forests charity supports the Children's Rainforest Project as well as the Bridge Project in Guanacaste. For more information, tel: 01733-563966 or go to www.tropical-forests.com

Rainforest Concern: an organization that buys and protects virgin forest, and also works with local people developing responsible ecotourism. It manages the Pacuare Reserve, just north of Limón, including a stretch of coastline that is the breeding ground for turtles. A small lodge can hold up to 24 people. Contact 27 Lansdowne Crescent, London W11 2NS, UK, tel: 020-7229 2093; fax: 020-7221 4094; e-mail: info@rainforestconcern.org Online at: www.rainforestconcern.org

World Society for the Protection of Animals: the Costa Rican branch of this society operates the only animal shelter and wildlife rehabilitation center in Central America, the Chompipe Biological Reserve (tel: 506-397 158) near Braulio Carrillo National Park. It has lobbied the Costa Rican government to adopt strict regulations on tuna fishing to stop the slaughter of nearly 100,000 dolphins per year. For more information contact WSPA, 34 Deloss St, Framingham MA 01702, USA, tel: 508-879 8350. Or WSPA, Apdo 516–3000, San José, Costa Rica, tel: 262 6129. The headquarters are in London, tel: 020-7587 5000, www.wspa.org.uk

Rural Tourism Guides

Eco-tourism is still the buzz word in Costa Rica and hotels can provide or recommend excellent guides. A fledgling organized rural tourism network is the latest way of guaranteeing a vacation that minimizes impact on the environment and maximizes benefits to those working in tourism. The new bilingual (English/Spanish) Rural Community Tourism Guide put out by COOPRENA, a national ecotourism network, lists several of these rural tourism projects. Tel: 248 2538, fax: 248 1659, www.agroecoturismo.net. The following are some options:

Active and Progressive Women's Association of Costa de Pájaros Gulf of Nicoya Tel/fax: 678 8205, Women's group that has developed tourism alternatives to the fishing economy. Butterfly garden, tours of mangroves and the Gulf of Nicoya, medicinal gardens, traditional fishing tours.

Finca Educativa Lodge Shiroles, Talamanca Tel: 373 4181, anaicr@racsa.co.cr. Lodge and meals in an indigenous Bri Bri Caribbean-slope community. Natural healing talks, traditional dances and plays, guided hikes through reserve.

Kekoldi Wa Ka Koneke Puerto Viejo de Talamanca Tel: 751 0076/751 0020. Association focusing on natural resource conservation and development of Kekoldi Indigenous Territory. Bilingual guides offer tours to observation platform, noted as the third best place in the world to observe migrant predatory birds.

Real Places, Real People Ticufres, 30 minutes west of San José Tel: 810 4444, www.realplaces.net. One-day or multi-day tours, immersion in rural community including basket weaving, bread making, pottery, and more. Recommended.

Birdwatching

Costa Rica has more than 850 species of birds, including macaws, hummingbirds, kingfishers, toucans, trogons, and the rather shy, resplendent quetzal. The following offer birdwatching trips:
Costa Rica Expeditions, tel: 257 0766.
Horizontes, tel: 222 2022.
La Selva Biological Station, tel: 766 6565, www.laselva@sloth.ots. ac.cr, has world-class birding.
Organization for Tropical Studies, tel 240 6696, www.ots.ac.cr, arranges bilingual group birding trips.
Savegre Hotel de Montaña, tel: 740 1028, www.savegre.co.cr, has excellent birding guides.

Language

Survival Spanish

Learn a bit of Spanish before you arrive, if only the simple courtesies: "Good morning." "How are you?" "I'm well, thanks." These seemingly inconsequential phrases are an important part of daily life in Costa Rica. English is spoken by many people in San José and in the larger hotels, and one can always get by without Spanish; but if your idea of a good trip includes some contact with local people, then speaking a bit of Spanish is the ticket.

If you are going on an extended trip, consider spending the first week enrolled in one of the many language schools. Tailored programs and schedules of all kinds, many with excursions and cultural programs, are available.

A pocket-sized English-Spanish dictionary is a good idea, and small electronic dictionaries are also available.

Numbers

1	*uno*
2	*dos*
3	*tres*
4	*cuatro*
5	*cinco*
6	*seis*
7	*siete*
8	*ocho*
9	*nueve*
10	*diez*
11	*once*
12	*doce*
13	*trece*
14	*catorce*
15	*quince*
16	*dieciseis*
17	*diecisiete*
18	*dieciocho*

19	*diecinueve*
20	*veinte*
21	*veinte y uno*
30	*treinta*
40	*cuarenta*
50	*cincuenta*
60	*sesenta*
70	*setenta*
80	*ochenta*
90	*noventa*
100	*cien*
101	*ciento uno*
200	*doscientos*
300	*trescientos*
400	*cuatrocientos*
500	*quinientos*
600	*seiscientos*
700	*setecientos*
800	*ochocientos*
900	*novecientos*
1,000	*mil*
2,000	*dos mil*
10,000	*diez mil*
100,000	*cien mil*
1,000,000	*un millón*

Common Expressions

Good morning *Buenos días*
Good afternoon *Buenas tardes*
Good evening *Buenas noches*
Goodbye *Hasta luego*
How are you? *¿Cómo está Usted?*
I'm well, thanks *Muy bien, gracias*
And you? *¿Y Usted?*
Please *Por favor*
Thank you *Gracias*
No, thank you *No, gracias*
You're welcome *Con mucho gusto*
How kind of you *Usted es muy amable*
I am sorry *Lo siento*
Excuse me *Disculpe* (when apologizing). *Con permiso* (when leaving the table or passing in front of someone)
Yes *Sí*
No *No*
Do you speak English? *¿Habla Usted inglés?*
Do you understand me? *¿Me entiende?*
Does anyone here speak English? *¿Hay alguien aquí que habla inglés?*
Just a moment, please *Momentito, por favor*
This is good *Está bueno*
This is bad *Está malo*

Shopping & Eating

What is the price? *¿Cuánto cuesta?* or *¿Cuánto es?*
It's too expensive *Es muy caro*
Can you give me a discount? *¿Puede dar me un descuento?*
Do you have ...? *¿Tiene Usted ...?*
I will buy this *Voy a comprar esto*
Please show me another *Muéstreme otro, por favor*
Please bring me ... *Tráigame por favor ...*
coffee with milk *café con leche*
black coffee *café negro*
tea *té*
a beer *una cerveza*
cold water *agua fría*
hot water *agua caliente*
a soft drink *un gaseoso*
a menu *un menú*
the daily special *el plato del día*
May I have another beer? *Puede dar me una cerveza más, por favor*
May I have the bill? *La cuenta, por favor*
[To get the attention of the waiter/waitress] *¡Oiga! Señor/ Señora/Señorita*
Where is the dining room? *¿Dónde está el comedor?*
The pharmacy *la farmacia*
the gas station *la bomba* (the pump)
key *la llave*
manager *el gerente* (male)/*la gerente* (female)
owner, proprietor *el dueño* (male)/*la dueña* (female)
Can you cash a travelers' check? *Se puede cambiar un cheque de viajero?*
money *dinero* or *plata*
credit card *tarjeta de crédito*
tax *impuesto*
letter *carta*
postcard *tarjeta postal*
envelope *sobre*
stamp *estampilla/sello*

Getting Around

Please call a taxi for me *Pídame un taxi, por favor*
How many kilometers is ... from here? *¿Cuántos kilómetros hay de aquí a ...?*
How long does it take to go there? *¿Cuánto se tarda en llegar?*
What will you charge to take me to ...? *Cuánto cobra para llevarme a ...?*
How much is a ticket to ...? *¿Cuánto cuesta un billete a ...?*
I want a ticket to ... *Quiero un billete a ..., por favor*
Where does this bus go? *¿A dónde va este bus?*
Stop (on a bus) *¡Parada!*
Please stop here *Pare aquí, por favor*
Please go straight ahead *Vaya recto, por favor*
right *a la derecha*
left *a la izquerda*
What is this place called? *¿Como se llama este lugar?*
I'm going to ... *Me voy a ...*
bus stop *parada del bus*
reserved seat *asiento reservado*
reservation *reservacíon*
airplane *avión*
train *tren*
bus *bus*
Where is there an inexpensive hotel? *¿Dónde hay un hotel económico?*
Do you have a room with... *¿Hay un cuarto con ...?*
bath *baño*
fan *abanico*
air-conditioning *aire-climatización*
Where is ...? *¿Dónde está ...?*
the exit *la salida*
the entrance *la entrada*
the airport *el aeropuerto*
a taxi *un taxi*
the police station *la delegacíon de policía*
the embassy *la embajada*
the post office *la oficina de correos*
the telegraph office *la oficina de telégrafos*
a public telephone *un teléfono público*
a bank *un banco*
a hotel *un hotel*
a restaurant *un restaurante*
a restroom *un servicio*
a private bathroom *el baño*
the ticket office *la oficina de billetes*
a department store *una tienda*
the market *el mercado*

Driving

Fill it up, please *Lleno, por favor*
Please check the oil *Vea el aceite, por favor*
Please fill the radiator *Favor de llenar el radiadór*
the battery *la batería*
I need ... *Yo necesito ...*
a jack *una gata*
a towtruck *una grúa*
a mechanic *un mecánico*
a tire *una llanta*
Help me, please *Ayúdeme, por favor*
Call a doctor quickly! *¡Llame un médico y prisa!*

Speaking Tico: Tiquismos

If you already speak some Spanish, learn a few *Tiquismos*, uniquely Costa Rican expressions. Tico (Costa Rican) Spanish is rich with them.

The familiar "*tú*" (you) is not used in Costa Rica, even with children. They often use an archaic form, "*vos*." The rules regarding the use of "*vos*" are tricky and elude even advanced students of Spanish: best to stick with "*Usted*," which is always correct.

When walking in areas outside of San José, people passing on the street greet one another with "*Adios*," or " '*dios*." "*Hasta luego*" is used to say "goodbye."

Costa Ricans love to use *sobrenombres,* nicknames. More often than not, the nicknames used have to do with a person's physical appearance: *Macho/Macha* if he or she is ever-so-slightly fair-skinned or fair-haired (not to be confused with *machismo*, an attribute of Latin males, used in Mexico); *China* if she has a slight slant to the eyes, or is actually Oriental; *Negro* if his skin is dark; *Gordito* for someone even slightly overweight; *Moreno* if the person is slightly dark-complexioned, and so on.

If someone asks, "*¿Cómo está Usted?*" it's always correct to reply, "*Muy bien, gracias a Díos*" ("Very well, thanks to God") or "*Muy bien, por dicho*" ("Very well, fortunately")

but you might want to try something a little more zippy and informal, such as: "*Pura vida*" ("Great") or "*Con toda la pata*" ("Terrific" – literally, "with all the paw") or "*Tranquilo*" ("Relaxed, or cool").

Spanish Language Schools

Whatever a student's language needs, whether merely conversational, for business, or to master the structure of Spanish, an appropriate language school exists in Costa Rica. Listed below are some of the better-known schools. Consult *The Tico Times* for others.

Centro Cultural Costarricense Norteamericano
P.O. Box 1489-1000,
San José, Costa Rica
Tel: 207 7500
Fax: 224 1480.
www.cccncr.com
Standard, intensive classes in Los Yoses, Cartago, and La Sabana. Special courses and individual tutoring. Conversation club. The center sponsors plays and concerts. Homestays. Academic credit available.

Costa Rica Spanish Institute
Tel: 234 1001
Fax: 253 2117
Toll free: 1-800-771-5184
www.cosi.co.cr
Intensive classes for groups and private tutition. Programs from 1–16 weeks. Classes start every Monday in San José and Manuel Antonio.

CPI
Tel. 265 6306
www.cpi-ddu.com
Classes, group and private, in Heredia, Monteverde, and Flamingo. Academic credit offered.

Instituto Británico
Tel: 225 0256
Fax: 253 1894
E-mail: info@institutobritanico.co.cr
www.institutobritanico.co.cr
Students are placed in the appropiate class through a written exam. General Spanish, technical Spanish, and Express Spanish.

Instituto de Español Costa Rica
Tel/fax: 283 4733
www.intensivespanish.com

Role playing, discussions, listening exercises, and videos are part of the classes. Courses at all levels for individuals or in groups. Also cultural programs such as Costa Rican cooking or Latin-American dance workshops.

ILISA
Dept. 1420, Box 25216 Miami, FL 33102–5216, USA.
Tel: 280 0700
Fax: 225 4665
E-mail: spanish@ilisa.com
Courses with a maximum of four students. Also one-to-one programs. Spanish for professionals available. ILISA uses a communicative approach rather than a method. Homestay and hotels. Free email and computer access.

Mesoamerica Language Institute
PO Box 1524
2050 San Pedro, Costa Rica
Tel: 253 3195
www.mesoamericaonline.com.
A department of the Institute for Central America Studies which is dedicated to the causes of peace, justice, and the well-being of the people and land of Central America. Offers a one-day survival Spanish class for tourists.

University of Costa Rica
Tel. 207 5634
Fax: 207 4296
www.espancr@le.ucr.ac.cr
Intensive group classes, four weeks, 80 hours. Placement exam.

Further Reading

Books

Because reference books are often unavailable or expensive in Costa Rica, consider purchasing books before leaving home. The ones listed below give a good insight into Costa Rican life.

The Children of Mariplata, by Miguel Benavides. London: Forest Books. Eleven fables from Costa Rica with local color and deep on human feelings. Translated into English.

Coastal Talamanca: A Cultural and Ecological Guide. History of the Talamanca region, both the indigenous and the African-Caribbean. Information on the area and hints on how to be a considerate visitor. Available in the office of the Talamanca Association for Ecotourism and Conservation (ATEC) in Puerto Viejo.

Cocos Island, by Christopher Weston. San José: Trejos Hermanos Sucesores S.A., 1992. Legendary treasures and the wonderful submarine world of the Pacific Costa Rican Island.

Costa Rica: National Parks, by Mario Boza. Madrid: Incafo S.A., 2002.

Costa Rica Nature Atlas, by Wilberth Herrera. Heredia: Editorial Incafo S.A. Notes, maps, and pictures of diverse sites, from mountains peaks and volcanoes to rivers and valleys.

Costa Rican Natural History, by Daniel H. Janzen. University of Chicago Press, 1983.

Costa Rica: A Traveler's Literary Companion, by Barbara Ras (editor). San Francisco: Whereabouts Press. A collection of 26 short stories by Costa Rican writers, skillfully translated into English.

Costa Rica: Wildlife of the National Parks and Reserves, by Michael and Patricia Fogden, for the Fundación Neotrópica, 1997. Gorgeous coffee-table book with easy-to-read, fascinating text.

A Guide to the Birds of Costa Rica, by Gary F. Stiles and A.F. Skutch. Cornell University Press, 1990. The bible for birders in Costa Rica; indispensable.

The Green Republic: A Conservation History of Costa Rica, by Sterling Evans. University of Texas Press, 1999. History of conservation ethic in Costa Rica.

A Guide to Amphibians and Reptiles of Costa Rica, by Twan Leenders. Distribuidores Zona Tropical, S.A., 2001.

The History of Costa Rica, by Iván Molina and Steven Palmer. University of Costa Rica, 2001. Dry but complete overview of the country's history.

Hostile Acts: US Policy in Costa Rica in the 1980s, by Martha Honey. Gainesville, Florida: University of Florida Press, 1994.

INBio Pocket Guides: Various easy-to-carry and complete guides on native ornamental plants, mammals, insects, butterflies, and mushrooms. Contact INBio (www.inbio.co.cr).

Life Above the Jungle Floor, by Donald Lire Perry. New York: Simon and Schuster, 1986.

Monkeys are Made of Chocolate, by Jack Ewing. Pérez Zeledón: Impresos Elimar, 2003. A collection of stories from a long-time conservationist on the southern Pacific Coast of Costa Rica.

Naturalist on a Tropical Farm, by Alexander F. Skutch. Berkeley and Los Angeles: University of California Press, 1981. An engaging account of naturalist Alexander Skutch's early days at Los Cusingos, his tropical farm near San Isidro del General.

The New Costa Rican Cuisine, by Isabel Campabadal. San José: Santillana, 1999. Coffee-table book full of beautiful photos, history, and natural information about Costa Rica's Caribbean coast and its people.

The New Key to Costa Rica, by Beatrice Blake and Anne Becher. Berkeley, CA: Ulysses Press, 2002.

A guide full of detailed, practical information on bus travel, hotels, restaurants and bars, and all tourist destinations.

Passion for the Caribbean, by Yazmín Ross. San José: Santillana, 2003. Coffee-table book full of beautiful photos, history, and natural information about Costa Rica's Caribbean coast and its people.

Potholes to Paradise, by Tessa Borner. Silvio Mattachione, 2001. Personal account and advice about moving to Costa Rica.

Pura Vida: The Waterfalls and Hot Springs of Costa Rica, by Sam Mitchell. Menasha Ridge Press, 1995. A self-published guide to 25 waterfalls, seven hot springs, and camping sites. Includes a variety of suggested excursions.

The Quetzal and the Macaw, by David Rains Wallace. San Francisco: Sierra Club Books. A history of Costa Rica's national parks.

The Ticos: Culture and Social Change in Costa Rica, by Mavis Biesanz, Richard Biesanz, and Karen Biesanz. Colorado: Lynne Rienner Publishers, 1998. A fluent, well-researched analysis of Costa Rican culture.

The Windward Road, by Archie Carr. Tallahasse, FL: University Presses of FL, 1979. The story of Tortuguero and the green sea turtle.

Newspapers

The Tico Times is the most important English-language newspaper in Central America. Print and PDF subscriptions are sent worldwide. Selected stories from the weekly edition (published Fridays) and daily updates are available at www.ticotimes.net. It publishes a tourist guidebook annually. The classified section contains valuable information. Staff can help direct you to the right resource if you e-mail questions to info@ticotimes.net.

Online

AM Costa Rica: (daily online tabloid) www.amcostarica.com

Chamber of Tourism (CANATUR):
www.tourism.co.cr
Costa Rica Internet Directory:
www.costaricainternetdirectory.com
info Costa Rica (has its own built-in search function):
www.infocostarica.com
Costa Rica Bruncas:
www.bruncas.com/aboutcr.html
Costa Rican Tourist Board (ICT):
www.visitcostarica.com
Sustainable Tourism Certification
www.turismo-sostenible.co.cr
Costa Rican Environmental Ministry: www.minae.go.cr
Costa Rican Foreign Relations Ministry:
www.rree.go.cr
Costa Rica General Guide:

www.costarica.com or
www.costarica.net
Gay and Lesbian Guide to Costa Rica:
www.gaycostarica.com
Grupo Taca (information about flights in Latin America):
www.grupotaca.com
La Nación Newspaper (has useful tourist information):
www.nacion.co.cr
The Tico Times:
www.ticotimes.net

Video and DVD

Costa Rica: Land of Pure Life PBS Home Video, executive producer Alex Gregory, 2000.
Southern Costa Rica: Directors Joshua Chambers, Bernadette

Castner, interactive DVD with links, 2003.

Other Insight Guides

Other *Insight Guides* that highlight destinations in this region include: *Insight Guide: Belize* offers a full portrait of one of the world's leading eco-tourism destinations, including its rainforests and coral reefs.

Feedback

We do our best to ensure the information in our books is as accurate and up-to-date as possible. The books are updated on a regular basis, using local contacts, who painstakingly add, amend and correct as required. However, some mistakes and omissions are inevitable and we are ultimately reliant on our readers to put us in the picture.

We would welcome your feedback on any details related to your experiences using the book "on the road". Maybe we recommended a hotel that you liked (or another that you didn't), as well as interesting new attractions, or facts and figures you have found out about the country itself. The more details you can give us (particularly with regard to addresses, e-mails and telephone numbers), the better.

We will acknowledge all contributions, and we'll offer an Insight Guide to the best letters received. Please write to us at:
 Insight Guides
 PO Box 7910
 London SE1 1WE
 United Kingdom
Or send e-mail to: **insight@apaguide.co.uk**

Insight Pocket Guide: Cancún & Yucatán Peninsula sifts through Maya history and Spanish heritage to unveil the mysteries of southern Mexico.

ART & PHOTO CREDITS

INSIGHT GUIDE
COSTA RICA

Cartographic Editor
Zoë Goodwin
Art Director **Klaus Geisler**
Picture Research **Hilary Genin**

Index

Numbers in italics refer to photographs

A
B
C
D
E
G
H
I
J
a
b
c
e
f
g
h
i
j
k
l